AT BREAK OF DAY

AT BREAK OF DAY

DAILY MEDITATIONS

By Fred Mitchell

Foreword by
J. OSWALD SANDERS
General Director, Overseas Missionary Fellowship

MARSHALL, MORGAN & SCOTT
London : *Edinburgh*

LONDON
MARSHALL, MORGAN AND SCOTT, LTD.
1–5 PORTPOOL LANE
HOLBORN, E.C.1

AUSTRALIA AND NEW ZEALAND
117–119 BURWOOD ROAD
MELBOURNE, E.13

SOUTH AFRICA
P.O. BOX 1720, STURK'S BUILDINGS
CAPE TOWN

CANADA
EVANGELICAL PUBLISHERS
241 YONGE STREET
TORONTO

U.S.A.
CHRISTIAN LITERATURE CRUSADE
FORT WASHINGTON
PENNSYLVANIA

First published 1959
Second impression 1960
Third impression 1961
Fourth impression 1963
Fifth impression 1965

MADE AND PRINTED IN GREAT BRITAIN BY PURNELL AND SONS, LTD.
PAULTON (SOMERSET) AND LONDON

FOREWORD

FIVE years ago I was travelling in the Far East with my colleague, the late Fred Mitchell, then Home Director in Britain for the China Inland Mission. Each morning "at break of day" I would see him with his well-thumbed Bible and the devotional textbook *Daily Light on the Daily Path.* After a period of meditation on the selection of texts for the morning, he would commit to writing the fruit of his study in the hope that the spiritual food which had nourished his own soul might some day bring similar blessing to others.

In the providence of God he had completed the three hundred and sixty-five meditations shortly before he was involved in the tragic "Comet" crash which brought to a sudden close his singularly fragrant and fruitful life.

While it is not intended or desirable that these brief daily readings should take the place of more serious study of the Scriptures, they can have a valuable function in pin-pointing a helpful truth with which to begin each new day.

There have been other commentaries on the headline texts of the readings of *Daily Light*, but not after this pattern. The author's method was to take, not the opening text merely, but the central theme of the whole morning's selection for his meditation, and this will explain many Scriptural allusions which might otherwise appear irrelevant. While the readings will be appreciated even if read alone, they will become much more significant if taken in conjunction with the morning Scripture selections of *Daily Light.*

Knowing the quality of Christian character and devotion to the Lord which lie behind these messages, I commend them to the Christian public with the utmost confidence.

J. OSWALD SANDERS

Singapore.

FOREWORD

[illegible]

A Single Objective

This one thing I do, forgetting those things which are behind.—PHIL. 3: 13.

THERE is power in a limited purpose and a single objective. Too many Christians suffer from a diffused and obscure purpose; it is the man who has a single aim who is a man of power. He who says, This one thing I do, is much more likely to accomplish something than he who fluctuates between two purposes. And what should be the single purpose of the child of God? Should it not be to do the will of God from the heart? Man's chief end is to glorify God, and in the pursuit of that end the lesser ends are most surely accomplished also.

This means that something must be renounced altogether; all weights must be laid aside. We are to forget some things in order to press forward. The gathering of wayside flowers is not to be the interest of the man running a race. His eye must be on the goal and all attention must be directed towards that end. While some things must be completely renounced, other interests must be definitely disciplined in order to run well; we must needs be temperate in all things. The Christian's body must be in subjection, and that calls for real moral courage. His time and talents must be harnessed, which calls for watchful care. The loins of the mind must be girt in order that we may run the course before us.

Most important of all is not the pace we set up at the beginning but that which we maintain throughout the coming days; we are to run with patience, to keep on pressing toward the mark. A crown awaits us, a crown which will not fade as did that given to the Greek athletes; to obtain such a reward given to us in that great day by such a Lord demands nothing less than our best and our all.

My Soul, Keep Up Thy Singing

Sing aloud unto God our Strength.—PSALM 81: 1.

HERE is a command of God to sing. It is good for us to sing. Singing opens up the soul not only to give outward expression to its inward thoughts and impulses, but also to an inward receiving of new supplies of grace from God. Singing is not always easy. Sometimes praise is a sacrifice, though it is never more helpful to us than when it is most difficult to offer, and it is certainly most acceptable to God when it costs us most.

We are to sing aloud lest the singing in the heart becomes quenched. We are to sing new songs and sing the song of redemption as they do in glory, as it were a new song. The subject of our singing is such as to demand new songs and new singing. There is singing up in heaven such as we have never known, but the praises of redeemed sinners is of all the most musical; and when we sing redemption's story angels will fold their wings, for they never knew the joy that our salvation brings.

But we must keep up our singing here; it is intended to brighten the pilgrim path, and there is such reason for it. We are the sons of God, the children of a King, our inheritance is reserved, our journey is guaranteed, our foes are conquered, we are in the best company earth can afford as we march to Zion. Then let our songs abound, let us sing of the majesty of the Lord, and of the glories of His Son Who was made man for our redemption. Let us glory in the Church of Jesus Christ, the godly company of all faithful people. It is God's remedy for sadness, so, my soul, keep up thy singing.

He Leadeth Me, O Blessed Thought

He led them forth by the right way.—PSALM 107: 7.

LIKE Jacob, God finds us in a desert land; we are travelling without a road or a track and with no guide. Each one of us is moving on towards eternity but have no idea of the direction or how to find the right way, until He finds us. Then He leads us, and when the Lord is with us we need only to keep close to Him, for the whole area of life, which is trackless desert and wilderness to us, is well known to Him and we are safe and our hearts can be at rest.

The Lord guides us by the right way that is the very best way. He is not merely concerned to bring us to the right destination but to lead us there by the way which is most profitable. The journey is meant to be an education and to afford us ample opportunity of learning spiritual lessons, and developing moral and spiritual qualities. The Israelites were not led through the wilderness by the shortest way; in the very first instance, a detour was made to avoid a foe which was too strong. Our God is utterly to be trusted to lead us by the right way; blessed are we if we trustingly follow.

He also leads us continually. We are not just guided in the great crises of our life, but in the daily duties and in those smaller decisions, which we are so apt to take without seeking guidance, but which are really of great importance because of the results which follow. Let us cultivate the habit of referring matters to our skilful loving Guide, for in following Him there is rest and blessing. No one can lead us like our Shepherd. He has crossed the desert first. He is continually guiding others and will guide us all the way. He leadeth me to-day, this year; O blessed thought.

We Are Travelling Home

In My Father's house are many mansions.—JOHN 14: 2.

THE temptation to settle down here has been a temptation to almost every generation of God's people; only perhaps in times of fierce persecution has the heart of His servants been truly separated from the earth scene. The thought of our being pilgrims too easily disappears and the whole tendency of thought during recent years has been against our being 'other-worldly'.

But the Bible is a book about another world and the living of an 'other-worldly' life in this one. If we are to live a heavenly life in an earthly environment, how can we do this unless our minds are set on heavenly things? The scriptures chosen for to-day's portion are a timely reminder of our pilgrim life and of the glorious country which is the Christian's real native land. To that we are not yet come, but we are journeying towards it and there are many arrivals there every day.

Our true home is heaven and heaven is a real home. The Father is there, and around Him, and His Beloved Son to Whom we owe all things, the family redeemed out of many nations is gathering. No sin can mar the fellowship, no limitation can possibly spoil the worship. To be with Christ there, is far better than anything could be down here. There are no more tears because no more sorrows and no more sins. The wicked who have troubled us here cannot disturb us there; we shall be at rest—not at rest doing nothing, far be such a thought, but at rest from trouble, division, sin. So let us lift up our hearts and fill our minds with thoughts of heaven and home; and our step will be lighter to-day.

My Strugglings are O'er

Come unto Me . . . and I will give you rest.—MATT. 11: 28.

THE passages of Scripture deal with one of the greatest problems which faces the believer. The joys of the first experiences of the Christian life have passed; the relief which comes through a knowledge of forgiveness of sins and the satisfaction of becoming a child of God have lost something of their newness, and the discovery is made that there is an inward conflict which was not anticipated. There is a law working in our nature which is contrary to the new life which has been imparted; the war within is very real and there is too often defeat; joy gives place to sadness and testimony becomes dull. What is to be done? Is this the best that a Christian may expect? Is there no deliverance and victory? The answer is that those who believe do now enter into a rest of faith.

This comes to us in the same way as all our spiritual blessings, it is a gift of God and is by grace through faith. Just as we believed on Christ dying for us and received pardon, so we believe that Christ is living in us and we receive power. The difference between the two great discoveries and experiences is that the first is in some ways critical and final while the latter being once received must needs be continually reaffirmed. If Christ liveth in us then we need not be continually defeated but we may enter into the rest of faith, the rest which comes through trusting Him to keep us from falling. The war rages when we ourselves are fighting sin in ourselves, the rest comes when we trust Christ to deal with our sin. The conflict is acute when we reign over ourselves instead of submitting wholly to our risen and indwelling Lord. "When the heart submits, there Jesus reigns: and where Jesus reigns there is rest" (J. Hudson Taylor).

That Beauty, Lord, is Thine

We all . . . are changed . . . by the Spirit of the Lord.—2. COR. 3: 18.

A CHRISTIAN is not one who believes differently from others but who is different. By the work of the Spirit of God deep changes have taken place in the heart, and these are the basis of great changes in the life. God is working in us to will the good and then to do it; first right desires and decisions, then right conduct.

This ultimately means that the Christian must be marked by certain moral qualities which make for beauty of character. There is to be about us an uprightness of conduct and a transparency of motive which make us stand out from others in this evil world. Then there is to be a sympathy and approachableness which are the marks of a follower of the Lord Jesus. All these and other qualities of character combine to give a true Christian testimony which is not in word only, but in disposition and deed and which speak loudly and unanswerably all the day long. The beauty of the Lord, the marks of His character, are seen in us. It is a real comeliness which is at once an absence of the ugly and a blending of the desirable into a true beauty of character.

Now all this which is to be seen by others is only possible because in the unseen depths of our lives God is working by His Spirit, imparting and renewing His own life in our spirits. It is His life which is in evidence; our personal and difficult traits of character are being replaced or sanctified by the features of Him, Who is altogether lovely. The beauty of the Lord our God is upon us because the spirit of life from the Lord our God is working within us; His comeliness is seen upon us because His life is growing up within us.

Loving Wisdom's Plan

I will visit you and perform my good word toward you.—JER. 29: 10.

BY His very nature God is pledged to do us good; His nature and His name is love. The only way which ensures His judgments is to pursue our own way and insist on our own will, in which case we must inevitably reap the fruits of our choice. He that soweth to the flesh, which means to ourselves, shall of the flesh reap corruption.

But God has thoughts towards us which are worthy of Him. They are the thoughts of Eternity and they are confirmed in an eternal covenant to all who are in Christ Jesus. They are thoughts of peace and form a plan which embraces the whole of our life and the whole of God's people. To this glorious end God is now working. The trouble often is that we do not know the deep thoughts of God, His loving skilful plan is at present hidden from our eyes; all we do see are the immediate workings which are often confused and sometimes painful. We are like the precious stone in the hand of the lapidary; we are on the wheel to be shaped or polished and cannot as yet foresee the pattern and the glory of our latter end. We are to be as jewels in His kingly crown and therefore must needs be prepared, though the processes are unwelcome.

The great thing is to be sure of God and of His loving purposes, to realise that He is working out the most skilful purpose for us. His thoughts for us are high and wonderful and to Him we can freely commit ourselves and our cause.

Some of us may already begin to trace something of the pattern even if faintly, as we review the past, and that should give us increasing assurance for the future. But the greatest peace will come as we rest on the loving wisdom of our God who knows His own thoughts toward us. And as His thoughts are higher than ours, so are His ways also.

Confidence in God's Character

They that know Thy Name will put their trust in Thee.—PSALM 9:10.

A NAME is given to a person to remind us who he is and instinctively the name and the character of the person become inseparably united; for that reason names become odious or precious. God's name therefore signifies His character.

Now they who know God's character do not find it difficult to put their confidence in Him. This reminds us that instead of faith being antagonistic to knowledge, it rather rests on knowledge as its basis. We can only trust God as we know the kind of Being He is; hence the need of studying for ourselves what the Bible teaches about God, and then of teaching others what we have learnt. Nothing is more needed in days of ignorance of God on the one hand or an undue religious emotionalism on the other, than a true knowledge of the character and ways of God.

God's character is such, that if it be known, His servants rest their whole need for time and eternity on Him. In times of trial of faith or persecution of mind or body they retreat into the stronghold of God's faithfulness. He has never forsaken His children and never will; He is pledged to support the righteous, and even if He allows them to experience much hardship or even die for the truth, He will yet vindicate them and in the meantime grant them His presence and peace.

Because of all this the Christian can both sing His praise and confidently testify to his confidence in God. The subject of our singing is The Lord Who is Himself our Saviour. And our confidence may be expressed to-day in exactly the way it was expressed in Bible times. Because He who is true and trustworthy has said that He will never leave us, therefore we may say that we are unafraid of anything our fellow-mortals can do to us. It is the character of God which matters.

Brightly Gleams Our Banner

Jehovah Nissi (The Lord my banner).—EXODUS 17: 15.

THE Church of God is committed to a warfare with the powers of darkness. Under the captaincy of Satan the whole world of evil spirits move to attack the Christian church as a whole, and in its individual members; and at its disposal are all men and women who do not serve the Lord Christ. But the issue of the warfare is settled, for the Captain of our Salvation has conquered the whole host of wickedness, and their continued resistance to His Kingdom is only by divine permission, for a wise purpose, until a coming day when the warfare will cease. In the meantime the warfare continues.

But the initiative is not really with the powers of darkness but with the Kingdom of light, the church of our Lord Jesus Christ. While we are not ignorant of Satan's cunning strategy yet we are not to be cowed by it; we are to go forth into the world which belongs to Christ by right and claim souls for His Kingdom. A banner has been given, around which we gather and under which we fight. It bears the Lord's name, for it is Himself Who rallies us to the conflict and victory. Truth is on our side and we can rejoice; even when the enemy's attack is a desperate one, our Captain leads us in conquest and puts him to flight.

Therefore all thought of defeat or yielding is to be rejected. The battle is the Lord's. We are to look to Him Who heads the armies of the Lord of Hosts, and be valiant. We are well supplied with equipment, if only we take it up and use it; we have the weapon of prayer, the Sword of the Spirit and the Shield of faith. Moreover we are in a campaign which is well conducted with correct strategy and adequate resources; but best of all the Lord of Hosts, the God of the Armies of Israel is in our midst and at our head. Therefore we go forth in strong confidence and as we go we sing. Later we shall gather up the spoil.

The Limitless Bounds of Grace

I pray God, your whole spirit, and soul and body, be preserved blameless.—
I. THESS. 5: 23.

THE whole being preserved blameless!—Such was the prayerful hope of the Apostle, as he wrote to the Christians at Thessalonica, who only a few months before, had turned from idols to serve the living God. The spirit, that innermost and deepest part of our nature; the soul, with its affections, desires and emotions; the body with all its faculties; all to be kept without blame; not faultless, but blameless. Such was and is God's ideal for us, each one; and such is the limitless grace of God that from His side the ideal is attainable. We must beware of belittling the power of Jesus Christ in a human life; rather we must be careful to allow the statements which are made concerning it, as being utterly sufficient, to have their full weight of meaning. Faith rests on the promises, and great faith rests on great promises. When we dilute the Word of God we dilute the faith which trusts it. So let us take these prayers and promises at their full value, and claim their fulfilment in our own lives.

The Scriptures chosen today speak not only of the process of preserving them but of the glorious consummation of presenting them before God, and that was something to which the Apostle Paul looked forward with joy. His teaching and praying was with this in view, and he speaks of presenting them complete, mature, without spot or wrinkle. Let us bring ourselves to God again as we read, and tell the Lord that we accept His ideal and present ourselves for an answer to these prayers and hopes of the Apostle.

So doing our hearts will be established in peace, and the process of our practical sanctification will be continued and deepened in preparation for the day when we meet the Lord face to face. There is sufficient grace for this and more.

Praise My Soul the King of Heaven

Let us offer the sacrifice of praise to God continually.—HEB. 13: 15.

IT is often more easy to pray than it is to praise. Our conscious need, the conflict with the enemy of our souls, the grinding pressure of difficult circumstances, all make prayer necessary; but praise must be cultivated. There are a hundred reasons why we ought to praise God, but there is not necessarily the adequate sense of its necessity; therefore let us remind ourselves today that we ought to praise God more, and let us seek grace to cultivate the attitude of thanksgiving.

Praise should characterise the saints below; believers passing through the world should do so with a song in the heart and often on the lips. It is glorifying to God; it enhances His reputation among men as well as satisfies His own heart. It is due to Him for the mercies He bestows, and we would do well to count our blessings oftener, then our hearts would surely praise more. The story of the nine ungrateful lepers who were healed and of the one only who returned to give thanks, is alas too true to life now. But wherever praise is offered, even though it be a sacrifice, then the soul is opened in the very act to receive further blessing. One translation of Psalm 50: 23 suggests that praise prepares a way by which God may shew us His salvation, that is, praise lays down the track on which further blessings may travel to us.

If praise ought to mark the saints below, then praise certainly does occupy the saints in heaven. The multitude in heaven have harps as well as white robes and palms. "The harps to praise withal" says Bunyan. There they stand from every nation and tribe praising God without ceasing. We shall be preparing ourselves for the engagements and service of the gloryland if we cultivate the habit of praise. Bless the Lord, O my Soul, and forget not all His benefits. My Soul, keep up thy singing. Praise pleases God and blesses us. It encourages Him to do yet more for us and prepares us to receive it.

All that I Need is in Jesus

The only wise God our Saviour.—JUDE 25.

KNOWLEDGE is the accumulation of facts but wisdom is the understanding of moral action; the wise man is he who knows how to live and conduct himself. It is thus that the fear, that is the reverent trust, of the Lord is the beginning of wisdom. Only when God is revered and His will and standards accepted, do we begin to learn wisdom and know how to live acceptably before Him.

The knowledge of God is deep for He is eternal and we are creatures of time. He is infinite in His glory and attributes, and our mind is bound by the finite. Mere human research or speculation will not reveal God to us; the discovery is not to the learned because he is such. God reveals Himself to the humble and contrite. "To this man will I look even to him that trembleth at my word."

To those who are penitent and trustful God reveals Himself in His Son. The Infinite and Eternal God has become man so as to reveal Himself to man; God Who is a spirit has in the person of His Son also become flesh so that all flesh may see Him. In His life, by His words and deeds, He has shown God to man, while in His atoning death Jesus Christ has removed the hindrance to fellowship and communion. All who believe in Jesus as Saviour are united to Him by grace and faith, and in Him they are at the very fount of wisdom. In ourselves we are ignorant of God and foolish in our ways, but in Christ we know God and are made wise in our conduct. The more we realise the blessing of this union and trust Him with Whom we are one, the wiser and godlier we shall be.

Conscious of our folly and ignorance if acting on our own initiative, let us ask of God Who giveth wisdom to those who ask and giveth liberally. Christians ought not, need not act unwisely.

Perfect Peace and at Such a Time

The peace of God which passeth all understanding—PHIL. 4: 7.

GOD promises to keep the heart of His children in perfect serenity, in a peace which is beyond description and for which there is no accounting, save that it is a gift of God. The saints have enjoyed the blessing all down the ages and in the most difficult circumstances; men have gone to the scaffold with an undisturbed mind; women have suffered the deepest sorrows, but in perfect peace.

This peace is described as perfect peace, that is, it is suited for every circumstance and adequate for all the strain which may be put upon us. This is possible because it is the peace of God, which means not only the peace which God supplies, but the peace which He Himself enjoys. It is His own peace, 'My peace,' as Jesus Christ described it. It therefore passes all understanding; it cannot be described, it can only be enjoyed; it is impossible to analyse it but it is possible to demonstrate it.

Now since this peace is from God, Who is eternal, and has been bequeathed to us by our Lord Jesus Christ as one of His legacies to His people, is it not dishonouring to Him not to possess it? In order to do this two things are necessary. First of all we are to cast our burden on the Lord. Things oppress and harass us; troubles gnaw at the heart with their corroding care; burdens weigh heavily and seem to cling. All these we are deliberately to throw off on the Lord, Who desires and is able to carry them. The second thing is that we ask for it, God gives it as a result of our prayer and supplication with thanksgiving. Are we aware of being disturbed? Is our soul anxious, burdened and fretted? Then let us take the burden and resolutely refuse to carry it and instead ask for God's own peace to possess our heart and minds. We may do this since we are in Christ Jesus.

The Father and the Family

When ye pray, say, Our Father which art in Heaven.—LUKE 11: 2.

THERE are many points on which Christianity shews itself completely different from the world's religions, such as for instance, the way of forgiveness it teaches, and the resulting peace of mind and heart it gives. But ultimately the greatest contrast appears in the views of God which the religions and Christianity present. The former mainly give us a haughty, touchy and offended deity who is to be feared and who is to be appeased by offerings, or by the infliction of pain and penance; while the Bible teaches us of a holy and righteous God who has Himself dealt with the sin that offends Him, and then offers Himself to us as a Saviour God and a Father. As we approach Him, our Lord Jesus says, "when ye pray, say, Our Father."

And this relationship is not merely one of benevolence, it is a vital one. That means that He has not adopted us into His family as an earthly father might, but that He has imparted to us His own life, so that we are truly of the family. This relation of life extends to others also, for Jesus said, "My Father and your Father," we are related to Him. It extends to all God's other children; they are the Father's children, partakers of His nature as we are, and we are therefore really one with them, vitally related to all who are the children of God by a second birth.

We are to cultivate this blessed and privileged intimacy of children and Father. Our Lord Jesus, when on earth almost invariably addressed God as Father, and He would have us enjoy the same sweet and intimate fellowship. As a child runs to its father in trouble, so should we; as a young man consults his father on plans and projects, so should we. He is accessible to all who are His, and loves us to abide in His love.

But our intimacy should not become familiarity. He is our heavenly Father of Whom our Lord said, "My Father is greater than I." Reverence becomes our approach and conduct.

Mounting Up with Wings

Set your affection on things above, not on things on the earth.—COL. 3: 2.

THE Psalmist was aware of a tendency in his life for his thoughts and desires to be occupied with earthly trivialities and it might have been with positively sinful things. Was he alone in this? Do we not find our own experience reflected here? Are we not too often like the man with the muck-rake grovelling in the dust when a crown of gold is over our head? The fact is, that although we have been born again of God's Spirit we are still in the body, and sin is still with us. There is a conflict of standards and powers in our lives. The flesh with its standards and attractions makes its appeal in gross or subtle forms.

But, thank God, there is in every believer the Spirit of life which is in Christ Jesus. This is our link with God; here is the strong pull towards heaven, the antidote to sin and the world. We are risen with Christ; heaven is our home; the command to set our affections above is possible of fulfilment because we belong there, our real home is there. All the tendencies are not downward as with the natural man, there is the life of God which soars and climbs, which longs for the pure air of heaven.

Now the choice rests with us as to whether we live responding to the one or the other. We may live after the flesh if we will, or we may live after the Spirit. If we intend to do the latter, then, like the psalmist, we need to pray to be quickened according to God's promises. In answer to such longings and prayers the Spirit of God will assert His power and lift us above. Longings for holiness and heaven will be strengthened, and ties and tendencies to earth will be weakened. The choice is ours as to which attraction will draw us today, shall we not acknowledge with the psalmist "My heart cleaveth unto the dust"; and then pray with him, "Quicken Thou me according to Thy word."

Let All Creation Worship Him

It pleased the Father, that in Him should all fulness dwell.—COL. 1: 19.

TODAY we are reminded of the deep things of God, of the place of the Son in the esteem of the Father. Let us think of Jesus Christ, the Son of God made man for our salvation, saying quite early in His ministry on earth, "The Father loveth the Son and hath given all things into His hands." Although Jesus had not anywhere to lay His head, and had to seek the tribute money in the mouth of one of His inconspicuous and innumerable creatures, yet all things are His by the Father's gift, because the Father loves Him. In Jesus Christ all the fulness of the Godhead dwells; in His body is revealed all the glories of the Godhead, though in such tempered light that we can behold them. And of such fulness we are made partakers by the infinite grace of God, for we are in Him and complete in Him. We lack nothing as we dwell in Him.

Now the glories shine out more clearly, for they are not being revealed alone in Judea or Galilee, but in glory. The limitations of His thirty-three years are removed, He is far above all, He is enthroned, worshipped and glorified. The whole creation is subject to Him and must serve His will. He is Lord of both dead and living. Master of the animate and inanimate worlds, men and angels serve His will and by Him kings and presidents exercise their power.

And the glories shine and the power extends not only to all spheres but to all ages, Christ is the centre of all, the Lord of all being. Time and eternity revolve around Him, for the Son Who is in the bosom of the Father, hath subjected Himself to suffer and redeem, and in so doing has eternally satisfied the heart of God as well as eternally saved the souls of men.

Love Lifted Me

Herein is love, not that we loved God, but that He loved us.—1 JOHN 4: 10.

THE reason and motive of our salvation lies in the loving nature of God. The reason certainly does not lie in ourselves, nor does it even lie in our need, but in God, Who out of His love met the need and used it as an occasion for the shewing forth of His mercy. It is not a case of our loving God but of His loving us and giving His Son for our redemption. We love God only because He first loved us, and He loved us so, so greatly, so very much. There is no god in the universe whose nature is love or who so displays his mercy. Other gods are to be dreaded and appeased; their nature is unpredictable and their wrath is cruel. But this God, the God and Father of our Lord Jesus Christ, is our God and our Father, blessed be His name.

In His love He hath delivered us from the pit of corruption, which means from both the power and guilt of our sins and from the eternal judgment to which we were hastening. With His strong cords of love He drew us out, and then He washed us and set us on our way. But some of the passages here are in the singular, Thou hast in love to *my* soul delivered it, Thou hast brought up my soul from the grave. He brought me up. There is a danger of considering truth in general instead of in particular, of thinking of Jesus Christ as the Saviour of the world and forgetting He means to be my Saviour. It is this personal application of truth which means so much, this personal claim on the Saviour's power which means salvation. Therefore let us make sure that what the Bible writers say of God lifting them in His love, is also true of us; then the psalms will not only be the psalms of David but mine too, for they will be the vehicle of my song.

He Comes the Prisoner to Release

Him that was to come.—ROMANS 5: 14.

THINK of Him as the Eternal Son of God, the One Who is God's Equal as He stoops down to our low estate. A bright seraph long before had sought to reach higher and in the pride of his heart had said, "I will be as God," and fell as he aspired, and was judged. But here is One Who is doing the very opposite; He is equal with God but He makes Himself of no reputation. The carrying out of the Father's counsel and plan means that since by man came death, by man also must come the resurrection of the dead; therefore since there was no man to atone and redeem, His own arm must do it and that means first becoming man. So He passed by the nature of Angels, and was made of the seed of Abraham, coming into this life of man on earth by way of the Virgin's womb and the obscurity of a Judean inn.

Here in this babe, boy and man, we see God manifest in the flesh. Here is the glory of the Lord revealed by Man to men; the exceedingly bright light is tempered for human eyes and the human mind. No man hath seen God in His pure essence at any time, but the only begotten Son hath unfolded Him, the brightness of God's glory and the exact expression of His nature.

In this Man, this last Adam, a new race is beginning. The former race bore the marks of its origin, fallen Adam; the new race is to bear the marks of its Founder and Fount, the last Adam, the Lord from heaven. In order that this may be possible it was necessary that Jesus should die, tasting death for every man, that by His ransom and obedience He might procure pardon for His own and share with them His own divine life. Behold what manner of love that we should be born of His Spirit, washed in His blood, and become the sons of God.

Active but Humble

Serving the Lord with all humility of mind.—ACTS 20: 19.

ALL Christians are servants of the Lord; it is expected that they will devote themselves in His employ. But there is a serious misconception which arises, namely that of assuming that God's service is necessarily or even primarily associated with what is sometimes called 'full-time service' or the direct service of the Church and Gospel. The fact is, that the Lord has called some women to be Christian mothers for the training of next-generation Christians, as well as His having called some women to be missionary pioneers and teachers. Some Christian men are appointed by God to a life in the world of business, science or art, where they may glorify and serve God. We serve God, if with our whole might and for His sole glory, we obey Him and do the work which He has appointed.

But such service wherever it may be is to be rendered in a special way and in a particular spirit. Christian service is not to be rendered by the piece; we are not merely to be concerned how much we can do for the Lord Jesus. The manner of service is fully as important as the service; the motive in which it is accomplished makes it either acceptable or unacceptable to God. The high service of God is to be offered in a lowly spirit, whether it be in an exalted or a humble sphere. We ourselves are only sinners saved by grace, the gifts we have are of His mercy, the office we hold is His appointment and He could easily withdraw the gifts or take away our office. We have nothing which we have not received, at the best we are unprofitable servants, we have done no more than our duty.

Therefore a true humility of mind, which follows a knowledge of our frailty becomes us. Let us cultivate the thoughts of God's greatness and His mercy; and of our own continual need. The resultant humility is pleasing to God.

O Come, Let Us Adore Him

They shall call his name Emmanuel . . . God with us.—MATT. 1: 23.

CHRISTIANITY is essentially miraculous. It is not just a matter of miracles being associated with the Lord Jesus Christ, but He Himself is the greatest miracle of all. The incarnation of the Son of God, the Second Person of the Ever-blessed Trinity assuming our manhood, is beyond our comprehension. How a Person of the Godhead could become a babe, could join in the most intimate union, His eternal wisdom with the innocence of a child; could unite infinite knowledge with a daily growth in knowledge; is beyond our comprehension. But it is so, and we can only bow and worship.

O Come, let us adore Him
Christ the Lord.

But He was not only wonderful in His birth but also in His life. Never man spake like this man, He was full of grace and truth; His every day, His every deed, His every word and way were such as to cause the Father in heaven to rend the silence and speak audibly, "This is my beloved Son".

But He was most wonderful in His death, when He Who was without sin, uncontaminated by our human rebellion and depravity, was made a sin offering for us and suffered, the just for the unjust, the guiltless for the guilty, that He might bring us to God.

And now He is wonderful as He is exalted at God's right hand, having received all power in heaven and earth, for He alone is worthy to receive power. He is far above all power and authority, human, angelic, or satanic and He reigns over the universe. Soon His visible and obvious reign over this evil world will be established, and that will be yet more wonder to add to all that is already. Much regarding His Person is as yet to us mysterious but with Isaac Watts we may sing

Where reason fails with all her powers
There faith prevails and love adores.

Only Good can Come from such a God

If ye endure chastening, God dealeth with you as with sons.—Heb. 12: 7.

There is a great danger in our modern presentation of the Gospel that we misrepresent the Christian life by suggesting that the Christian life is so full of joy that there is no place in it for sorrow. The fact is that sorrow is an indispensable and invaluable ingredient in the experience of the child of God; its sanctifying, sweetening and ennobling effects are of just as great value, as are the results of other more exhilarating experiences. We are reminded today of some of the purposes of suffering.

The first is fruit, that is, the fruit of righteousness and the fruit of the Spirit. If we long for patience we must needs learn it through tribulation, through pressure of circumstances, and when tribulation is having its gracious results in our character then a number of other graces are also being encouraged, and the understanding love of God is shed abroad in our lives by the Holy Spirit.

The second result is that of purity of heart and life. The fires of affliction and adversity test life's motives and reveal life's pollution. We only discover the resentment and rebellion against God latent in our hearts, when He sends us periods of frustration, or denies us the service which we so urgently desire. It is at such times that we have the opportunity of being refined by the fire, of being ground by the mill-stones. In such circumstances we either crack with the heat, or become refined and smooth; we either break under the grinding-stone or become fine-flour for bread for the hungry.

Let us exercise ourselves so that when God, in His love, dispenses to us the seemingly hard and harsh trials of life, we do not resent them but kiss the hand that sends them. In eternity we shall bless the hand that guided and the heart that planned—why not now?

Grace, Guidance and Glory

This God . . . will be our guide . . . even unto death.—PSALM 48: 14.

THIS God is our God—this God Who is the Creator of the ends of the earth, Who hangeth the earth upon nothing, to Whom the nations are as a drop of a bucket and Who taketh up the islands of the earth, including the continents, as very little things—this God is our God. If God be for us who can be against us? If omnipotence is with us, what lesser powers need we fear?

O Lord, Thou art my God; the sense of relationship is brought nearer. This Lord, Jehovah, is my very own God. Grace has made Him thus; of His own will He saved me with the word of truth; He it was Who bound me to Him with the cords of love, and by His nature and His promises engages Himself to care for me and even to serve me, for ever.

This God will guide me unto the end. He knows the way; He knows the foes which beset; He knows the tendency to stray; but He will guide. Whether I need refreshment or rest, whether I pass through the dark valley or the enchanted ground, He knows the way He taketh and I will walk with Him. He leadeth me in the paths of righteousness for His name's sake.

And He will continue to guide until I dwell in the house of the Lord for ever. Enemies may be about me but He will spread a table before me in their presence, and then one day He will call me to His immediate presence where no enemies dwell and we shall need no more correction or protection, guidance or grace, but all will be glory. The Saviour's prayer for His own that they may be with Him where He is and behold His glory will be accomplished. Amen, so let it be.

Let there be Hope Today

Blessed is the man . . . whose hope the Lord is.—JER. 17: 7.

THERE is always so much in the Christian's present circumstances and in the world in which he lives, to distress. The injustices, the suffering, but most of all the neglect and rejection of God by the many, and the ignorance of Him by the millions who have never heard, that the servant of God could easily be depressed. It is in these present circumstances that hope has its great ministry, in brightening the sky and lifting up the spirit which is cast down.

But hope is not just an optimistic outlook, it is a Christian grace and is based on certain stable facts. First of all it rests on the nature of God; it believes that He is fundamentally good and wise and that all that He does is for the best. This means taking a long view-point and looking ahead to the final consummation. For that, the Christian has the promises, promises of the judgment of the wicked and the blessing of godly, promises of a creation all subdued under the Lordship of Christ, and of a heaven in which there is nothing unclean.

Thus hope rests on God's character and promises. The believer makes the Lord His trust and finds His hope in Him. So fixing his mind on the Lord his heart is not unduly moved with passing events and human failure and he is unashamed because of the ground of his expectations of better days. The Lord has really need of nothing more than promising such a future of glory but in order to accommodate Himself to our low level of faith and to encourage us to hope in Him, He has confirmed His word with an oath and so bound Himself to us by two unchangeable and unbreakable things, that our confidence in Him and in His complete Sovereignty and triumph, might be strong and unshaken. Jesus hath died and hath risen again; He sits at God's right hand till all His foes submit; and hope rejoices in the prospects.

He is Both Present and Coming Again

Wherefore comfort one another with these words.—1 THESS. 4: 18.

THE Lord is at hand, or near, this is a statement of Scripture which may mean one of two things. It may mean that His coming is at hand, or more likely, that He is Himself near at hand all the time. Let us take both these meanings of the text and rejoice in them.

His coming is near, the events of history suggest that He cannot be far away and that soon He may break the silence and bring in his glorious reign. Then will come to pass the age for which the Saints have waited with long patience, the time for which God has waited too, when evil shall no more trouble the children of men nor rear its rebellious head against God. We should encourage ourselves and others to pray, "even so come Lord Jesus"; and test our love of Him by our readiness to welcome His appearance.

But possibly the second meaning of the Scriptural statement concerning our Lord's being near at hand is that He is now and always close beside us, according to His promise. Lo, I am with you even to the end of the age. Not a thing will transpire today but that He will be at hand. This ensures His readiness to help, to advise, to restrain or encourage. The fact of His nearness will cheer the drooping spirit, or it may check the hasty word. It is a wonderful and yet a solemn thing to live in the near presence of the Lord Jesus. If this word and truth be apprehended and applied, then today must be a great day, for no day can be mean which is spent with so august a Guest and Friend.

Both these applications of the text, "the Lord is at hand", call us to godliness, to lay aside every weight, to renounce every sin and to walk in holiness and love. Let us seek to live this day in His presence and expectation.

Thy Righteousness My Glorious Dress

The righteousness which is of God by faith.—PHIL. 3: 9.

OUR righteousnesses are as filthy rags, says God through Isaiah the prophet. The truth is not very flattering to human pride and if human judges and judgments were concerned then the statement would appear exaggerated. But the estimate is God's, and it is His estimate of our best and not our worst. The fact is that the best human righteousness is far from satisfying God and so we are disqualified from any hope of acceptance or justification on the ground of our own merits.

But the Gospel brings the news of a righteousness which is adequate and acceptable to God. It is His own righteousness, the righteousness of God. This is available to men because the Son of God was made man and offered Himself without spot to God. The righteousness, which is God's is mine by faith, because by receiving Christ Jesus as Saviour I am made one with Him and all His merits and acceptance become mine also. He Who knew no sin was made sin for us, that we who have no righteousness might be made God's righteousness in Him. It is the story of a wonderful exchange and by faith this means that we lose our sin and receive His righteousness. This is not by works, that is by our struggling to be better, but by faith that is by receiving the Righteous One, Jesus Christ, as our own personal Saviour. This is possible for all who believe the good news.

Is it not incumbent on us to reject all other grounds of confidence and refuse any other supposed basis of our acceptance with God.

Jesus Thy blood and righteousness,
My beauty are my glorious dress;
Midst flaming worlds in these arrayed,
With joy shall I lift up my head.

So we may calmly stand in the presence of God because our righteousness is now the righteousness of God.

Reproached but Rejoicing

Partakers of Christ's sufferings.—1 PETER 4: 13.

THE true Christian soon discovers that following the Lord Jesus is not a popular calling, for Christ was crucified by the world and the world loves Him no more now than then. His standards are so different from those of the world and His objective is completely different, for while men of this world serve and please themselves, Christ lived only to please God—and the Christian is called to do likewise.

Here then is a challenge which confronts the Christian soon after his conversion, if not before; and indeed it may be a constantly repeated challenge all through life. It is this, am I a follower of the Lamb of God which means living a life which is very different from that of my neighbour and my business associate, or am I content to be little, if any, different from the unsaved. If we purpose to be true Christians then our path is with the Lord, in separation from the world. This means something of shame and reproach; we shall be dubbed old-fashioned, slow, awkward and unsociable; and while we must not seek to be such yet if we are true in our life and witness we shall certainly find ourselves marked men and women, both in the office and the shop or wherever we may be. But the comfort which is ours is that we are sharing the reproach and rejection of Christ, and that means we are near Him and pleasing Him.

If we are at present being ostracised and reproached for Christ's sake let us rejoice. Are we called old-fashioned? Then so is the sunshine, and old well-tried things are not lightly to be discarded. Are we unsociable? It is only because we are living in a fallen world which lieth in the evil one. The Spirit of glory and of grace rests upon us, on their part Christ may be rejected and disowned but on our part He is glorified. Let us count it a privilege and not a shame to be associated with the Lord of Glory.

Following Holiness for Love of Jesus

He hath made Him, to be sin for us, Who knew no sin.—2 COR. 5: 21.

JESUS CHRIST was sinless; His manhood was holy; no taint of human failure or rebellion soiled His pure nature. In order that it should be so it was necessary that He should be born miraculously, a break in the line of the generation of fallen sinners was essential. So He was begotten by the Holy Ghost of the Virgin Mary and was without spot, undefiled. This was necessary because He was God as well as man and the thought of the God-Man being associated or defiled with sin is abhorrent, and the fact is impossible.

But the mystery deepens and the miracle grows; for after thirty years and more of a sinless life, not only sinless by its freedom from sinful acts but by its freedom from sinful omissions, our Lord Jesus Christ was made sin for us. By the most stupendous act which God ever undertook, in the most unfathomable mystery of the ages, the Lord caused to meet on Him the iniquity of us all. He became for three hours our Sin-bearer and Substitute, and carried our sinful nature and our sinful acts to the death for judgment.

And now, since His offering was accepted and He is risen again we may be made righteous in Him. This is most wonderful and constitutes an irrefutable challenge to us to live as those who were identified with Christ in His death to sin, and in His heavenly life in righteousness and power.

Lord Jesus are we one with Thee
O height, O depth of love.
Thou one with us on earth below,
We one with Thee above.

There is every reason why, since we were redeemed by the sinless Saviour and are now represented by such a High Priest, we should hate sin in every form, and make it our chief concern to live holily and unblameably before God and men.

Strong in the Strength which God Supplies

As thy days, so shall thy strength be.—DEUT. 33: 25.

GOD is the source of strength for His people; He it is that giveth power to the faint, and if there is a special weakness or special need then He sendeth special supplies. His strength is always matched to our weakness and whatever may be our need, however keen the sorrow or heavy the trial, we are reassured by the fact that His grace is sufficient.

Like all God's gifts and grace, the Lord's strength is ministered to us as we need it. He does not supply us with a deposit of strength, a sort of spiritual battery from which we may draw for a while until it runs down; but He supplies a continual flow which is received by faith and as required. Our life is divided into days and each day should see us experiencing an adequate supply as we look to Him and wait on Him. This means that we do not need to be laying up stores for the morrow for to meet tomorrow's needs we shall have tomorrow's supplies, offered by grace and received by faith.

This all means that the Christian can face his future and his foes, his work and his weakness, in a spirit of confidence. He knows that the cross is not greater than His grace, the burden not heavier than His strength can carry. Indeed He knows that He giveth more grace when the burdens grow greater, and if heavy hurdens become heavier then great grace will become greater. It is this which makes Paul say, "Most gladly therefore will I glory in my infirmities, that the power of Christ may rest upon me. Therefore I take pleasure in infirmities, reproaches etc."

With such sufficient promises of God's strength mediated to us according to our need and guaranteed by promises for every demand, we too may say "I can do all things through Christ Who strengtheneth me."

Living in the Presence of God

The eyes of the Lord are in every place.—PROVERBS 15: 3.

THERE is no place where God is not present. The Psalmist expressed the truth of God's everywhereness (His omnipresence as theologians call it) in Psalm 139, when he asks and answers, Whither should I flee from Thy presence? If I ascend up into heaven, Thou art there; if I make my bed in hell, Thou art there, and so on. There is nowhere outside the presence of God, where His eye does not rest upon us.

But the Lord's knowledge of us is as much a thing to be welcomed as to be dreaded. To the man bent on his own ways then God's presence is unwelcome indeed; like Adam he seeks to hide himself from the presence of the Lord. But to the godly the presence of God is home; only there the heart is at rest. The true believer pants for God as harts heated in the chase pant for cooling streams; he rests there as birds nest in the sanctuary. We may well test ourselves by asking if we love to dwell with God and live our lives under His eye. It is true that the eyes of the Lord are in every place beholding the evil and the good; but they also run to and fro throughout the whole earth to bring deliverance and help.

Today, and again every day, let us face this truth afresh, that God is very near, acquainted with all our ways. If we are intending to please Him we can rejoice in Him, for His presence is salvation and His scrutiny is such that He can send help just when and where we need it. But if we have plans on which He cannot smile, if we practise habits which He cannot approve, then the eyes of the Lord are unwelcome and conscience seeks to evade them. But let us remember there is no place in this world or another, no place in office or kitchen, in secret or in public, where His eyes do not behold us. Let us then think twice before we sin.

Keeping Up the Pace

Let us run the race with patience . . . looking unto Jesus.—HEBREWS 12: 1, 2.

WE are pilgrims travelling onwards to the Celestial City, but we are also viewed in scripture as athletes on the course. This means not only that we must be sure of our direction and keep steadily going on, but we must also bend all our energies to the journey and make progress swiftly.

A runner must needs make a good start or the race may be lost at the beginning. He must then keep up a good pace with his eye on the goal and in order to win he must do better than others. Many are content to think they are as good as others, some are even content with being in the race, but the true Christian is to attempt to be first in humility, service and love.

Now for this race our goal must be clear. It is Jesus Who has gone before us and given us not only a track to follow but has given us a start through His grace. Likeness to Him in character in word and deed is our objective and that means earnestness and prayer and the exercise of faith every day during our all-too-short life. Then we must needs strip ourselves for the race which means laying aside all we can do without. It is of all things most necessary to renounce sin, and it is essential that we should also lay aside doubtful things which are as encumbrances to our movement. We need to keep our bodies under, to conserve our time and strength and give ourselves wholly to the race.

But the race is a long one. It is not a short sprint on the course but a test of endurance, and so we need to keep up the pace. Many make a good beginning but do not continue. We may not always have an appreciative audience but we do have the Lord Jesus to encourage us, and as a Christian said in her old age, the last lap may be done at a sprint.

Continuing the Battle

Fight the good fight of faith.—1 TIM. 6: 12.

THE Christian life is not only a pilgrimage and a race but also a battle. There is a war in the spiritual realm which began with the revolt of the angels and which entered the sphere of human life when our first parents chose their own will to God's. From then until now the fallen spirits under the Chief have sought to draw man away from God and to deny to God the creator of both orders of beings, the right and pleasure of fellowship with man. So the battle is set between the spiritual forces of light and darkness, between good and evil, and we must take sides in the conflict. The believer has already done this when he became a Christian but he must needs maintain his position all the time.

The war calls for an all-out campaign. We cannot fight effectively unless we turn out the foes in our own ranks. So all known sin must be renounced and all parleying with evil must cease forthwith, otherwise by subtle argument they will weaken our side and become traitors in the ranks. Our weapons too must be the right ones. We are not in a physical or human conflict fighting with men of differing views; if we were, we could use natural weapons such as human arguments, plans, craft, propaganda, etc. No, we are in a spiritual war where only spiritual weapons avail. So we have only recourse to prayer and the Word of God, that is to the power of God manifest in answer to prayer and effective in the truth of God.

This conflict is not only being fought in the world but in our souls, where the flesh and the Spirit are at war. To the flesh we are to give no quarters; it is to be starved and denied; but to the Spirit we are to yield a full and glad obedience, so that He Who is the believer's life and holiness and power, may win the battle in us and then use us in carrying the victory into other lives.

A Life of Faith and Love

Whom having not seen, ye love.—1 PETER 1: 8.

THE Christian life begins with an act of faith; we accept the record God gives of His Son; we commit ourselves to Jesus Christ for time and eternity; the receiving and the giving are both phases of the one act of faith which brings us out of sin into salvation. There was nothing to see and at first nothing to feel, but we rested on the truth of God.

Now the Christian life continues on the same principle of faith; the just live by faith, day by day. Whereas in our early Christian life there was much that appealed to our sight, and there were many feelings which were pleasant, as the life progresses it appears to be God's way to withdraw little by little the things of sight and feeling to teach us to walk more by faith. Our guidance becomes less spectacular and dramatic and our spiritual life becomes more regular as we walk with God. We are called upon to trust God much more, and to be content without the external and evidential.

What does deepen, however, is our love for the Lord; our life is lived in quiet, humble daily fellowship with God. Instead of unusual guidance we begin to have the mind of Christ, to think His thoughts on things and situations. Christ in us becomes our anchor much more than the external things of the Christian life. And our love to God becomes more graciously expressed in love to others. We see Christ in them, we remember that the same Holy Spirit dwells in them, and that they are travelling towards the same city, trusting in the same Saviour and having in their hands the same book.

Thus we may join the company of the blessed who having not seen the Lord Jesus, believe in Him, who without external evidences continue to put their trust wholly in His character and word.

Deliver Us from Evil

The Lord knoweth how to deliver . . . out of temptations.—2 PETER 2: 9.

IT is one of the marks of a Christian, one of the proofs of his being born again, that he hates evil and longs to be delivered from it. It is a mark of our growth in grace that we are concerned about our own evil, rather than another's, and most of us have sufficient trouble with our own failings and sins that we need not be unduly watchful and critical of our brethren. Our flesh is weak, that is, we ourselves, our wills, are not sufficiently strong to cope with temptation. The good that we would we do not, and the evil that we would not that we do; our desires are far beyond our achievements.

It is therefore good that we pray for ourselves, asking that we be delivered from evil. It is desirable that we should pray God in His mercy to remove us from circumstances which might prove too much for us, whether they be circumstances of want or of plenty, and the latter is usually the more perilous.

To those who are concerned to live a godly, righteous and sober life, God has given many promises. He engages to keep us from evil, and to deliver us out of the hand of our Strong Enemy. He knows how to do this for He is stronger than our strongest foe, more than a match for our worst circumstances and mightier than our most sinful tendency.

And what shall we do to experience His delivering and keeping power? We are to keep the word of His patience, that is, the promise which He has made in His patience and which is made as a match for our weakness, we are to hold; we are to cling to the promise in faith, resting our souls upon Him Who promises. Further, we are to seek Him much and often, praying Him to keep us from evil. Then we are reverently to expect Him so to do.

Go in This Thy Might

Be strong . . . and work, for I am with you.—HAG. 2: 4.

THE two commands, to be strong, and to work, stand together, and we separate these which God hath joined at our peril. There is even a tendency in our lives to one extreme or another. Like Moses, killing the Egyptian, we are either hastily going about our work with consequent peril, or like him we are shrinking and giving excuse that we are not eloquent. The Christian who would be healthy must needs attend to both duties.

The command to be strong presupposes that this is possible and in order to its obedience, God hath made available all the resources of grace. We are to be strong in the grace that is in Christ Jesus. Here then is the source of our strength, in Christ Jesus. This means that if we abide in Him, that is live in Him, we shall grow strong and His strength will become ours. This is no merely passive state, for abiding means not only resting on Him but feeding on Him and learning of Him. It calls for Bible Study, prayer and the discipline of life, but it means especially and ultimately that we realize that our strength is in Him and we wait upon Him to receive it.

But we must beware of thinking that we are not to work until we have accumulated a certain amount of strength. A baby begins early to exercise itself and with the exercise there is a development of strength. So work is not only desirable for the use of accumulated strength, but is in itself one of the ways of increasing it. The outflow in service makes way for the inflow in communion. Slack hands do not make for a ready mind. Renewed, therefore, by waiting upon God we are to go out into the world and work for Jesus Christ. We must work while it is day, and there is much to do. While we are not to fall into a modern peril of working beyond our strength, neither are we to fail to use our strength. What God hath joined, let not man put asunder.

Neither Going Back nor Looking Back

The Lord hath said . . . ye shall . . . return no more that way.—DEUT. 17: 16.

OUR severance in spirit from the world is once for all; we cannot go back. First there is that which is natural and afterwards that which is spiritual, but the order is not to be reversed again. We have said in the words of the old hymn, "My old companions, fare ye well." This is not done in a spirit of pride which would be utterly unworthy of the Christian, because if we have left the world which is under judgment, it is because of grace. But left it we have, and we cannot think to return to its fellowship and its ways.

The world has nothing which the disciple of Jesus longs for or needs. We desire a better country, we have been given a taste for heavenly and better things. The presence of the Lord, His people and His service are our attraction now. The world offers only the pleasures of sin for a season, while we have found true pleasures which last, and we are ready to suffer affliction for our inevitable testimony against the world, if needs be. As the justified we are living by faith, that is we are trusting Jesus Christ and relying upon God's word and we will not turn back from such a blessed life to sinning with the world which rejected our Lord. Having put our hand to the gospel plough we cannot even look back with longings as Israel did in the wilderness, when forgetting the taskmaster's whip and the bricks without straw, they longed for the savoury foods and loathed the simple life of the pilgrim.

But we confess our desires to make progress to Zion and refuse to turn back or look back, with a true sense of our need of the continuing grace of God. We ourselves are not able to keep ourselves and we need to walk humbly with our God. Our glorying is in the cross of Christ and in the Christ of the cross. It is what He is and in what He did, that our whole confidence rests. But we do trust Him who first turned our faces towards God and heaven to keep us travelling in that direction.

Eternal Life, Abundant Life

I am come that they might have life.—JOHN 10: 10.

DEAD in trespasses and in sins. Such is the divine description of us all apart from Christ. It is not very flattering, but it is true, and it is with the truth we are concerned. Could any words more faithfully depict our state by nature or make real our inability to recover ourselves from the power of sin.

But God in His great mercy hath done something for sinners and what He has done is the message of the Gospel. As death came upon the human race by the fatal choice of its head and representative, so Another has come into the world to impart life to those who believe and so begin a new race within the first race. Jesus Christ has come as the Son of God and the Son of Mary and He has died to make possible our forgiveness and also that we may be grafted into Him to become partakers of His divine and everlasting life. God hath therefore given to believers the gift of the Eternal life which is in His Son, and the moment we believe, that moment we receive the life of God. Blessed miracle of grace! All the glory must be to Him Who has taken the initiative and worked this great miracle in our lives.

But the full purpose of God is that we should share His life in abundant measure; Christ came to give us life abundant. It is therefore the will of God and the desire which He is ever seeking to realise that we should be cleansed from everything which hinders our receiving the Holy Spirit, the Giver of life Who proceedeth from the Father and the Son. Moment by moment in a stream of power and grace the Blessed Spirit is meant to communicate to us the fullness of life, moment by moment we are meant to be receiving such fullness. What doth hinder? Ignorance of what is ours, unbelief which closes the heart, and sin which hinders the flow.

Grace, Abundant Grace

The exceeding riches of His grace.—EPHESIANS 2: 7.

GRACE is the unmerited favour of God; it is such favour adapting itself to our personal needs. It therefore describes the disposition of a loving but holy God towards His sinful and undeserving creatures; and is expressed to us in the person and work of Jesus Christ.

Let us think for a moment of this grace, for if we begin to understand it we shall appreciate it, and if we appreciate it we shall all the more adore and love the God of all grace. Is it not wonderful that the holy God Whom our sins have so offended should be otherwise disposed to us than in wrath? When once a sinner sees the enormity and guilt of his own sins he can understand the wrath of God, but here is the God Who might be angry with us disposed to forgive us. On what ground can He be so disposed? The answer is in the fact that His Son has become man and for us men has offered up Himself as a substitute. All this has been made possible by the grace and obedience of our Lord Jesus Christ Who stooped down to become a sin offering for us. His offering is accepted, our sin has been judged and now God can be our justifier while still remaining just.

So God has taken the initiative and dealt with our sins. He now offers pardon and peace and power to the rebellious sons of men. None can boast for no man can make himself acceptable to God, but humbly accepting God's way of pardon and receiving God's gift of His Son, all the merits of the Son are accounted to the believer. God's grace is abundant, there is no hesitation or limitation in the pardon; there is no shadow about the acceptance: And there is no restriction in the resources which are now ours in Christ Jesus.

And all God's gifts to me I claim
I dare believe in Jesus' Name.

Let Us Give Thanks Unto the Lord

Beware that thou forget not the Lord thy God.—DEUT. 8: 11.

IT is an easy thing, as well as a base thing, to receive everything at the hand of a loving God and seldom stop to thank Him. His mercies come so regularly, they are so many and varied, they arrive so thick and fast that we need to cultivate the habit of giving thanks. Many of us refuse to take a meal without a grace, but what about the kindness of God in the receipt of a letter from a friend, the opening of a book to cheer the soul, the listening to some sweet music, the delight of a hot bath. Should we not make it a point of honour to thank the Giver of every good and perfect gift?

Few of us have missed a meal because there was nothing to eat; yet think of all that is involved every time we sit down at our breakfast or dinner-table. The dairy-farm has been made a ministry of God to us, and the transport services have delivered it before it became sour. Farmers in another country have provided our meat and sailors brought it to us; and there has been gas prepared to cook it. There is an awful danger lest we think all these are our rights because we pay for them. They are all gifts of God about which He may have often to say "Where are the nine?" or, "Where are the ninety-nine?" There is only one found who has returned to give thanks.

The cultivation of this grace of thanksgiving is a necessary discipline for thanks are due to God our Father. And in addition, a thankful spirit is of great price. It is conducive to joy, it is destructive of criticism and grumbling. Thankfulness to God lifts the heart and mind up to the purer regions of heaven, and sets the mind of the Christian on the Giver as well as His gifts. When thou hast eaten . . . thou shalt bless the Lord. Let us give thanks unto the Lord. It is meet and right so to do.

A Privileged Intimacy

The secret of the Lord is with them that fear Him.—PSALM 25: 14.

IN this as in so many other ways Christianity stands far apart from the religions of the world, or to put it more exactly, the way which God has revealed is so different from, and superior to, the ways which men have devised. In other religions God is feared, in the Bible way of fellowship God is to be reverently loved; indeed He longs to draw men into a privileged intimacy with Himself, as He did with Abraham and others.

We are reminded therefore that God is not looking for servants only, as though His chief concern was to get a certain amount of work done. The Scriptural view is that He has undertaken the work but is allowing His children the privilege of sharing; and sharing, not in the work merely, but in the plans. Is God longing to share something with us, while we are too busy to listen and learn? Happy is the man whom God chooses and draws into His counsel; happy indeed is the man who responds and is drawn into the inner circle of His loved ones. For the secret of the Lord, the deep things of God are open to such. God's acts are seen by all but His ways are only understood by His friends.

It is by communion and obedience that this sacred intimacy is fostered; we prove ourselves His friends by doing whatever He asks. Rebellion, even in the heart, and disobedience disqualify even a Christian from becoming a friend of God, and all who would know the high honour of becoming members of the Lord's Privy Council must needs deny themselves the privilege of doing as they please and of making their own plans.

God is longing to have at His side and in His presence men and women who wait upon Him, who tarry His leisure and learn His plans. Is it not above all, our duty as well as our privilege to meet such a longing?

Glory Dwelleth in Immanuel's Land

There shall be no more death . . . for the former things are passed away.—REV. 21: 4.

HERE we have no permanent abiding place and have constant reminders that we cannot settle down. We are pilgrims travelling to a better land, to an eternal city. The tendency of thought during recent years has been to centre the thoughts of Christians on this earth rather than on Eternity, and we have become unfitted for the task of witnessing because we have lost the joy of anticipation of heaven. Today we think of the comfort of glory.

There will be no night there, the sun shall not go down. This means that everything which is dark and perplexing will have gone for ever in the light of God's presence.

There will be no more tears, either tears of repentance or grief. We shall not weep because of our failures or the failures of others, neither shall we weep because of cruelty or oppression.

There will be no more death. The last enemy has been destroyed; no longer shall we look upon the cold form, the vacant chair, the open grave; all will be life and light in the glory of the heavenly home.

There will be no more pain, either physical, mental or spiritual. No man will torture another, no disease will rack the frame, no oppression will crush the soul or torture the body.

All these, and every other thing which is contrary to the best and most satisfying experiences of the human soul will be banished for ever. They came as a result of sin, they will go as a result of redemption and will have no place among the redeemed in glory.

So our loved ones who have departed in the faith are comforted; we need not sorrow for them, for theirs is all joy.

Light has Chased the Darkness

God . . . hath shined in our hearts.—2 Cor. 4: 6.

YE were once darkness, wrote the apostle. Not only did we walk in darkness without but there was darkness within. Our souls were without the true knowledge of God, we neither knew Him nor had we the capacity to discover Him. We were, indeed, like the earth in the first chapter of Genesis, chaotic and void, with darkness over the whole of our moral world.

But God Who commanded the light to shine out of darkness hath shined in our hearts to give the light of the knowledge of the glory of God. God in His Sovereign mercy ended our darkness and scattered it by giving light. The transformation was complete like being in a darkened room when the lights are switched on; once darkness, now light. We are like the blind man who had become the centre of controversy regarding Jesus Christ; we can say with him, "One thing I know, whereas I was blind, now I see." It is beyond dispute even though we may not understand all that made our spiritual sight possible.

Now we are to live in the light and the promise is that if our eye is single, that is if we have only one intention to glorify God, then our whole life in its every part will be bathed in light; we shall have knowledge as to God's will in every part of our life. Such a life will be transparent to others and shining as a light in a dark place. Men will see us not governed by the dark principles of the world but by the knowledge of God and eternity.

And as we live in the light which shines in the person and character of Jesus Christ we shall reflect the same light and be changed into the same glory, the Holy Spirit working in us constantly to make Christ real to us and known through us. May God give us to know what high privileges are ours and to what a high destiny we are called.

Out of the Abundance of the Heart the Mouth Speaketh

They that feared the Lord, spake often one to another.—MAL. 3: 16.

A PHILOSOPHER may live in solitude, but a Christian's place is in society. The former may keep his thoughts to himself but the believer shares them with his brethren. The New Testament knows nothing of the hermit or recluse and one of its characteristic words is fellowship. It was so even in the first dispensation as the text reminds us today.

They that feared the Lord—that is the Old Testament's description of the godly; they lived in the solemn yet glad sense of God's presence all day long. Such had an experience of God's mercy, and so many tokens of his love as they travel on, that they must needs tell their fellow-travellers on life's journey. And as they told, so they listened to others who had similar and different accounts to give; they spoke one to another and the Lord overheard their conversation which to Him was so precious that he had notes made. This makes us believers of a later day ask ourselves whether our hearts are so full of Christ as to long to declare the glorious matter. Are our experiences of His mercy so numerous and varied as to afford us a fresh occasion of testimony to God's faithfulness whenever we meet a friend?

Or another question presents itself; is our conversation unworthy gossip? It is written that we shall be judged by our words, we must give account of every idle and profitless conversation. Jesus is still drawing near to the twos and threes as they travel together; does He hear that which makes Him glad or sad? The two on the way to Emmaus were talking of Christ and His resurrection despite their confusion and darkness; this gave the Lord Jesus an opportunity to open to them the Scriptures. Are we ready for the opening of the Holy Book or is our conversation petty and worldly?

A Great Privilege and a High Destiny

They shall be Mine . . . when I make up my jewels.—MAL. 3: 17.

WE are Christ's now; we belong to Him on three accounts. First, we have been given to Him by His Father; secondly, we have been purchased by His blood; and thirdly, we have given ourselves to Him. No one can dispute His claim to me, He is mine and I am His for ever and ever. Let us meditate on this precious truth that we are the Lord's, bought with a price far beyond gold or silver or precious stones. Let the high price He paid remind us how dear we are to Him and then let us be reassured that no harm can come to us since He is keeping us as the apple of His eye.

But in a special sense we shall be His when He makes up His jewels. As Lord of Hosts, as Director of all angelic and human companies, He says that when He is crowned we shall be specially His own possession. No evil power will be able to tempt or touch us, no foe come at all near us; we shall be wholly at His disposal and for His glory. Heaven will consist not of streets of gold and gates of pearl; they are the metaphors of something infinitely more precious, something spiritual; heaven will consist of being with Christ and being like Him. And lest we should think only of our own enjoyment of the celestial home, let us remind ourselves that it will mean more to Him. We are there as a result of His sufferings and death; He loved the church and gave Himself for it. He is waiting with long patience for the crowning day; and longing expectantly for those whom God hath given Him to be with Him where He is.

In view of what we are now, and what we shall be hereafter, what manner of persons ought we to be in all godliness. We should disdain to act or speak other than as a King's consort, intended for a high destiny.

A Man on the Throne

The man Christ Jesus.—1 TIM. 2: 5.

"GOD, of the Substance of the Father, begotten before the worlds; and Man, of the Substance of his Mother, born in the world; Perfect God, and Perfect Man." So reads the Athanasian Creed, that noble statement of our faith; and these two facts, Christ's perfect Godhead and Manhood we must needs hold with conviction and courage in all times. Today we are reminded of His Manhood; He is the Man Christ Jesus, made in the likeness of men.

It is as Man that Ezekiel sees Him on the throne of heaven and indeed since God rules over all, upon the throne of the universe. He is there now having taken His Manhood back to heaven. He represents redeemed mankind there and His presence reassures our hearts that we shall be there. But He is not only in heaven, He is on the throne of heaven. The Perfect Man, the One Who suffered for men, is now enthroned. Judgment is committed to Him and all authority is His. Could any other person be so suited to rule and to judge?

And we who are redeemed are united to Him. He joined Himself to us in His incarnation, represented us in His death and then by the work of His Spirit enabled us to be linked by saving faith. We are one with Him now He is enthroned and faith daily draws strength and joy from such union. Let us lift up our hearts; though they so often cleave to the dust, let us lift them up unto the Lord.

He lives at God's right hand
He all His foes shall quell.

This is our hope for the ultimate recovery of a ruined world, that Jesus Christ hath conquered every foe and now lives to bring in His glorious Kingdom.

Thou Sweet Beloved Will of God

I delight to do Thy Will, O my God.—PSALM 40: 8.

HERE is a life unlike every other life lived upon the earth, and that because He who lived it was unique. For Jesus Christ the Son of God and Son of Mary never once concerned Himself to do His own will, He was ever saying not my will but Thine be done, I delight to do Thy will.

Such a life was lived in sharp contrast to those about Him in the days of His flesh, and is just as different and superior to our lives now. No self-seeking, no self-pleasing, no strong desire to pursue His own course; all was submitted to God His Father. What God desired He must do and do gladly and promptly, even though it meant being despised and rejected, a Man of sorrows and acquainted with grief.

Such a life gave infinite pleasure to His Father. At last there was One on the earth who did not seek his own will. There was One who was obedient and loving. Well might the Father rend the heavens and say, "This is my beloved Son, in Whom I am well pleased." Day by day in Nazareth and then in other cities and villages in Galilee and Judea He was magnifying the broken law and shewing what a life lived perfectly according to His statutes was like. Here was One who was fulfilling all righteousness, and answering fully to all the prophets said.

Such a life being laid down in sacrifice was acceptable to God as our sin offering. It condemned sin in us but brought hope and salvation to us. And now by His Spirit the Risen Christ lives in us to repeat and reproduce His life; to enable others, that is us, to fulfil not merely the letter of the law but its spirit, which may be summed up as doing the will of God from the heart. So help me, God.

We Cannot—but God Can

Who can say, I have made my heart clean?—PROV. 20: 9.

SIN is a very defiling thing. It is a state of rebellion and disaffection towards God which has been passed down from one generation to another, and which grows both as men grow older and become more bound together by social ties. It has affected every part of man's nature; the mind is blinded and cannot understand; the heart is defiled and cannot desire God as its sole Object; the will is warped and weakened so that we cannot even do the things which we know are right. We are all as an unclean thing, and are unable to cleanse ourselves. This evil principle in our nature is beyond us to eradicate and thus if anything is done for us, it must be done by Another.

Now the message of the glorious Gospel exactly meets this situation. It tells us that God has done something for us in that His Son has borne this sinful nature to its judgment and that all who believe in Him are free from its curse and may be set free from its dominion. We on our part do not have to play some mental trickery and persuade ourselves that we are free from sin but rather to acknowledge its presence and power, and to confess our sinful nature and acts. If we do this and turn away from ourselves to our Substitute and Saviour then we are set free, pardoned and restored to God's favour.

And the promises of the Gospel include cleansing. It is the will of God that we should love Him with all our heart, that our minds should be renewed and know Him, and that our wills, now empowered, should choose to do His will rather than our own. Let us explore the Gospel promises and humbly claim them for ourselves. Who can say I have made my heart clean? We cannot cleanse ourselves but God can.

His Name shall Shed its Fragrance Still

Unto you therefore which believe He is precious.—1 PET. 2: 7.

CHRIST has become our offering and sacrifice unto God. As with the Old Testament sacrifices His sacrifice of Himself is acceptable to God, only infinitely more so, for they were all and only types and foreshadowings of Him. Such an offering was an offering of a sweet savour to God and for ever retains its virtue in His sight. To us, who by grace have believed on Him, He is also most precious.

This self-offering of Himself, made on Calvary on behalf of sinners, is perpetually preserved for our memories in His name Jesus. Other titles remind us of other qualities and offices which he has, but when we call him Jesus we are reminded that He saves us from our sins. This name, more than title which He bears, is fragrant as the Old Testament ointment or anointing oil which was poured on the heads of priests and kings. The name attracts us and moves us.

Jesus, the name that charms our fears
And bids our sorrows cease;
'Tis music in the sinner's ears,
'Tis life, and health, and peace.

But all Christ's names and titles combined are insufficient to interpret what is meant by "the name of the Lord". This great phrase means God's character as revealed by these names and all other means. The name of the Lord which is a strong tower in His unchanging character; His truth which never changes, His love which never dies. His holiness which never darkens, His mercy which endureth for ever—and these all combined. To such a God may we flee, on Him we may rest our whole weight of need both for time and eternity.

Jesus, I My Cross have Taken

Let us go forth . . . without the camp, bearing His reproach.—HEB. 13: 13.

"WITHOUT the camp"—there the lepers were sent to cry, unclean, unclean; and there the sacrifice for sin was burnt and the ashes poured out. Outside the city wall went our Lord Jesus Christ to His death for a world of sinners, and there He was offered up as a sacrifice for sin for ever on a place which has now become the pivotal place of history. "Without the camp" is a phrase which reminds us of the loneliness of Christ. He was separate from the sinners yet in the midst of them until at last they could bear His pure presence no longer and they cried "Away with Him, crucify Him."

Now the Christian's principal concern should be to be like His Lord, which means that we are to desire to be as close to sinners in their need as possible, but as separate from them in their sin. And this may mean for us a similar rejection, for our holiness should convince sinners of their sin. "Without the camp" meant for our Lord outside the religious camp of Israel in which He had been born and which, despite its corruption, was dear to Him. And many Christians who have sought to live only for Jesus have found that the enmity of Christendom can be more acute even than that of the world, because there can be religious sin as well as other forms, and there has often been religious persecution.

But while we are not to make ourselves martyrs we are to be loyal to our rejected and risen Lord. If we are reproached for His sake then we are privileged indeed, and instead of shrinking from the shame we are reminded that it is but the precursor of an unusual weight of glory. No cross, no crown.

We Shall be Brought Through

Thou art my hope in the day of evil.—JER. 17: 17.

TRIAL is the lot of all, for man that is born of woman is full of trouble; the Hill Difficulty certainly occurs in every Pilgrim's pathway and usually comes frequently. It is through much tribulation that we enter the Kingdom of God, and it is wise for us to realise this and to be prepared.

In the midst of our difficulties it is of the greatest comfort and help to know that we shall be brought through, our troubles will have an end. It is most demanding and challenging if we cannot be assured of a happy issue out of our affliction. The tunnel is dark and may be long but is made more bearable because we know it is leading us somewhere and that the daylight awaits us at the other end. In the meantime while we await the light let us reassure our hearts that God is too wise to err, too good to be unkind, and that this present trial is meant for our enrichment in the first place, and afterwards for the blessing of others whom we shall be able to comfort with the comfort we ourselves have received from God.

Then comes the morning, the day-break after the darkness and we shall sing aloud as we see in retrospect the mercies of the Lord in the very time of trial. We shall know then that our affliction was transient, but for a moment, and light, while the benefits of it are eternal and weighty. Weeping may lodge just for a night but joy comes for a longer stay when the sun shines again.

In the meantime let us trust and not be afraid, and do our best to sing, with Paul and Silas, at midnight.

God Giveth True Wisdom

If any . . . lack wisdom, let him ask of God . . . —JAMES 1: 5.

By nature we are ignorant and unwise; sin has affected both mind and heart and we are alienated from God's life and therefore from the knowledge of Him. This accounts for the fact that man, by searching, cannot find out God. The scientist may be moving, all the time, among the handiwork of God in creation but fails to see the Creator. By processes of logic we cannot lead one to Christ, though of all things faith in Him is the most logical. Man, left to his own resources, and though knowing many things, does not know God or behave wisely.

But when a soul is born again then he becomes the possessor of Christ, Who is made unto us wisdom from God. The reverent trust of the believer leads him to the source of wisdom and knowledge, and he knows what the scientist without God can never know. The entrance of God's truth makes even the simple and unprivileged to become wise, to understand God and man, and to know the power of God's redemption.

Thus it is expected in the New Testament that the Christian shall behave himself wisely and always act with understanding. Folly is unbecoming and often ignorance is inexcusable. So we are to walk in wisdom, our speech is to be always with grace, our manner of life is to be as becometh the Gospel. High ideals are placed before us because the Spirit of Christ dwells within us. Low ideals and low achievements are unworthy of such a Guest and Lord. When He was on earth gracious words proceeded out of His mouth, and may not gracious words proceed from ours if we commit our hearts and lips to Him?

The Fruits of His Dying

That we might be made the righteousness of God in Him.—2. COR. 5: 21.

THE purpose of Christ's dying was a great and worthy one. Had it been our forgiveness alone, the reinstating of sinners in the favour of God, the result would have been eternally worthwhile; but it was much more than that. Today we think of some of the fruits of His passion and death, which make the Son of God satisfied.

The first mentioned here is our being justified or made righteous in God's sight and this because we become partakers of the righteousness of God in Christ. He who took our sin imparts His righteousness. Next He has a people gathered out of the nations of the world who are to shew forth His praise both by their lips and in their lives; they who have received so much are to be both living advertisements and advertisers of the mercy and power of the Lord. And such is to be the result of God's grace in them, that the heavenly powers are to look down and see the many-coloured wisdom of God in His diverse people; while in the eternity which awaits us we shall still continue His praise.

But we are also to be those who are filled with His own Spirit, the Spirit by Whom Christ was incarnate, by Whom He lived and by Whose power He was enabled to die. Such a Spirit living in the hearts of God's people is to sanctify them, and keep them evermore extolling the virtues of Him Who died and rose again. These results bring joy to our Lord—but does He actually see them in us?

Thine Utterly and Only

Ye shall be holy unto Me.—Lev. 20: 26.

Fundamentally our holiness is our being set apart by God for His own possession and glory. Thus we are intentionally sanctified immediately we are justified and the blood of Jesus which saves us at one and the same time makes us a different and separated people. Our motto is to be "Holiness to the Lord" and this is to be applied to every part of life.

But there follows from this a process of practical sanctification. It is carried out by the Holy Spirit who uses the word of God. The intention is to make effectual the separation which was first effected; now we are to be not merely set apart for God but we are to be morally fitted for such a position. We are not only to be set apart by God but by ourselves also, and this means that we co-operate with God in His gracious work of making our lives more Godly, more like the Lord Jesus.

In this process there may well be times of real crisis. Often the pathway begins with a crisis, when recognizing the Lord's will for us, we accept His complete Lordship of life and hand ourselves over to Him as His willing bondslave. This is often a matter of real conflict, for it involves matters of daily and practical conduct as well as the ultimate issue of who is to determine our life and actions. But the Holy Spirit has been given to every Christian in order to make the will of God the good, acceptable and perfect thing that it is. So accepting the will and plan of the Lord for the whole of life as well as for the details of conduct, the Spirit is set free to work in us a holiness which is not only intentional but actual.

Lead Thou the Way, Thou Knowest Best

Thine ears shall hear a word behind thee saying—This is the way.—ISAIAH 30: 21.

IT is not always a lesson which is easily learned and it may need to be learned again and again, that the way God chooses for us is the very best way even if it should run counter to our personal wishes. But the Christian who has settled the matter in intention and purpose that life is to be directed by God has gone a long way towards a life of blessedness. Such a man or woman is one who fears the Lord and who is thus in the path of wisdom.

In order to guide us God will use His word. The Bible becomes alive, its messages become relevent to personal needs. It is not merely an account of how God spoke to Abraham but it is a medium through which He is now speaking to me. The Scriptures not only speak directly to the heart but they also shape the thought—life, which more and more becomes renewed and fitted for a life which pleases God; the spiritual man has the mind of Christ and in measure reacts towards situations and teaching as Christ, Who is indwelling, reacts. Because of this there is often an impulse within which corresponds to the Scriptures without, and the believer has a double light upon the path. Such a one needs not to be continually directed by circumstances and checked by events, he moves under the controlling signal which he finds in Christ His Lord.

In order to continue in the God-guided life, which is so blessed, it is necessary ever to remember that we must have a single eye, that is a pure motive to know and do the will of God, and to recognise that it is not in ourselves to guide our own life. Let us wholeheartedly commit our way to God and closely follow Him.

Precious, Precious Blood of Jesus

The blood of sprinkling.—HEB. 12: 24.

ALL through the Bible this scarlet thread runs linking the whole together. According to the Scriptures it is the blood of Christ not his life which makes atonement for our sins. By the term "the blood of Christ" we mean the life of Christ offered as a sacrifice for sin; and the term is not to be understood literally but as a graphic and simple way of reminding us that it was necessary for the Son of God to save us, and that He did this.

The blood of Christ is here described as "the blood of sprinkling". This reminds us of the Old Testament practice of killing the offering, catching the blood and then applying the blood to the person or the people. It is another way of saying "the blood which is applied", for it is one thing to know that Jesus Christ died for us but it is another to trust that sacrificial death and so to apply it to our needs. The blood which is applied to us is much superior to that of Abel's lamb because the blood of his sacrifice could never take away sin, but only serve as the basis of a trust which looked forward to a better sacrifice. Now we know the better Sacrifice Whose blood has removed our sin completely.

Relying wholly upon God's acceptance of the sacrifice of the life of His beloved Son we are accepted also. The full identification of Christ with the sinner's sin made its judgment possible when Christ died, and the full identification of the sinner with Christ when he trusts Him as a Saviour, makes it possible for him to have a righteous standing before God. Our hearts are thus sprinkled and we may draw near to God with a reverent boldness.

God's Way of Doing Things

Ask, and it shall be given you.—MATT. 7: 7.

GOD has ordained that prayer shall be the means of blessing. He might in His sovereignty have chosen to work otherwise but in His loving wisdom He has planned that His people should co-operate with Him in the fulfilment of His designs. This lifts the godly exercise of prayer on to a very high plane, and we may say concerning any unfulfilled purpose of God that He is looking to us to ask Him to do it. This means that there are some things which we do not yet see because we have not yet asked, and today we are encouraged to ask with the promise that it shall be given us.

Obviously there are things which God cannot or will not give to His children; the giving of such answers would not be good for us and others and would not be for the completing of the wise plans of our God and Father. Prayer is not the means by which wayward children may get all they want but the way by which the Sons of God may help prosper with eternal prosperity the best interests of the family of God. Within that wide sphere however prayer should be simple, sincere and expectant for God means His promises to be taken literally.

Today we are facing great problems in the world and in the Church; it may be that our own lives are themselves in desperate need. Let us then take today's message as God's answer to today's problems. The Father loves us; He has ordained that we should draw largely on His power and wisdom; one reason for our poverty is that we have failed to ask; the Lord is bending down to hear us ask. Let it not be true of us today that we have not because we ask not.

Stand Then in His Great Might

Resist the devil, and he will flee from you.—JAMES 4: 7.

WE have a strong and subtle foe whose purposes are dark and whose experience is vast. In league with him is a great host of fallen spirits and he uses as his tools both sinful man and the present world system. His methods are varied and changing; at one time he is openly attacking God's servants, at another he is subtly working in a Christian heart or assembly, sowing discord and division or leading believers away from the will of God. But behind all his cunning and his skill is his avowed enmity against God and against His Christ whose Lordship he refuses and Whose crown he seeks to wear.

It is necessary therefore that while we must not be always looking out for the enemy we must yet be well aware of his devices and be ready to stand against them. We need to know the Lord sufficiently well as to detect that which is against Him, and He has promised to make us quick to scent evil by filling us with His Spirit. We are to know, also, that Satan is a defeated foe and a usurper. It is not merely that he is to be defeated sometime, but already at the Cross his power has been broken and his claims on men cancelled for ever. We may therefore live, work and pray with the assurance that no one needs to be held captive by him.

Our attitude towards him is to be one of quiet strength. We are to resist him; we are to stand against his wiles. For this we must needs be clothed in a complete Christian armour and know how to use both sword and shield. But we fight one who is weaker far than our Captain and whose wisdom is far less. Let us therefore go forth with the assurance of victory and take spoil from this age-long foe of Christ.

Clean Vessels

Examine me, O Lord, and prove me.—PSALM 26: 2.

THERE is a place for self-examination in the true Christian life. While introspection may become an unhealthy practice yet we must from time to time consider our ways in the presence of the Lord. Especially are we enjoined to do so before we take the Lord's Supper, lest we eat and drink unworthily. The self-examination which is taught in Scripture is really the submitting of ourselves to examination by the Lord; it is conducted in His presence, and the testing is in the light of His word. Moreover we are reminded that if we so judge ourselves we shall not be judged of others.

Self-examination must concern the whole of our life. Our outward conduct is to be tried; we are to commend ourselves to every man's conscience in the sight of God. Our inward personal life is to be tested, for God looketh on the heart and desireth truth in the inward parts. Thorough and radical dealing with God in the secret place has been one of the secrets of the holy life of many of God's saints. No excuses for sin are allowed in God's pure presence and while all extenuating circumstances will be understood by God, we are to avoid exonerating ourselves. We must allow the truth of God to have full play upon our whole being.

Such searching of our hearts is to issue in a godly repentance, a turning from every known sin. This will not only mean avoiding evil which appears to others but the refusing to give place to such inward sins as jealousy, pride, bitterness. They are to be hated as much as the grosser sins of the flesh. Having so dealt with ourselves as God shall lead and help, let us draw near to Him with a true heart, and walk in the light as He is in the light.

Living with Jesus a New Life Divine

Reckon ye also yourselves to be dead . . . unto sin, but alive unto God.—ROMANS 6: 11.

ALIVE unto God! the three words are filled with glory. We were once dead in sin, alienated from the life of God, unable to bring forth any fruit in our lives but the fruit of sin and death. But now by the grace of God it is otherwise, we who were dead are alive—alive unto God.

This great miracle of regeneration came about by God sending His Son and by the Son giving His life for us. Then He caused the message of this great gift and deed to come to us in the Gospel and we were enabled to hear His word and believe on His Son; and life, eternal life, became ours. At the time we understood little but we did trust in Christ and God effected much. We were made alive unto God.

Thus the Christian life began, and its continuance and development depend upon our continually reckoning on these historic and experimental facts. We have passed from death unto life, we have been crucified with Christ, we do now today live unto God. That being so, life must be completely different from what it would otherwise have been. We are no longer to live unto ourselves, we are the Lord's, and must live for His glory, giving chief concern for His interests. We are to seek the things of heaven and eternity, rather than the things of time and sense. Ours is to be an other-worldly life, lived on a different principle from the life of the unconverted. We have died to much which the world counts valuable, we live for the things which it tends to despise. The sports meeting is displaced by the prayer-meeting, the ball for the open-air witness; how odd it all seems! The explanation is that with Christ we have died and risen again, and life must be changed.

Love So Amazing, So Divine

If God so loved us, we ought also to love one another.—1 JOHN 4: 11.

OUR salvation had its origin and fount in the deep, deep love of God; God so loved. It was He Who planned our redemption before ever the world was, or before ever the first man and woman sinned. It was He Who gave His Son to die with all that means as an expression of His love.

For an earthly father to give his son for some good cause is a great achievement, but God the Father giving God the Son is something of which the earthly and human is only a faint picture, for in the Blessed Unity of the Holy Trinity, the Father and the Son are one God. The Son bearing the sin of the world therefore, means some deep suffering in the very Godhead, a suffering which is beyond our understanding, being completely outside our experience.

Well might the sun in darkness hide when the awful, yet glorious act was enacted on Calvary's hill. It was during those hours, which at present remain veiled, that God in Christ reconciled the world to Himself, the Son becoming a Sin-offering, the Father laying upon Him the iniquity of us all. In this, not in His life of healing and preaching, but in this was manifested His love toward us.

Now we Christians who have been so loved, and come to know of it, are called upon to love one another. Any other attitude is condemned outright by the love of God shown on Calvary. It is impossible for us who have begun to appreciate and enjoy the Father's love to harbour grudges, jealousy and bitterness in our hearts. Whatever men may do to us, let us cultivate the divine enduement, the love of God shed abroad in our hearts by the Holy Spirit, as we love one another.

Consider the Fowls of the Air

Boast not thyself of tomorrow; for thou knowest not what a day may bring forth.—PROVERBS 27:1.

THERE is a deep and innate desire in man to be independent of others. In the case of the ungodly it also includes a desire to be independent of God, which is of the very essence of sin, and it was on this point that sin first reared its head. In the case of the Christian it is not always easy to determine where the attempt to reach a justifiable position of not being a burden to others when sickness or old age comes on, and the state described for us today which tempts one to say, Thou hast much goods laid up in store; eat, drink and be merry.

It is foolish however to feel that goods can ever be really secure especially in a world where riches may become an embarrassment, or most dangerous, or on the other hand disappear in the night. And boasting either in ourselves, our position or possessions, is of the essence of folly, when we are so frail and unable to foresee the future.

The best use of today is to be sure that we are right with God; that will ensure that we are spiritually safe both for time and eternity. After that the next concern is to do the will of God as it is known today, and do it well. We are each appointed to our varied spheres and God will be glorified and satisfied if just where He has put us we do heartily as unto Him the meanest task assigned.

The future, unknown to us, is all known to God, Who is our Heavenly Father. Simple trust in His love and promises, will bring rest of mind and heart, and anything which causes us to be either anxious or unbelieving is to be rejected as unworthy.

E'en let the unknown tomorrow
Bring with it what it may.

The Highest Love

The fruit of the Spirit is love.—GAL. 5: 22.

GOD is love. This profound statement in three words baffles the mind and yet comforts the heart. Is God love and something else? That is, is love one of many qualities in His nature, or are the other qualities expressions of this one fundamental, all-inclusive quality? This is just one of the problems which has puzzled thoughtful men and theologians during the centuries. However the fact remains that God is love.

But we must seek to be delivered from unworthy views of love. Our poor human love at its best can easily deteriorate into selfishness. A mother's self-giving love for her child can quickly and unconsciously become a self-seeking love. But the love of God is just a pure going out of His thought and care in seeking the very best for each one of us. His love is strong and not sentimental, hence He sometimes denies what we ask and appoints what we would evade. But He is working for our highest good and not merely for our present pleasure.

Such a loving God stopped short of nothing in saving us from our sins, even though it meant the sending of His Son, Whose down-stooping, incarnation, rejection and death must have cost God that which is beyond our knowledge. And such a love once appreciated can only beget love in us in return, and a love for Him which enables us to reckon ourselves as having died with Him to everything petty, selfish and sinful.

Moreover the New Testament everywhere lays upon us a special obligation, namely, that being so loved by God we should love one another. If God sought the very best for us even at the cost of giving His Son to death, then we must put the good of others before us as our highest responsibility and privilege. Our love to God is to be expressed in loving others whom He loves. We are to live our lives, loving others with a pure sacrificial love.

Suffering's Worthwhile Purpose

Blessed be the God . . . Who comforteth us in all our affliction.—2 COR. 1: 3, 4.

SUFFERING is the common experience of all men and the child of God is not exempt from it. Our minds accept the fact that we should not be spared what is part of the inevitable experience of our human family. It may be that certain forms of suffering become much more acute for the Christian, especially that which is concerned with the state of the world.

Suffering is of various kinds and on various levels. There is that which afflicts the body of which we are all aware and of which our hospitals are a sufficient demonstration, reminding Christians that we have this treasure in earthen vessels. Then there is mental suffering which can be much more painful in its various forms. There is the pain of cruel misunderstanding, anxiety for the welfare of unconverted loved ones, remorse over personal sins and a sharing in the grief of the sins of others. And is there not a spiritual suffering which touches the very depths?

But all this is permitted to come to us with a view to blessing. For ourselves it would be unhelpful if we always had a plain course, and for the sake of others it is most necessary we should learn to sympathise, which is only really possible when we ourselves have passed the same way. As we have shared the sufferings which come to us so we are made partakers of the consolations, and the two cannot be separated.

For our help in bearing the sufferings of the present, or in facing those of the future, let us remember that it is in love we are afflicted. The heat of the flame is mercifully and tenderly controlled by the hand of the Son of Man, Who was in all points tempted like as we are. Let us therefore, without hesitation or restriction, commit ourselves to God our Father, Whose purposes for us and others are infinitely wise and good.

Guide Me, O Thou Great Jehovah

I will guide thee with mine Eye.—PSALM 32: 8.

IT is not in man that walketh to direct his steps; his knowledge is limited, his wisdom is inadequate. We do not know the future, nor the effect of our actions and decisions upon others. Our human nature is all too likely to make choices which are in some way selfish, so that it is unwise to trust our own hearts. The only safe way, and it is safe, is to trust in the Lord wholly. He cannot fail us if we refuse to choose our own way. Choices we must make, decisions we must take, but they must be made and taken with a sincere desire not to do our own will but the will of Him Who has saved us. This means that in all our ways, in every department and crisis of life, we should acknowledge His right to direct us. This is the pathway of safety and blessing.

For God has promised to guide all such, teaching them what His will is, guiding them in a personal and intimate way. Those who are concerned only to do God's will do not need to be continually restrained as does the horse; they are gently led as a child and are spared the many sorrows of the self-willed and self-directed. When in perplexity the message comes to them from God, through some appointed channel to shew them the right path and in that way the Lord Himself is a constant companion.

The choice is simple but clear. Do we wish to take our own way and walk alone or to live in God's plan and enjoy His company? In the first instance we shall find there are many sorrows of our own choosing; in the latter our sorrows will be only a share of the afflictions of Christ as He suffers still with His church and grieves still over sinning men; but it means deep fellowship with Him.

Lift Up Your Hearts

Set your affection on things above, not on things on the earth.—COL. 3: 2.

LIKE David our hearts all too often cleave to the dust. We become unduly occupied with the things of earth and of this life, at the expense of the interests of the world to come. Our affections too easily become taken up with houses, which are insecure, and with goods which corrupt. Houses and goods are in themselves right but not when they claim our affections and fill our hearts.

We need therefore continually to lift up our hearts. This calls for deliberate and purposeful acts, and it is good that we are often reminded to do this. The more often we lift up our hearts and set them on the Lord in glory, the more habitual it will become, and in due course we shall possess a heavenly-mindedness which leaves its stamp on all our conduct. Where our treasure is there our heart is also, and we are weaned from the treasures and pleasures of this sinful world.

So the Christian is called to a life of faith, that is, one which is determined and directed by the reality of unseen things. Heaven becomes more real than earth; eternity more certain than time, and our lives are therefore affected both as to our choices and our bearing. Losses of earthly things begin to count little and affliction is borne more easily, because we are confident that we have untold wealth in Christ and our temporary sorrows are only being made to work out for our eternal enrichment. Beyond this passing scene we have enduring foundations whose architect and builder is God. This place is prepared and reserved for us, and we are being prepared and reserved for it. Lift up your hearts, we lift them up to the Lord.

Weighed Down and Lifted Up

Unto Thee I lift up mine eyes, O thou that dwellest in the heavens.—PSALM 123: 1.

It is perhaps more common as life advances than in youth to feel the burdens of life; things press us down. There is ill-health which is so wearing; the matter of support of ourselves or others is a matter for constant consideration; the competition of life becomes keen or the pace of living too much, and life loses its joy. Or there may be spiritual problems, personal failure or concern for others, and a battle against Satan seeking to depress and discourage. O Lord, I am oppressed, may summarise the experiences of many days. Now, what is to be done?

The Bible remedy is to look away to Jesus and ask Him to undertake. We are to look as Eastern servants looked; their whole life being taken up by giving their attention wholly to their masters. We are to look up definitely and make known our desperate need directly, Hear my cry, O God, attend unto my prayer. And we are to remember for ourselves, and to remind God, that He has heard others and ourselves before. This godly exercise puts our hearts and minds in the right direction, turning them away from ourselves and our circumstances to God above, to God Who cares.

And is it not full comfort to remember that He Who sits on the throne of Heaven has Himself suffered being tempted, sat weary at the well, had nowhere to lay His head, and been despised and rejected of men. We have an High Priest Who is fully acquainted with our human weakness and infirmities and He is engaged to minister grace to us for our time of need. He, when He was oppressed, committed His soul to His Father Who judges righteously, now He asks us to do the same. Just now let us bring our burdens to our understanding Lord, He will carry them.

Guided and Protected

He preserveth the way of His saints.—PROVERBS 2: 8.

OUR way is preserved as well as our goal; every stage is marked and protected as we journey on to the Celestial City for our Lord has gone before us to ensure that all is well, then He accompanies us lest we should miss the appointed path. The path is lit up by night and overshadowed by day because our safety and blessing are bound up with our being in the way.

Then God has made sure that we are kept travelling. There is a great danger lest we settle down, we are all too prone to this and especially as life advances and changes become less welcome. An eagle refuses to leave the eaglets in the comfort of the nest because she knows that each must learn to fly, so she stirs them up and puts them through the same disturbing discipline she herself went through, with the result that the young exchange the nest for the open sky and the high altitudes. Are we settled down as pilgrims or are we travelling, making progress in the heavenly life. We are sure to stumble sometimes in the pathway, but the Lord of pilgrims has promised to lift us up. It is bad to fall but it is worse to remain fallen; for us who trust and obey, however, we are promised not to be utterly and hopelessly cast down. For the Lord knows how to help us both in our battle against ourselves and our foes.

For our complete assurance and comfort God has said that not only will He bring us through but that every incident on the journey will make its contribution to our eternal enrichment. So that we need not be anxious or fearful, even when the way is hardest. What can trouble us when God, the Almighty God, is ours.

We Are One for Ever

As the bridegroom rejoiceth over the bride, so shall thy God rejoice over thee.—ISAIAH 62: 5.

As Christians we are brought by grace into a most privileged and wonderful relationship with God. As sinners we were under judgment and shut off from God but now in Christ Jesus we are made nigh. Even that, however, does not represent our intimacy for we are now one spirit with the Spirit of God, and He fills our spirits and unites us to the Father and Son as a wife is made one with her husband. This is a grace indeed of which a king marrying a beggar would only be the faintest picture.

This deep fellowship and eternal relationship are meant not only to move the heart and mind in adoration but also to affect the whole life and service. The bride of the Lord cannot live as she once did, she must be queenly in all her ways, and bring credit to the throne—and so must every individual Christian who forms one of the vast number which together constitutes the bride of the Lamb. As royalty, therefore, we are to be glad. We must put off the spirit of heaviness, as unbecoming to our rank, and put on the royal robe of praise.

From this exalted position none can drag us down, though we may fail to enjoy our office. From the Father's heart none can separate or pluck us from His hand. Righteousness has united us to Him since Christ has died and borne our sins; judgment has made us His since all its force has fallen on the One Who took it in our place; loving kindness has joined us to the Lord since He has pitied us and lifted us out of the pit; mercies have made us one with the Lord for ever for God has worked in us by His Spirit a true repentance unto life and a living faith in the Son of God.

"I am His, and He is mine; For ever and for ever."

Ransomed, Healed, Restored, Forgiven

Who is a God like unto Thee, that pardoneth iniquity?—MICAH. 7: 18.

WE have become so used to the thought of God's pardon that the cost and wonder of it tend to be forgotten. That God Whom we have so offended in thought, word and deed should forgive us at all is wonderful, especially when we remember His moral government of His creatures and that He must, in forgiving us, satisfy the whole creation that He has not lightly passed over our rebellious attitude and acts. But by the substitution of His Son, or shall we not say Himself, to bear the due punishment of our sins, God can now be just and yet the justifier of Him that believeth in Jesus.

That Thou shouldest love a wretch like me,
And be the God Thou art;
Is darkness to my intellect,
But sunshine to my heart.

And God has not only forgiven us but does it with a generosity which is so attractive and exalting that we can only worship and adore Him. He delighteth in mercy, with great mercies He recovers us, with ever-lasting kindness does He pity and pardon us; and when He forgives it is with completeness and finality, "I will remember their sin no more".

Happy indeed are we whose wilfulness is pardoned and whose sin is removed. Happy indeed are we to whom guilt is no longer charged. We are forgiven for Christ's sake, we are reinstated in the favour of an offended God, nay more, we are adopted into His family and graced as His sons. Our hearts should indeed be singing, for the Lord hath done great things for us whereof we are glad. Our sins are behind His back but not behind ours, if we are looking unto Him; He forgets them, but the remembrance of them by ourselves is very salutary, both keeping us from pride and helping us to be truly understanding with those who are still under God's judgment.

All Things Come of Thee, O Lord

The living God giveth us richly all things to enjoy.—1 TIM. 6: 17.

CONSIDER how wonderful is the Giver of all good gifts; He is the living God, the Lord thy God. As the living God He is not only the Creator of all things visible and invisible, but also the Sustainer and Supplier of all life. He is actively operating in every sphere of life in all realms and worlds; there is nothing static or inadequate about Him.

Then consider the manner of the giving. They are given with such grace and freedom; He giveth richly, freely and generously. There is no meanness in God's giving. He that spared not His own Son will certainly not be restricted and niggardly after that: though we must remember He is too wise and loving to give us that which is harmful and which would tend towards pride, indulgence and worldliness.

And the gifts. These are so varied that no phase of our intricate life is neglected. We often say grace before meals, ought we not also to do so before reading a good book, when seeing a beautiful view, when privileged to enjoy an hour of relaxation; these are all His gifts. And should we not oftener remember His good gifts of health, loved ones, homes, friends; all these are included in the all things richly to enjoy.

The purpose of His giving to us so freely is that on our part as His children we may enjoy them, and then acknowledging Him as the bounteous Giver, praise Him and be careful to give Him all the glory. How many, even of God's children, have assumed too easily, in days of success and plenty, that it was their business skill or foresight which brought such large results.

Should one read these lines who is in need, let him now remember God the Giver of all good gifts, and ask Him simply to meet the need.

Why Should I Be Anxious?

My God shall supply all your need, according to His riches in glory . . . —PHIL. 4: 19.

THE heart of man is easily anxious about the future. It is all unknown and so unpredictable. A hundred unforeseen eventualities may occur, so that we can never be sure of supplies, even with the more careful assessment and provision. Wealth may disappear in a night, a country may change governments or lose its identity, or health may go and leave us helpless dependents. Against such possibilities men take many precautions but the Christian's all-inclusive guarantee for time and eternity is the character and promise of God. We are His for ever.

In the first place the Lord has provided against the more serious thing which could befall us, namely, our coming into judgment. This He has done by providing a Sacrifice for sin in the person of His Son. This guarantees every other spiritual supply and is the promise of God's willingness and ability to save us from sin's power as well as its guilt.

Then God has promised to save us from the hand of our enemies. His eye is everywhere to search out those who would do us harm. They are His enemies if they are ours and He will take care of them. Happy shall we be if we rely confidently on His protection.

His promises cover all the varied and possible needs of our future. "My God shall supply all your need" is an inclusive word which will be variously interpreted in different lives and at different times. But there it stands as a divine insurance against every adverse and threatening experience in the future. Because of such promises made by such a God, we can rest and be quiet from fear of evil. Nay more, we can go out into the days singing.

Why should I charge my soul with care
  The wealth in every mine
Belongs to Christ, God's Son and Heir,
  And He's a Friend of mine.

Blessed and Made a Blessing

Thou, Lord, wilt bless the righteous.—PSALM 5: 12.

THE blessing of the Lord is all of things most to be desired. With it we are made truly rich, without it we are poor whatever our possessions. With God's blessing upon our lives we move amongst men as dispensers of His mercies, without it we contribute little of value to a world in need.

The Lord's blessing is His favour enriching our life. It is like the continual supply of oil to the bearings of a machine, the continual stream of water through an otherwise arid tract of land. By such favour we are safeguarded in our walk, being kept from the evil that surrounds us, and the temptations which abound. But more than a deliverance from evil the Lord in blessing makes us the means of a positive life of goodness and holiness. In His favour is life and by the daily renewing of His Spirit there is life more abundant. We are both kept and blessed.

The Bible puts before us, and we have examples in the portions for today, both promises of blessing and prayers for blessing. In other words God, from His side, makes overtures to us and proffers His blessing; while we on our side are provided with prayers which we may bring and so respond to the divine initiative and promise. The Lord shall deliver and preserve me; "Holy Father keep through Thine own name". So we may be bound to the Father in a life of daily blessing by both promise and prayer, and blessed ourselves become a blessing to others, as Abraham was in his day and way. For no life is blessed by God but the blessing overflows to others. Let us wait upon Him not only that He may give us things, but that He might enrich our lives and endue us His servants with His heavenly grace.

Enlightened and Rejoicing

The brightness of His glory and the express image of his person.—HEBREWS 1: 3.

THE modern view that the Bible is a story of the historic process of man's discovery of God is fundamentally wrong and has produced much evil. Rather is it that the Holy Scriptures give us the record of an increasing revealing of Himself which God has given to His people. This revelation has been gentle and progressive as man was able to bear it, but it is a revelation and the activity has been on the part of God.

The full revealing of the Godhead has finally come to us in Jesus Christ. The only begotten Son of God was with the Father in eternity, but came forth to be born of a virgin, to assume our nature, and to disclose the character of God expressed in a human body, in human words and in the circumstances of ordinary human life. To know Christ, that is to appreciate Who He really is in the unity of His two natures, and in the finality of His atoning work, is to be illuminated with light from heaven. Whether the light comes in a blinding flash, or in a gradual dawn and development, the light is from God and is given by Him.

It is the increasing knowledge of God, enlightening the mind and sanctifying the soul of man, which is so much needed and so earnestly sought and promised in the passages today. Happy indeed, and certain to be a blessing to others is the man on whom this light of knowledge shines. It makes for true happiness and deep peace for we understand God's character and ways and are satisfied with His atonement for sin. The strong and cheerful Christians are they who know their God, and of such we have far too few. So, be of good cheer, for the Lord has not only revealed Himself in Christ, but by His Word and Spirit is revealing Himself to you today.

There is a Way Back to God

. . . We have an Advocate with the Father, Jesus Christ the righteous.—1 JOHN 2: 1.

THERE is one God, that is, there is only one true and living God. There are many false gods; some are reared in heathen temples, others in heathen homes, but most are set up in human hearts, whether heathen, atheistic or Christian. For, alas, it is possible for a worshipper of the true God to have gods of money, pleasure, power, etc. Let us allow this simple statement, "There is one God", to search us.

There is one Mediator Who said, He that hath seen Me hath seen the Father, and, "No man cometh unto the Father but by Me". Christ Himself and Christians after Him teach an open way to the Holy God for sinful man, but it is an exclusive way only through Christ. There is no place left for a second mediator or for a compound of other religions. The One Mediator, Jesus Christ hath fully accomplished what was needed, namely, an atonement which made possible a relationship of love and peace between the offended but pitying God and fallen, sinful man. Now He lives at the right hand of God to intercede and bless.

This only Mediator, seeing He was to mediate between God and man, being God also became man. So as to understand to the full the needs of both. Retaining His deity He assumed and retains our humanity and so is the unique God-man. He it is Who has brought us near to God, and is now able to mediate to us the ministry of His indwelling Spirit all the fullness of God, seeing He is risen from the dead and ever lives to make His salvation actual and vital in the life of His people. We looked to Him to save us when we first believed; shall we not look to Him to save us from all sins today seeing He ever liveth to make intercession for us?

The Beauty of the Lord Upon Us

Adorn the doctrine of God . . . in all things.—TITUS 2: 10.

THERE is revealed truth concerning our Lord Jesus Christ which is the saving faith. It teaches us that He is God and Man; that He was born of a virgin and sinless; that He died in our place, and rose again. These, and it may be certain other truths, constitute the doctrine of God our Saviour. To them we hold, and for them if necessary we must contend, for they are dear and must be preserved.

But we are not only to believe these truths once for all delivered to the saints, we are to adorn them; we are to so live by them that our lives commend them. Others are to see that such saving truths actually produce Christian character and make the men and women who believe them like the Saviour of Whom they speak. It may be that we who long that others should believe the Gospel, have estranged them from it by our unChristlike, uncharitable conduct. So our whole manner of life is to be in keeping with the Gospel.

We must avoid things which, though right in themselves, may give the appearance of being wrong. There are things which others may do which we who profess faith in Christ cannot. Our ambition must be to live blamelessly in this critical age, so that the Light of the World Who dwells in us may shine forth through a clean lamp.

This will call for care and discipline. We must even beware lest we abuse our Christian liberty. Paul, who, more than any other New Testament writer, boasted in our blood-bought freedom, put himself under all kinds of restrictions that he might win men. We are Christ's representatives and witnesses, it behoves us therefore to remember our high and responsible position and to seek daily grace that we may daily shew forth the excellencies of Him Who has called us out of darkness into light.

The Way the Master Went

The Captain of their salvation made perfect through sufferings.—HEBREWS 2: 10.

IT appears at first sight that our Lord Jesus Christ needed nothing to perfect Him; was He not true God and perfect Man? He was indeed, but it was in the counsels of eternity that He should become more, namely, Saviour and High Priest.

As Saviour He must needs suffer for sin, the Just for the unjust, that He might bring us to God. This was suffering indeed and we are reminded today that the sufferings which hurt and atoned were not the physical sufferings merely but the agony of His soul when He gave Himself to be made a sin-offering for us and to be forsaken of God for our sakes. See Him in the garden; what is this cup which is so bitter? It is the cup of God's hatred against sin, against the sin of human hearts with whom He was now identified and for whom He was to become a substitute. Being in agony He prayed . . . and His sweat was like great drops of blood. Reproach broke His heart but it was not the taunts and reproaches of men, difficult to bear as they were; it was the reproach which came upon One Who was standing in the place of rebels and bearing their guilt and punishment at the hands of a holy and offended God, Who was also His Father. Oh mystery of mysteries!

> In vain the first-born seraph tries
> To sound the depths of love divine.

But He was also perfected through suffering to become a sympathetic High Priest. He must needs suffer in every way, on every plane, before He could minister true comfort and strength to His needy people. Is it not a comforting thought that when we are suffering either in mind, body or spirit we know that He understands and is fitted to help? So today, on the throne of heaven, there is One Who has died for our sins to become our Saviour, and Who suffered that He might also sympathise in our sorrows. Jesus understands.

Time is Passing but God Remains

The world passeth away and the lust thereof.—1 JOHN 2: 17.

HUMAN life is brief at the longest. Generations come and go; and while each one thinks it is the most important it soon passes away and is forgotten. A few individuals leave their mark on history and their names are remembered for good or evil, but most are soon forgotten and in due course even their tombs and epitaphs crumble. Life is like a cloud of steam, swifter than a courier or even a bird in flight. Man is like grass or a flower and there is every reason why we should walk humbly and not be proud and boastful. The Caesars, Napoleon and others are gone and now stand stripped of human glory in the presence of God their Judge.

We therefore should pray with the Psalmist that God would teach us to number our days that we apply our hearts unto wisdom. If human life is brief and is the prelude to eternity, if our eternal destiny is fixed by our decisions and conduct here, then we should treat this time of probation as one of serious purpose and not fritter away our life in aimless pursuits. Wealth will soon disappear, how foolish to give ourselves to its accumulation. Honour will soon drop away, how unwise to make that our chief concern. But the doing of God's will means that our life here is related to eternity rather than to time and therefore it takes upon itself a more permanent aspect. When our call comes we shall see a change of scenery rather than of company for even down here we have walked with God.

Change and decay in all around we see, but there is One Who changes not. His years have no end, that means He never grows older because He is the Eternal. If in Him we have put our trust, if to Him we have committed our souls as our Saviour, then time and eternity need bring us no anxiety; we are safe in the arms of Jesus.

Lord Jesus are We One with Thee?

Not redeemed with corruptible things . . . but with the precious blood of Christ.—1 PET. 1: 18, 19.

WHEN the Israelite of old laid his hand upon the head of the Sacrifice it was symbolic of his complete identification with the victim. The animal to die was to die in his stead and therefore for his sins; if therefore the animal was accepted so was he. Now that Christ has died on Calvary, having offered one sacrifice for sins for ever, all we need to do is to identify ourselves with Him; this means that we trust Him as our sinbearer and so doing we are accepted as He was accepted. We are saved by His death, redeemed by His blood. Grace on God's part united us with Christ in His death nineteen hundred years ago, faith on our part links us with Him now and makes the sacrifice efficacious on our behalf. Let any in doubt say now,

My faith would lay her hand,
On that meek head of Thine,
While as a penitent I stand
And here confess my sin.

That death has, however, not only made possible our pardon by the transfer of our sins, but has also made necessary the transfer of our sovereignty. Hence Christ must surely be our Master as well as our Saviour. We are called to commit ourselves, Spirit, Soul and body, to God by Jesus Christ. Because we are in Christ we are committed to God as He was; this is but our logical response and offering.

To all who respond to Christ's self-giving for us by giving themselves wholly to Him, He has promised to keep. He is able to keep us from falling, and though on account of our weakness we may stumble, God in grace will lift us up again. He is strong and trustworthy; let us give ourselves to Him without reserve and serve Him in holiness and righteousness all our days.

Looking Upward, Pressing Onward

O Lord, I am oppressed: undertake for me.—ISAIAH 38: 14.

THERE are times in the lives of God's children when all is black, the way is dark, the soul feels to be sinking. No promise is made that we shall be immune from such experiences. What is promised is that we need not bring them about by our own folly; but our common inheritance and relationship with our fellow-beings ensures that we shall pass through such seasons; and indeed it would appear necessary that we should, both for our own sanctification and training as well as that we may be able to sympathise with others. So if not now, it will be sooner or later, our soul will be vexed, our heart sore pained, and our spirits overwhelmed.

The Bible records what men of old did in such trials; they looked upward. Instead of regarding the waves they looked away to the stars which were set to guide and light their darkness. A look, a fixed gaze upon the Lord of darkness and the storm, that is the Bible way of deliverance. And we may need to look for a long time, to look steadfastly; but in answer to our appeal and expectation the Lord will come for our deliverance. Faith will not be tried beyond its strength.

To those who look for Him Jesus Christ will appear one day a second time for our full salvation. It may be at morn when the day is awaking, it may be in the evening when the shadows are deepening, or again in the dead of night or heat of day; but one day He will come again to receive from the world His own. O Lord Jesus, how long? The appearing will be glorious; it will finish His work in us, and He will bring us home to glory and we who may be living then will go there without dying. Blessed hope for a pilgrim church and for tried believers. Let us lift up our hearts, our redemption is nigh. Is our deep interest in the world fixed horizontally, or is it upward?

Christ Jesus Lives Today

God, having raised up His Son Jesus, sent him to bless you.—ACTS 3: 26.

IT is not only true that Jesus Christ rose again on the third day but that He is alive for evermore and lives today to save His people from their sins. His resurrection is not only a fact of history and a fundamental truth of the Christian faith but, like all doctrine, has a very real practical effect and experimental application.

Jesus Christ is risen indeed, and He is now imparting His resurrection life to all who are His, but only in the measure in which they abide in, or live in communion with Him. The life of the vine pours into the branch which is one with it; in the same way the Christian lives his life because Christ liveth in him by the Spirit. We are therefore not only called to be holy, but are holy, and become increasingly holy as we abide in Christ. It is here that evangelical Christianity demonstrates its distinctive features, namely, that holiness is not achieved as taught by Roman Catholics, by the repression of every natural instinct but by a life of faith, that is, of receiving and relying. True there must be a discipline of one's life but that is the negative side of holiness and it is the positive believing of the promises and the expectation that the Spirit of Grace will work in us, which makes it possible for the Spirit of life in Christ Jesus to form Christ in our life and reveal Him, though He is in heaven, in our mortal bodies.

In such a relationship of life, the Christian on earth made one with the Christ in glory and the union maintained by the Holy Spirit Who proceedeth from the Father and the Son, we may reverently look to Christ to make us like Himself, and to minister to us of His fullness, grace upon grace, and grace upon grace. Let us cultivate the attitude of being good believers and good receivers.

Thy Word is a Lamp unto My Feet

The entrance of thy words giveth light.—PSALM 119: 130.

GOD is light for He is the fount both of truth and knowledge. There is no darkness in Him for there is no lack of knowledge and no phase of truth is absent or deficient in the being of God. This perfection means that the light is undimmed and is indeed "the burning bliss".

Our true conversion comes when the light of God shines into our darkness and gives the light of the knowledge of God in the person of Jesus Christ. Then darkness gives place to light and we become children of light. The dawning may be gradual or sudden but however it comes it is due to the mercy of God and is an utterly transforming experience; we pass from darkness to light.

Afterwards we are called to walk in the light, that is to welcome from God all knowledge and truth concerning Himself and concerning ourselves. This means that when His truth shews us our error we accept the truth, when His light reveals our darkness we renounce the darkness. On this principle the Christian walks in the light as God is in the light and there is fellowship between God and His child.

The light, or the truth, generally comes to us from God's Word, hence the importance of a daily, prayerful reading of the Scripture. The Bible is God's instrument for correcting our ways, stimulating and guiding our consciences, so that we need not only to look at it with our eyes in some hurried reading, but also to commit it to our memories, to meditate upon it in our hearts, to receive it into our hearts. The entrance of God's Word is like the shining of the light into our minds and hearts. If we are obedient to it we shall be cleansed and kept clean as we pass through a dark world and live in the midst of a sinful generation.

Be Prepared for Every Attack

Be ye therefore sober, and watch unto prayer.—1 PETER 4: 7.

EVERYWHERE through the Bible there is the same call to watchfulness. The Christian is a pilgrim passing through enemy country, and, as dangers lurk along the way, he is to be watchful lest his feet be taken in a net or some foe openly attack him. Or he is a soldier in the King's army and his foes are everywhere and all the time waiting to attack when he is least ready to fight.

Principalities and powers
Mustering their unseen array;
Wait for thy unguarded hours
Watch and pray.

Those who returned to Jerusalem and built the walls of Jerusalem followed the advice, so that with one hand they built while the other handled the sword. This reminds us that whatever we may be doing, we must be prepared for attack, either open or subtle, and watch.

But we are not left alone in the pilgrimage or the battle. By our side always, in fair weather and foul, is the Lord. To Isaiah he is the Lord our God, but to us His name is the Lord Jesus, for He has now come down from His high dwelling in heaven and for thirty years and more has lived in the very land through which the pilgrim's journey lies, and He has fought the same battles as we now fight and, thank God, wounded to death the foe who is the arch-enemy of all the King's friends and followers. He is with us to-day holding our right hand. With such exalted and powerful company, let us step out into to-day, determined not to be careless but to watch and pray.

Danger and Deliverance

Lot . . . beheld all the plain of Jordan, that it was well watered . . . —GENESIS 13: 10.

TO-DAY we have given to us a solemn word of warning. A righteous man became covetous and ambitious; so his vision of God and eternity became dimmed and he set out upon the slippery path of seeking wealth and honour. The seed of all that followed was in his heart before he took one step towards the cities and pasturage of the plain; the lifted eyes, the straining gaze, the ultimate decision were all the result of a heart which could not or did not trust God to give the best to those who leave the choice to Him. So Abraham and Lot parted because their spirits were different. One looked for a city whose builder and maker was God; the other looked for a city whose principles were otherwise. Now all this is written for us also upon whom the end of the ages are come. Many a Christian, full of promise and zealous for God, has followed Lot's course because he first of all had Lot's ambitions. Let us remember where it led Lot; for it was not only to the pasturage of the plain but to the patronage of its cities with their sin. It may have been that Lot thought to improve the city and its society as it has been often thought in recent days, but let every man who thinks to join a worldly society remember Lot. And let him also remember Lot's wife who failed even more miserably than he did.

But there is mercy in the Bible account of this man who made mistakes. God calls him just Lot . . . a righteous man, who was vexed with the unclean life of Sodom. And not only so but in mercy God called him out of the wicked city before it was too late. Let every Christian whose conscience is troubled about his association with a worldly society and who has made the same mistake as Lot also make the same final choice and escape, refusing to tarry longer. There is mercy and blessing still in store.

Only Thou Art Holy, There is None Beside Thee Perfect

Holy, holy, holy, Lord God Almighty.—REVELATION 4: 8.

IF there is one failure more serious than another in the Church to-day it is the failure to preach and to worship the true and living God. By that is meant that the God Whom we worship is not the God of the Bible, but One Who is so loving as to be indulgent and so weak as to require all kinds of human inventions and activities to carry on His work of calling out a church for His Son.

To-day we have a timely reminder of the holy character of God. He is One before Whom the sinless seraphim veil their faces, and in Whose sight the heavens are unclean; before Him Moses shrinks and takes off his shoes. Isaiah cries out "Woe is me for I am a man of unclean lips," and both Daniel and John fall down as dead. This is largely forgotten to-day and we enter and leave the place of worship and prayer with chatter; we draw near to God without due preparation of spirit; we have ceased to hold Him in awe and tremble in His presence.

The result of this has been a growing laxity of conduct and a lowering of moral standards both in the Church and the world. Christians practise to-day what would have been regarded with shame years ago; while in our domestic and national life the growth of sin of every kind makes one shudder if God be holy.

There is no cure for our declining morals or our lowered ethical standards but a fresh realisation of the holiness of the God with Whom we have to do. If we bear His name then we ourselves must be holy, there can be no escape from such an obligation. But whether we profess faith in God or not, He is still the Holy, Holy, Holy, Lord God Almighty and before Him we must one day stand—indeed before Him we stand to-day.

Faith is a Living Power from Heaven

Abram believed in the Lord.—GENESIS 15: 6.

THE Christian lives by faith. He begins his Christian life by trusting and continues it all the way through on the same simple principle. Of this we are reminded to-day and Abraham is set before us as an example.

The precise subject on which the promise, which was to afford Abraham his opportunity of exercising faith, was that of a son being given to Sarah and himself in their old age. Whether or not there was a long struggle in Abraham's heart or not we do not know, but ultimately, and apparently quickly, he believed the Lord. Abraham had learned the lesson that God is not only able to fulfil His promises but that He is righteous in so doing, and the reliance on God's character and word was reckoned to Abraham for righteousness; he was justified by faith. Now our Christian life begins in the same way; we hear the Gospel of God concerning His Son and the promise that if we receive the Saviour we shall be saved. When we truly believe this promise and commit ourselves to Christ for salvation, we too are justified by faith. To many of us, the day when we were enabled to trust in this way is well-defined and a memorable day indeed.

But the justified continue to live on the same principle, that of resting on and claiming the promises of God. He has committed Himself to caring for all our needs and carrying us through all our temptations, and we are called upon to believe that He is just as faithful in keeping the other promises as the one on which we first relied when we were converted. God Who made the promises is faithful to them and to us as we claim them, let us then take the words of Scripture as they are severally applied to us, and let us tell the Lord with all humility and boldness that we are counting on His fulfilling all He has promised. The Lord loves to be held to His word, and it is by so doing that through faith we obtain the promises and become strong.

His Presence is Salvation

I will never leave thee, nor forsake thee.—HEBREWS 13: 5.

OTHER helpers fail and comforts flee, well-known and well-tried friends are taken up in other friendships or pass away. So that no human friendship is in itself sufficient and satisfying but there is One Who never disappoints and it is about His unchanging love and never-failing presence that we are reminded today.

Let us note how absolute and all-inclusive His promises are. The Lord undertakes to be with us in all places where we go, and unto the end of the world. This means that there is no time or situation within our life and experience which is not covered by His promise and guarded by His presence. Whatever difficulty we are in today, therefore, we are in it with Him Who does not leave us comfortless or without peace; so that we may confess now in this present situation, The Lord is with me, His peace is my present experience.

Some, who read this page, may be passing through a bitter trial as was Paul in his last imprisonment; some Christian brother or sister may have failed us just when we needed them and just as Demas failed Paul; we may be left almost to bear our burden alone; nevertheless the Lord—yes, that is always the case—nevertheless, whoever may fail us, the Lord stands by and strengthens us.

God's unchanging presence has been proved by millions of God's people in all generations, but we may face the present trouble or the future loneliness not alone on the experiences of the past, but on God's own pledged word, "I will never leave thee nor forsake thee." It is God Who commits Himself to us in such words and because He is God and is unchangeable and reliable, we may boldly say, I will not fear what man can do unto me. What men do to us is strictly limited but God's presence is unlimited and is guaranteed to us all the days and all the way.

Faithful Stewards of Manifold Grace

As every man hath received the gift, even so minister the same . . . —1 PETER 4: 10.

WE are committed to Christ to be His faithful followers and soldiers unto our life's end. From our first act of faith, from our first entering into covenant with Him we have been accepted and regarded as His servants in a loyalty of service which has no reserves or regrets.

To each of His servants the Lord Jesus Christ gives gifts. To some, gifts which are to be exercised in a public ministry of service but to most gifts, which fit them for the hidden life of helping others. To each of us some gift has been given, and such a gift has been chosen with infinite love and care. The ministry is suited to us, for the One Who made us has also appointed us. The ministry is also fitted in to the whole complex service of the Church of God on earth. It is not therefore left to us to choose our work or sphere; it will not do for one called to public office to choose private service, or vice versa. Each is to be in his own appointed place discharging faithfully the appointed duty.

With the calling and the gift of the Lord comes the accompanying responsibility; if much is given much will be required, if less is given less will be required. But every appointment and bestowal is meant for the profit of all and any failure not only disappoints God but others also and the whole testimony of God's people is inevitably affected. It is therefore necessary for us to ask ourselves today, whether or not we are really doing that to which God called us and for which He fitted us. The way may be hard, but if we know we are in the place of His choice then most certainly our hearts will be kept in peace. If on the other hand we are disobeying what we know to be the will of God then let us acknowledge the fact immediately and confess our sin of disobedience. Where there is true penitence and a hearty desire to do the will of God, then God will see to it that we are led into His plans, or if already in them, that we are kept in the same. In His will there is peace.

Workman of God, O Lose not Heart

To him that soweth righteousness shall be a sure reward.—PROVERBS 11: 18.

APART from those great occasions of revival when God sweeps multitudes into the Kingdom, most servants of God know what it is to labour on without much evidence of blessing and with few evident results. This is the case of both minister, Sunday School teacher, or Bible class leader. The weeks come and go demanding prayer and preparation which is regular if not routine; and while sometimes the heart glows both in musing beforehand or in sharing eternal truth with others in the service, yet there is not much to show.

Now such appearances tend to discourage but there are two corrections to such a tendency which ought to be noted. The first is that sowing the seed of truth is a work calling for patience and plodding, but if the seed be the word and truth of God then it must bear fruit. So let our confidence in the living character of the seed be undiminished. The other correction is that which is brought before us in these passages today, namely, God's promise of a sure reward. He is not unrighteous to forget our labour of love and will give a corresponding compensation. He has not called us to a service without first planning to use it. He has deeper interest in our congregation or class than we have, so we must refuse to think that we care for their souls and if only He did so as much, then He would bless us and save them.

Our service is not only for the purpose of producing results. It is first of all an expression of our love to our Lord. After that it is a means of developing our spiritual life and character as we share with Him His sorrows and concerns. To all who are faithful, rewards are sure and these will include the ability to do more, to possess and use more talents because we used well the one we had. Besides this there will be honours such as are suggested by crowns when the day arrives for our service and suffering to be assessed and rewarded. For that purpose He will come again and receive us to Himself.

Be Not Afraid, Only Believe

The Lord is the strength of my life: of whom shall I be afraid?—PSALM 27:1.

FEAR is a powerful emotion and, being God-given, is of great value. It is natural that we should shrink from danger and evil; the preservation of life is often only possible because of fear. But when a right thing is in a wrong place, and an emotion which is normally healthy assumes a function for which it was not given then we must needs beware. It is against fear exercising a wrong function that we are warned so constantly in Scripture and that the words, Fear not, occur so frequently.

One of our chief concerns must be to avoid the fear of man. Such fear is a snare and brings us into a bondage which can be very crippling. We fear to be known as Christians, to conduct ourselves as such and so be regarded as odd; we are afraid to witness as we should. Or we may fear earthly rulers and their executives so as to deny the Lord; this is appearing again and with new force in parts of the world where it has not been known for centuries, and in many countries a Christian is a marked man and lives dangerously. The cure for the fear of man is the true fear of God; God being God and our Saviour and Judge is the One to fear, man is after all greatly restricted in his powers and can do no more than kill the body. Of whom shall we be afraid?

Or we may be afraid of the future. Its indefiniteness and unpredictableness make us shrink; it may hold sorrow, loneliness, poverty, pain or death. These are all unwelcome to us and we shrink from a future which is hidden from us. But with such a Saviour and Friend in control both of our life and of the future, should we not go into whatever awaits us singing,

> E'en let the unknown tomorrow
> Bring with what it may.
> It can bring with it nothing
> But He will bear us through.

Inheritors of the Promises

Come . . . inherit the Kingdom prepared for you.—MATTHEW 25: 34.

GOD has made so many promises in His Word and they have not yet all been fulfilled. It is true that the promises of the first coming of the Lord Jesus have long since been realised, but there are so many concerning His second Coming and of the glory which is to follow, that the heart looks onward and upward in glad expectation to the time when these too will all be fulfilled. And especially is this so because we ourselves are very much concerned in their full fulfilment.

In the first place we are to inherit a Kingdom of which by grace we are already members. At present the Kingdom is largely hidden in the hearts of God's children and only realised in the smallest measure in the Church of God's Son. Then the kingdoms of this world will have passed away and become the kingdoms of our God and of His Christ. Only one kingdom will remain and that the one prepared for us from the foundation of the world; and it will be the Father's pleasure to give it to us.

In the second place there are particular rewards to inherit. Crowns of righteousness and glory are to be given to those who have been faithful. The great honours of which these crowns are the signs we shall doubtless lay down at the feet of our Lord by Whose mercy alone they have been won, but is it not wonderful to anticipate the Judgment Seat of Christ where we shall receive the rewards?

But the basis of all expectations is that we are blessed of the Father, Who Himself loveth us and that He Who first began a work of grace in our souls is continuing His work until it is finished and we are with Christ and like Him. Welcome day of Jesus Christ! Let us hasten it by earnest consecration to walk the narrow way.

Keep Thy Heart with All Diligence

Isaac went out to meditate . . . at the eventide.—GENESIS 24: 63.

As a man thinketh in his heart, so is he. It is in the thoughts and intentions of the heart where both the springs of life rise and where true character resides. When serious trial arises it is not what we have said in public but what we really think and believe in our hearts which really holds us and which is ultimately disclosed. It was the fact that the imaginations of the thoughts of men's hearts were evil which grieved God in the early history of fallen man.

Now the question arises as to whether we can control the thoughts and imaginations of our hearts, and, granted that the reader is a true Christian with an experience of the grace of God, the answer is yes. St. Paul, writing to the Philippians said, whatever is true, whatever is honourable, whatever is just, whatever is pure, whatever is lovely, whatever is gracious, if there be any excellence, if there is anything worthy of praise, think about these things (Phil. iv: 8–9, R.S.V.). To some degree at least whatever we put into our hearts and minds remains there to form character and issues in conduct. We are therefore to occupy our thoughts with noble and lovely things; we are to meditate, to think carefully and deliberately, on the highest things, as Isaac did in his evening walks. The Word of God is to have a special place in our reading and meditation and we should commit it to memory. So the meditations of our hearts will be acceptable in the presence of God.

With hearts and minds so filled, our walk, that is our general behaviour, will almost take care of itself. With God's Word in our memories as a preventive and corrective we shall want to avoid walking after the counsel of the ungodly or becoming involved in the conversations and plans of the wicked.

Comprehensive Promises

He that spared not His own Son, . . . shall He not with him also freely give us all things?—
ROMANS 8: 32.

"ALL things"—these are the words which recur all through the selections of Scripture chosen for today. The promises and statements made offer the most satisfying assurance that nothing is overlooked or excluded in the provision made by our Heavenly Father for His children; therefore we shall want nothing which is good for us.

The promises include first of all, all things temporal which we need. It is here that many of us become anxious; we have sufficient today but the shadow of a possible need of tomorrow haunts us; we are troubled lest old age should find us unprovided for and in need. To such, God says that if we seek His Kingdom and concern ourselves with living righteously before Him, He will make much more adequate provision for us than for the lilies and the sparrows; all these daily necessities will be added to us. If God promises them they are assured to us indeed, for no person or government can truly speak with such confidence, since deep changes in the life of a country may destroy the resources of either. The guarantee and proof that no good thing will be lacking is that God has given His own Son for us, and in view of such a gift no smaller gift will be overlooked or omitted.

Ours is not to worry but to trust and obey. Our concern is not to be whether in the future we shall be short or in plenty but rather to walk uprightly before God and seek His favour. The living God Who controls both men and nations, times and tides, seasons and harvest, is our Heavenly Father, and through Christ is lovingly disposed to us. Because we are Christ's and Christ is God's all things are ours.

Why should I charge my soul with care?
    The wealth in every mine,
Belongs to Christ, God's Son and Heir
    And He's a Friend of Mine.

My Soul Keep Up Thy Singing

Exceeding joyful in all our tribulation.—2 COR. 7: 4.

THIS is a sad world, sin has made it so. Burdens on the conscience, troubles in the home, cares in business, misunderstandings, insecurity and other undesirable things make the world a place of sadness, despite so much apparent gaiety. It is necessary therefore that the Christian should be filled with joy. While it is true that we are in the midst of the world and must of necessity share its sorrow, yet the whole of life in its every aspect has been changed for the one who is born of God.

Think again of God's mercies to us. We were burdened with sin and fearful of judgment but, like Bunyan's Christian, when we came to the Cross our burden was strangely loosed from off us and tumbled into the sepulchre. Then God's loving care for us is dealing now with our problems in home and business, and He certainly intends that we should cast them upon Him rather than carry them ourselves. Misunderstanding hurts but if there is none between our Lord and us we can be thankful, while insecurity is an unknown word for the child of a King.

Are there not a hundred reasons why we can rejoice and if we can rejoice ought we not to do so? Is it not due to our Lord that we bear witness to His love and care by being glad and living without care? If indeed the Spirit of God is dwelling in us and exercising control then we shall certainly exhibit this fruit and rejoice greatly. If for a season we are in heaviness yet even now we must tune our harps for there is joy set before us and the very anticipation of it is thrilling.

If good people are needed in this bad world then glad people are also needed in this sad age. There is all the difference in the world between an empty jollity such as the worldling sometimes knows and the joy of the Lord, which is our strength; and the worldly man recognises it.

Strange Gods may be Familiar Gods

Thou shalt worship no other God.—EXODUS 34: 14.

IDOLATRY is not alone associated with heathen lands, where gods of wood and stone, paper and brass, are set up and worshipped; it is, alas, too prevalent in all places and among all sorts and conditions of men. Strange gods may appear in strange places and we need to guard against idolatry in every form.

There are idols of pleasure as demanding as any idols in false religion. Life moves round the centre of some sport or pastime. Instead of God being supreme, the arrangements of life and the main interests of the mind, are adjusted to this idol and homage is thus paid to it. Keep yourselves from idols.

There are idols made of homes. A modern home or an ancient one—with its equipment, furnishings and conveniences, assume such a place in life as to control us. We study it and serve it, and instead of the home being our servant and becoming for us a place of repair and relaxation, it becomes a master. Women, who are naturally homemakers, need to be specially careful. Keep yourselves from idols.

Many a business has become an idol and demanded that a man fall down and serve it. Here is a snare for men as the home may be for women.

A church, a denomination, social life which is made up of visits, parties, clubs, or even the social life of a church may easily displace God from the central and supreme place in the heart of a man. These are only a few of the many more possible idols.

What God asks is that we should love Him with all our heart, giving Him undivided loyalty and unquestioned obedience. All other claimants to the throne must be rejected and we must watch lest any one of them climb the steps of the seat of authority in our hearts. Keep yourselves from idols.

God's Strange Ways are Wise Ways

My thoughts are not your thoughts . . . saith the Lord.—ISAIAH 55: 8.

GOD'S thoughts and ways must ever be beyond our poor human minds to grasp. In His mercy He shows us sufficient of them for our salvation and godly conduct and no one need be in error concerning these. The wayfaring man though unlearned need not err therein. Our attitude to God for this great mercy should ever be one of adoring gratitude.

But His ways with men and nations are often beyond us, and at this time God does not always attempt to explain them. Why He permits wicked men to trample on the rights of the poor and defenceless; why He suffers His church to be harassed and persecuted we do not understand and God does not wholly explain. His thoughts and ways are different from ours—and we are reminded, not only different, but above all we could design or do.

What then is the way to interpret these mysterious events and strange happenings? The answer is surely, that God has revealed Himself if not His ways, and that all we know of Him as revealed in His Son and Word, is good and wise, infinitely good and infinitely wise. In the light of His pure goodness and His perfect wisdom, may we not leave the unexplained ways of God with the world, the Church and ourselves as being the very best, though at present most incomprehensible? If we had the knowledge which God has we should all do as He does; and we may be sure that nothing better could be. God is dealing with a race of rebels which is slow to see how costly and hard a thing self-will and self-rule is; yet out of that race He is still drawing a people for His Son and saving those that believe. Is not this in itself a help in appreciating, if not interpreting, His judgments and His ways.

He Will Carry You Through

Fear not; I am the first and the last.—REVELATION 1: 17.

WHAT an unspeakable comfort it is to know that the Lord Jesus is both the One Who initiated our salvation and the One Who brings it to completion. Had it been necessary for man to take the first steps to save himself, he would have been lost for ever. The first thing Adam and Eve did when they fell was to run away from God and hide themselves, and the human race has been busy doing the same thing ever since. But God took the initiative by seeking for the sinning pair and He too has been doing the same ever since.

But the Lord was also bring our salvation to completion for He is the last ill well as the first. He will not cease until He has accomplished all that He has spoken of to us. He is working in us now. He will continue until the work of sanctification is complete and glory begins. Had it been left for us to continue and complete the work, had salvation been of grace in the beginning but left to works for its continuance and completion, then we might well have sunk in despair, but no, He Who began the good work will perfect it.

This mighty God and Saviour, Who is from everlasting to everlasting, has entered into a covenant with all who are in Christ to bring them to glory and to perfect all that which concerns them. We need not, must not, fear because the Lord is both before us and behind us. There is none like Him; He has no equal; all the hierarchies of hell so well trained and skilfully directed are no match for our Lord Jesus Christ. To all the hosts of evil and to the combined forces of this evil world we can humbly throw out the challenge, Who is a rock, save our God? The answer is, None.

Oh, for a Faith that Will Not Shrink

I will not let Thee go, except Thou bless me.—GENESIS 32: 26.

GOD loves the grace of importunity—of pertinacity. It is of course possible to be determined to get one's own way which is a serious spiritual condition. We have turned everyone to his own way, is the Bible description of sin and therefore it is best to describe selfwill as sin; even though, alas, sometimes it is expressed in doctrinal and ecclesiastical affairs.

But we are thinking today of obtaining not our way but God's blessing. It is not so much a case of our insisting on God's giving us something but rather of His giving to us more of His Spirit and of His blessing. We want me nof faith and prayer, we long for more love for Himself and for others and we find that such precious gifts are not given just for once asking. God tests our desire and increases it by the waiting. He sifts our motive by the delay but whenever the motive is pure, then in due course and at the best time God will say to us as to the woman, Be it unto thee as thou wilt, or as unto the two blind men, according to your faith be it unto you.

It is just in this grace of importunity that so many of us fail. We are too easily discouraged and we fail to persist, just when God is waiting to see how much we really long for Himself and His blessing. What is needed is a new generation of men and women who know how to wrestle with God, how to take hold of the skirts of the Almighty and to besiege His throne. The way to learn this art of importunate prayer is to practise it, and seeking a daily renewal of God's Spirit for this ministry to wait on, refusing to be discouraged or denied until God grants our petition. Then what rejoicing there will be!

He Ever Lives Above for Me to Intercede

Christ is entered into heaven itself, now to appear . . . for us.—HEBREWS 9: 24.

IT is passing wonderful that our Lord Jesus died for us, taking our sin and its guilt to Calvary, that we might be reconciled to God. It is wonderful also that He should rise again for our justification, but today we are reminded that He is living in Heaven for us, giving Himself to intercession and praying constantly for all Who are His. The Old Testament priest went in to intercede for Israel at the golden altar of incense but he also came out; there were periods when the tabernacle was not set up and there were times when there was no priest in the holy place; but not so with our Lord Jesus Christ Who intercedes for us continually in the heavenly sanctuary.

Again the high priest of old, while he was touched with the feeling of their infirmities was also affected with their sins, while our Intercessor being Man as well as God is both touched with sympathy with us and is at the same time sinless. He never fails, His prayers for us are always heard. These are some of the reasons why we should come boldly to the throne of grace; a welcome is assured; grace will be given.

But so coming we too are become intercessors and fulfil our function as priests. Are not all the redeemed called out of darkness into light to become members of a royal and a holy priesthood. This means that as Christ in glory bears our needs on His heart and prays for us, so we should carry upon our hearts the sins and needs of others and intercede for them. Let us come boldly and ask largely, for we have an entrance to the Father through the Son, as the Spirit leads us in to pray.

Strangely Contradictory—Yet True

As sorrowful, yet always rejoicing.—2 COR. 6: 10.

THE apostle describes the Christian life by a series of paradoxes, as sorrowful, yet always rejoicing; as poor, yet making many rich, etc. Opposites are joined together in the Christian; both are wholly true.

It is so in God Himself Who is both exalted yet very near; Who is at the same time the Centre and Soul of every sphere, yet to each loving heart how near. When we turn to the Incarnate Son we observe the same apparent contradictions. He is both God and man; He is possessed of all knowledge yet He grows in wisdom as in stature. He is the Man of sorrows but is filled with joy. The stranger to the Lord Jesus assumes that this cannot be, but the friends of Christ know that it is so and they find a confirmation of the fact in their own experience, which, as St. Paul says, is also strangely and apparently contradictory.

We rejoice with joy unspeakable, how true this is if we know the Lord Jesus! We rejoice in His pardon and in His presence. All we know of His wonderful Person and work makes the heart to sing. At the same time we are sorrowful as we think of men despising Him to their own temporal loss and eternal peril. We rejoice that Christ rules over all but we sorrow that in some countries it appears as if Satan has sway.

These two phases of the Christian life need ever to be recognised. We must not cease to rejoice and become sad; we must not cease to care for and sympathise with those who are in need and danger. To do this we need to continue in communion with our Lord Who will so share His life with us that what is true of Him will also be true of us.

All That I Need is in Jesus

In everything ye are enriched by Him.—1 COR. 1: 5.

THERE is not a problem of the human soul but what Christ is able to meet it. All the various and deep needs of our intricate personalities and our involved circumstances were anticipated when God planned our redemption in Jesus Christ.

Our past, of which we are made so ashamed, its guilt before God and its failure in our own eyes, was adequately dealt with by our Lord Jesus Christ. Its guilt He bore on the Cross so that our conscience may be stilled and our hearts at peace. Our present, with fears within and with foes without, may all be put into His strong hand so that both we and our circumstances are held and controlled by Him Who is holy and loving and wise. Our future, so unpredictable on earth and so indescribable in heaven, is in His keeping and we need never fear. All that would tend to distress and alarm as we look out into the unknown is well known to Him, Whose name we bear.

Do we need peace, power, purity? They are found in Christ and we are in Him. Our need therefore is to maintain communion with Him. This makes possible a full supply of the Spirit of our exalted Lord, and His risen life ministered to us by the Spirit as the life of the vine is conveyed from stem to branch by the sap, will keep us fresh and make us fruitful. The most important thing in life is to remain in fellowship with Christ. This will call for prayer and the daily devout reading of Scripture; it will mean obedience to His revealed will and a careful eschewing of anything contrary to His desires and designs. If, however, we abide in Him we may be sure that He will be glorified, we shall be satisfied and others will be blessed.

Free from Corroding Care and Fear

Fear not, . . . I have called thee by thy name.—ISAIAH 43: 1.

THE number of times the believer is commanded to be unafraid is surely proof that this, one of the most common temptations which has presented itself to man all down the centuries, is to be fearful and apprehensive. It is suggested that there are almost as many reminders not to be anxious or afraid as there are days in the year. It is therefore a daily temptation.

In the world advice is given to be unafraid but often without any good reason. In the Bible a reason why we should be unafraid is appended to the injunction. We are not to fear because we are redeemed by the Lord; because He has become to us as a husband who provides and protects; because our sins are forgiven and judgment is passed; because the Lord of Hosts will undertake our cause; and so on.

Here then again today, we face the Lord's own words which so frequently meet us; and it is good to ask ourselves of what and of whom we should be afraid. Many of us fear the future; the unknown tomorrow may bring with it distress and want, loss of health or wealth. But the answer to that is that the Lord is our Shepherd and we shall not want. Many fear men and movements; there is a dread lest evil men or some evil system will sweep over our country as it has done over others. The answer to that is that God is on the throne and so long as we humble ourselves and seek Him, He will bless us either by means of a friend or foe. Or again want, sickness, old age are things which produce fear and apprehension in other hearts and minds. The Lord would remind such that He has promised to carry His own down to old age, that in sickness He will make His own arrangements ("make their bed" is the Lord's tender way of putting it). Indeed there is no cause for fear and anxiety which is not already met by a specific promise by Him Who never fails.

My Shame and My Glory

I am black, but comely.—S. OF S. 1: 5.

THE page is filled with a series of glorious contrasts; first there is a self-portrait as one appears in his own sight when the Spirit of God makes a man realise his own sinful condition and then there is the statement as to how God sees a soul which has been washed in the blood of Christ and sanctified by His Spirit.

The soul which has been made aware of its inward depravity says, I am black, because born with a sinful nature, and aware of the fact that apart from grace no good thing can spring from such a sinful heart. Experience has proved that when there are better desires they are unrealisable and so there is self-abhorring in the presence of God.

But the Lord Jesus carried such a nature to its death when He was made sin for us, and when by grace we are enabled to trust the Saviour, we become regenerate, all fair and without spot; it becomes known that this great change has taken place and others are caused to give glory to God.

It is in proportion as we see ourselves really sinful that we are able to appreciate the exceeding great grace of God in pardoning us. And if we see ourselves as black and abhor ourselves, how much more sinful does the Holy God see us, and how much more is His grace magnified when we realise His love to us who are so unworthy.

And from my smitten heart, with tears
Two wonders I confess,
The wonders of His glorious love
And my own worthlessness.

Words Which Help and Heal

Set a watch, O Lord, before my mouth.—PSALM 141: 3.

THERE is no more common failure among Christians than that of unguarded and unwise speech. The tongue is an unruly member which few of us check as we should. Too easily the harmless joke passes into a doubtful remark, observations turn to criticisms, and before we are aware of it we have sinned with our lips. We are enjoined, therefore, to be slow to speak and swift to hear. The wise man listens more and speaks less, while the unwise does the exact opposite; therefore the wise man grows wiser and the foolish more foolish, for he who knows much learns more and he who knows less learns less.

The control of our speech is a matter of great necessity. Its accomplishment is compared to the capture of a city, the mastery of an untamed horse. Well might we pray that God would guard our lips from speaking shame. Many a good man is spoiled with this weakness, and often a person with many excellent qualities is disqualified from service because his brethren are doubtful about his keeping silent or his speaking discreetly.

In this, as in all matters, our Lord Jesus Christ is both our Example and our Helper. In His mouth there was no guile; His contemporaries wondered at the gracious words which proceeded out of His mouth. Neither flattery nor criticism made Him speak unadvisedly; He knew when to speak and what to say; and when to remain silent. In this His true wisdom was revealed and He now dwells in His people by His Spirit and desires to control their lips as He controlled His own. Shall we not pray—

Let me no wrong or idle word
  Unthinking say;
Set Thou a seal upon my lips,
  Just for today.

Free from the Law, O Happy Condition

By Him, all that believe are justified.—ACTS 13: 39.

THE Apostle Paul who best knew both the contents and the limitations of the law, said that he agreed that it was good. No fault could be found with its moral and ethical standards. Its prohibitions were such as are absolutely necessary for the maintenance of the best life of the individual, the home and the nation. The two tables which regulated man's relations with God and with his fellows were clear, inclusive and adequate, so far as laws were concerned.

But the fault with the law was that while its commands were good no power was provided for their being kept. Sinful man, instead of keeping them, found himself provoked by them to further sin—much as a command not to walk on the grass, may make it more inviting for us to do so. Here then was a simple perfect code of conduct but insufficient moral and spiritual power to keep it.

There was One, however, who fulfilled its every demand; He was the One Who had made it and Who now came down to earth and kept it. Not one jot or tittle passed from the law until all was fulfilled by Him, Who made it honourable. Having kept it He then took the curse which it imposed on those who broke it, upon Himself. Cursed is everyone that continueth not in all things of the law to do it; cursed is everyone that hangeth on a tree; He made the curse of the broken law His own and was hanged on a cross, so removing the curse from us who have failed so miserably to keep the law of God which was written both in stone and in conscience.

Now the law is satisfied and we are justified. Its commandments no longer threaten but guide. They suffice to curb men's liberties where such will offend God or intrude upon the liberties of others. The law forms still a basic expression of the will of God but not the means of salvation.

How Can I Shew My Love to Thee?

Honour the Lord with thy substance.—PROVERBS 3: 9.

ALL things come of Thee, and of Thine own have we given Thee, said David; every good gift and every perfect gift is from above, wrote James; and all the other writers of sacred Scripture remind us in one way or another of the loving kindness and lavish generosity of our God. But His gifts become our responsibilities; we are accounted stewards of His mercies. They are not only sent to us for our pleasure personally, but that we may prosper spiritually by using them aright.

Our giving then must be to the Lord Whose gifts to us they are in the first place. We must beware of merely giving to churches, missionary societies, the poor etc. as such. The true way is to give to the Lord as He shall direct us, and always making sure that the gifts are an expression of our love to Him.

Our giving must be regular. On the first day of the week the Corinthians were to set aside their gifts. It may be that we receive our salary monthly or quarterly in which case we may need to give ours to the Lord then, distributing it week by week as we are guided.

Our giving is to be proportionate, as God hath prospered us. A larger income necessitates larger giving, and faithfulness in this is pleasing to the Lord Who often commits more to those who are faithful stewards.

Our giving must be hearty, bountiful. We are to give gladly and as generously as possible in view of God's great love to us in Christ. We shall find real joy in giving to the Lord if we keep in mind that when we give it to one of the least of His brethren it is given to Him. And none of us should give Him our gifts and withhold ourselves. Present your bodies as a living sacrifice and as a definite gift.

Jesus, Thou Joy of Loving Hearts

How precious are Thy thoughts unto me, O God!—PSALM 139: 17.

HOW utterly beyond our expectations have been our discoveries of the Lord Jesus! We came to Him in our need daring to believe He would meet it and give us pardon or peace, or that which we then knew we needed, but since then almost every day has seen fresh discovery of His fullness and mercy so that now we are lost in wonder. Is it not so? If not then let us ask that it may be.

The Psalmist joined together such an experience of satisfaction of God's fullness with his meditations, and is not this just where we lack? In accordance with western ideas and modern ways, we are too busy to meditate on Jesus Christ in Whom dwells all the fullness of the Godhead bodily. We need to take time to think, to ponder the Person and work of our Saviour, to take note of His words and His ways. It is to such that the Spirit reveals Jesus and it is to such only, who find His thoughts great and precious, and His words sweeter than honey or anything natural. Once a Christian really sees the glories of Jesus Christ he will certainly ask whether there is anyone else to be compared; indeed he will quickly answer that there is no person and no thing which is comparable.

Samuel Rutherford who wrote such seraphic letters from his prison in Aberdeen to his parishioners in Anwoth, and to his correspondents elsewhere, was in raptures of delight as the Spirit, Whose ministry it is to reveal Christ, revealed Him to His servant. So His Lord was to Him a Running-over Lord Jesus and in the cellar of affliction Rutherford looked round for the Lord's choice wines. What mattered it to him to be imprisoned, because it was with his Lord in Whom He found new glories. Lord Jesus, save us from being so busy that we do not know Thee as Thou art.

He is Abundantly Able to Save

Their Redeemer is strong.—JEREMIAH 50: 34.

OUR sins are mighty and strong to hold us; our transgressions are of many kinds and we need a Saviour Who is strong to deliver us. No mere teacher can help us for we already know more than we can perform. No social reformer will suffice for our social confusion springs from sin within. No good man, no perfect man, can break the power of evil or atone for its heinousness and guilt before a holy God. But One has come Who is able; able to save to the uttermost and able to keep. He is the strong Son of God joining in Himself both divine and human natures and so is eminently fitted to reconcile us to God and to deliver us from evil.

Is there then a sinful habit from which He cannot deliver us? Is there a difficult situation from which He cannot extricate us? Is there a trying circumstance through which He cannot bring us? The answer to all such questions is strongly in the negative. Let us then look to Him in quiet confidence to bring us through in triumph.

And as we think of others, is there a sinner whom He cannot save? Is there a deluded person whom He cannot enlighten? The word of salvation is divine, never less. A miracle is needed for the deliverance and regeneration of any person, old or young, moral or immoral, religious or irreligious. But can we not expect Him to save such? It is He Who cast seven devils out of Mary Magdalene as well as taught Nicodemus? He it was Who arrested the chief persecutor of the early Church and made him chiefest of the apostles.

Do we think sufficiently of our Lord's great strength? Do we expect Him to do great things? Do we not too easily despair of men and women, when all the time their Redeemer is strong and waits to save, both them from their sins and us from our unbelief?

A Serious Mistake

I said . . . I am cut off . . . nevertheless Thou heardest . . . my supplications.— PSALM 31: 22.

IT is easy to come to conclusions too early and on insufficient evidence. Judges in a court of law are trained to avoid this serious mistake, but we ordinary folks commit the blunder often; we do it in our daily affairs and, alas, in our experience of God.

It may be a comfort to us to know that it has evidently been a common fault for centuries, for the Psalmist fell into this same mistake on a number of occasions. Notice some of these in today's portion for twice he confesses that he has spoken unadvisedly. Some delay in the providence of God made him say in haste, I am cut off from before Thine eyes. When trouble came over him like a flood he said, I am cut off. When his prayers for deliverance were not answered quickly he came to the hasty conclusion that God had forgotten him or did not hear. But both assumptions were wrong for God cannot forget His servants and He does not fail to hear their cry.

What then are we to do when delays become trials and when apparent denials disquiet our souls? We are to follow the Psalmist in this, that on one occasion to which reference is made today he said, in the midst of his perplexity, I will remember. He called former mercies to mind and found lessons in them and especially this lesson that God had never failed, and he drew this correct deduction that He would not fail him in his present distress. This kept him from fainting in the day of adversity and sustained his faith until a fresh deliverance came. Are you in difficulty today? And are you tried up to the limit of endurance? Remember God's former mercies and expect His help again.

Praise the Saviour Ye Who Know Him

Whoso offereth praise glorifieth Me.—PSALM 50: 23.

IT is becoming for the creature to offer praise to the Creator for His countless blessings; it is also surely the desire and delight of the saint to praise the Saviour Who has redeemed him at such infinite cost. Such praise both extols our God and Saviour and also satisfies Him, for the appreciation of His mercies by His people is welcome. Part of our ministry as believer-priests is to offer up the sacrifice of praise to Him Who hath called us into His light and love and we are therefore to be engaged in offering up such sacrifice continually, not only feeling thankful in our hearts but expressing our praise with our lips.

In order to praise God worthily, we are enjoined to allow the word of Christ to dwell in us richly. The words our Saviour spoke and the words which the psalmists and prophets before wrote, as well as those of the apostles after Him, are to be hidden in the heart and mind. These will then become the worthy vehicle of praise when we offer up our sacrifice. Have we not met those whose prayers and praises are enriched with Holy Scripture, who find the Psalms as helpful in their praising God as David did so long ago. Do not the paeans of praise in the Revelation come to mind when we desire to extol the Lamb upon His throne?

Here then is our need. Our hearts are to be filled with the spirit of praise and our minds with the words of Scripture, so that praise may be expressed and God may be glorified. We have so much for which to praise that we should be proud of our God and make our boast in Him Who has saved us and keeps us. Let us encourage one another in a life of praise saying, "O magnify the Lord with me, let us exalt His name together" in speech and song, in private and in public, in prayer and in praise.

The Mediator of a Better Covenant

A Prophet . . . like unto thee.—DEUT. 18: 18.

THREE qualities in the character of Moses are considered here as being the marks and qualifications of his prophetic office and as being repeated and perfected in the Lord Jesus Christ in His ministry as Prophet.

Moses was Mediator standing between the Lord and Israel to show the Word of God. This our Lord Jesus Christ is, only in a perfection of character which was beyond Moses. For Christ not only mediated the truth of God but also the grace of the Lord ("The law was given by Moses but grace and truth came by Jesus Christ"—John 1: 17) Jesus Christ also mediated between man and God, representing man and atoning for sin on the Cross.

Moses was meek, indeed the meekest man in all the earth. That is surely a wonderful testimony, for it was given by God Who knoweth all things, and to a man with possibly more power than any other man in Israel or in surrounding nations. The temptations to self-advancement and the opportunity of becoming a great nation were rejected by this meek man whose only concern was the reputation of God (*see* Exod. xxxii and Numb. xiv). But the Lord Jesus was in His divine nature far above all creatures, yet He humbled Himself to the lowest shame and did it deliberately, substantiating His claim "I am meek and lowly in heart".

Moses was faithful, discharging his offices with a due sense of responsibility to God. All slackness and weakness, alas so often characteristic of God's servants, were rejected so as to be well-pleasing to God. Our Lord could say at the end of His brief but wonderful life, "I have finished the work that Thou gavest me to do" (John 17: 4). And these qualities found in the man who mediated the First Covenant, and perfect in the Mediator of the Second Covenant, should be found in all ministers and prophets in these days of grace.

Entering the Sanctuary of God

No man cometh unto the Father but by Me.—JOHN 14: 6.

ALL through the Scriptures we are reminded of the privilege and cost of a man's approach to God. Sin has excluded us from His holy presence; we have neither right nor fitness to approach the throne of God. But a way has been opened by which we may come, for Christ hath suffered for our sins, and through Him we have access to the Father.

In the Tabernacle in the wilderness a series of doors of curtains shut out the Israelite from entering beyond where he had the privilege. The impenitent must remain outside the white curtain with its many-coloured door, but the penitent might enter with his sacrifice. He, however, could go no further than the brazen altar and only a consecrated priest could go into the holy place, while into the holiest of all entered the high priest only once a year when he carried in the blood of the atonement.

But the doors are open to the believer under the New Covenant. He is a priest able to enter the holy place where he may worship, and the veil beyond, has been torn from top to bottom, so we may draw near to the Shekinah glory. How privileged we are since Jesus died for us! We have this great honour of being able to draw near to God to enter with boldness into the holiest place.

The privilege is ours as God's children and priests, but are we using it? Do we tread this way often? Are we those who spend time in unhurried worship? Ours is not only to believe but to belong; we are not only to be workers but worshippers. The Father seeketh those who will worship Him in Spirit, in the deepest depths of their being, beyond the emotional and the artistic; and in truth—that is, without unreality, pretence or sin. The Father seeketh such; may He find us drawing near.

Holy, Happy Separation

Every man that hath this hope . . . purifieth himself.—1 JOHN 3: 3.

THERE is something absolute and final about the demands of Holy Scripture. Today it is the call for absolute separation from things evil. There is a danger of thinking that separation is a call primarily to separation from people, whereas it is principally a command to eschew evil. Let the Word of God have full power in our hearts and consciences as we search them today, for "nought of the accursed thing" is to be retained, we are not even to touch the unclean we are to keep absolutely clear of things that are carnal and unclean. These are words of command and entreaty as though by one means or another God is concerned for the spiritual purity of our lives.

On the positive side we are reminded of our high calling as sons of God, that in view of His return we are to seek purity of life and utterly refuse to give place to anything unsuited to a life of godliness. We are to live soberly as touching ourselves, righteously as touching our neighbours, and godly as towards our God; and all the time we are to be expecting the return of the Lord Jesus from heaven.

Finally, we are reminded that when our Lord Jesus Christ died for us on the Cross, it was not only that we might be forgiven, but also that He might deliver us from all iniquity and so cleanse our lives that we might be evidently His very own people, anxious above all else to live a holy life in this sinful world. Should we not remember this more and teach it to men? Is not purity of life as much a part of the Gospel message as pardon for the past? Let this call to absolute separation from all evil and complete dedication to God come home to us today, and let there be a full response to its authority, as we say, "Be it unto me according to Thy Word".

Living by Faith and Continuing by Grace

Stand fast in the Lord.—PHIL. 4: 1.

THE Christian is called to steadfastness. The world around is changing with its fashions of thought and conduct, but the servant of the Lord must stand fast. The enemy from below is constantly changing his methods of attack upon us, but clothed with the armour of God we are to stand. The heart within may melt with fear or the mind may be perplexed with providence, but faith must still hold on its way saying, "What time I am afraid, I will trust Thee".

This is the life of faith which the justified live. We began our Christian life by trusting the Saviour's finished work, both in heaven and in the heart. So, come what may, we must not and will not draw back. We intend, by God's grace, to remain steadfast. This proves that we are true disciples, that our faith is saving faith, and will endure; and that at the last we shall be clothed in white raiment as victors who have overcome.

Lest, however, we should think that all this is due to our own determination and moral strength, we are reminded that it is primarily due to the Lord Who Himself stands fast and does not forsake His saints. It is because He has promised to preserve us that we are preserved; it is because He is able to make us stand that we continue to stand fast.

God's power and our own renewed purpose are both required to remain upright and alert. Let us cast neither aside.

He Was accepted for Us; We Are Accepted in Him

Behold the Lamb of God, which taketh away the sin of the world.—JOHN 1: 29.

MY sin is condemned and I am doomed. I am not merely sinful but guilty, not only weak but rebellious. My sins deserve eternal death, and mind and heart agree in accepting the condemnation and confirming the doom which is pronounced.

My sin must be atoned for if I am to be pardoned, for God is not only a loving Father but a righteous Judge. There can be no light dismissal of the punishment or the whole universe would run riot in its rebellion and ultimately condemn such treatment of sin. Insurrection, the refusal of God's will and the choice of self-rule must be put down and judged. This means that a substitute must be provided, an offering without blemish—in short, a Man without sin. Only God can provide such a sacrifice, and He Who wondered that there was no intercessor, Himself brought salvation, for the Son of Man was made flesh.

Our Substitute must die; His life lived is not sufficient; it must be laid down as a ransom for many. It must be yielded willingly, so although outwardly it appears that He was taken by wicked hands and crucified and slain, yet He never rebelled against their crude and cruel handling, but went like a lamb to the slaughter and offered Himself at the Cross as an oblation once offered to make a full, perfect and sufficient sacrifice, oblation and satisfaction for the sins of the whole world. This Jesus did and finished the work.

But I must lay my hands on the Sacrifice, that is, I must make the sacrifice my own, I must commit my sins and my soul to Him. "My faith would lay her hands, on that meek head of Thine, while as a penitent I stand, and here confess my sin." So doing, I am accepted by God.

I Am Weak, but Thou Art Mighty

The Lord was my stay.—PSALM 18: 18.

WE need someone on whom we may lean for we are weak. We have tried many things and many people but all have given way and it was in vain we ever looked for security and help.

It would appear that we ought naturally and first of all to lean on God, but our fallen nature tries other things and people first, until we realize that it is vain. It is only then that we discover how reliable the Lord is, how secure His protection and how adequate His support. When we do this then we certainly feel like shouting, for the Holy One Who is the Defender and Commander of His people, is in our midst.

Reverent, personal trust in such a God ensures His continual presence. He is watching over us like an army sentry moves round the camp, and when we need to cry for help He comes swiftly to our rescue.

And He is not only around us as a sentry, but underneath us as a support; and as He has said that He will never leave us undefended or unsupported, we may courageously confess that we are unafraid of all our foes. We should never be so free from fear were we left to ourselves, for we are weak and timid and our foes are strong and aggressive, but grace has changed the condition. Alone we are beaten, but with such a Commander and Defender we are safe, and knowing this we are calm.

Lord, Thy Word Abideth, and Our Footsteps Guideth

The Lord visited Sarah . . . and did unto Sarah as He had spoken.—GENESIS 21: 1.

GOD hath spoken to His people. The Bible is not the story of a people groping after God, but of a continual and progressive self-revelation on the part of God. His Word contains both precepts and promises, poetry and prophecy, and it is the promises and prophecy which are principally in mind here.

If God has promised something then we may be sure He will be faithful. He was to Sarah, for He visited her "as He had said" and did "as He had spoken". The Lord was just as faithful to the people of Israel in Egypt, though the implementing of that promise was a much greater thing. Indeed, God's people in all ages can join with the writer of the history of Israel in the land and say, "There failed not ought of any good thing which the Lord had spoken . . . all came to pass".

It is just because of God's faithfulness that His word of promise or prophecy is so sure and certain of fulfilment; and it is because His promises will most certainly be fulfilled that we, like David, may in our present perplexity encourage ourselves in the Lord our God. Just as certain as this present earth and these present heavens will give place to the new earth and heavens wherein dwelleth righteousness, so surely will the Word and promise of God not pass away, but will stand for ever.

Faith finds its basis not in passing events, or fluctuating feelings, not in human schemes or hopeful programmes, but in the immutable God, Who has spoken in His unbreakable word. If we believe not, yet He abideth faithful; He cannot deny Himself; and what remains yet unfulfilled, will one day be "as He had said" and "as He had spoken".

A Prince and A Saviour

He appeared to put away sin by the sacrifice of Himself.—HEB. 9: 26.

JESUS CHRIST came into the world expressly to meet our greatest need. This was not, as some imagined, to heal the body or to heal society though He is able to do both, but to save men from their sins. So to the sick of the palsy he said, "Thy sins be forgiven thee" before He said, "Take up thy bed and walk". Our greatest need is to be delivered from our sin, to be delivered from its guilt and power, and only Jesus can do helpless sinners good.

In order of our understanding and acceptance the forgiveness of our sinful acts comes first; and with what joy and relief we receive the joyful news of sins forgiven. Like Bunyan's pilgrim, the burden rolls from our back and we go on our way rejoicing. But we must remember that what brings so much joy to us, brought unspeakable suffering and death to our Lord Jesus, when He was wounded for our transgressions and bruised because of our perverse and rebellious acts. It was necessary, in view of the nature and government of God, that Christ should suffer, in order that remission of sins may be preached.

But later, often much later, we realize the burden of our sinful nature, the defilement of our hearts, and we need to learn how Christ has taken our nature to the Cross for God's judgment and for death, when He Who knew no sin in His own nature was made sin for us. For Christ died as our Representative as well as our Substitute, and there is deliverance from the dominion as well as the guilt of sin We have died, when He died; we have been crucified with Him that the principle of sin may no longer dominate us; let us wait upon God to make it clear and real.

So today we think of His name Jesus, the Greek and abbreviated form of Jehoshua, for the Lord's deliverer of His people Israel from their bondage, is a type of our greater Joshua-Jesus.

Safe in the Arms of Jesus

Underneath are the everlasting arms.—DEUT. 33: 27.

THERE are times when we fear lest we should slip. Indeed such a fear may be a healthy thing and a sign that we are those who "worship God in the spirit and have no confidence in the flesh". Others have fallen, their fall warns us, and we wonder if we may similarly fall.

But we are not meant to be weakened by a constant fear of falling which is unrelieved and without compensation. We are meant to "rejoice with trembling". If the trembling is concerning our own frailty, then the rejoicing is to be in His strength and constant care. His arms are underneath to support us, and on the very first awareness of falling we have recourse to Him Who hastens to the help of His servants. And if we have actually stumbled we are not to remain down for He is at hand to lift us up again.

We are the beloved of the Lord. He has loved us with an everlasting love and with loving-kindness has drawn us. The cost of our redemption was stupendous for it was in blood, the blood of His only-begotten Son. Is it thinkable that we to whom such grace has been shown and on whom such love is lavished, will be left to sink in trouble?

> "His love in time past forbids me to think
> He'll leave me at last in trouble to sink."

Moreover, His very support is gentle and understanding. The lost sheep He lays not on one shoulder, but on His two shoulders in comfort, and the strong supporting hands are under our heads and around us. We may therefore rest in Him in deep contentment, casting any anxiety upon Him, for we have His guarantee that we shall not perish.

True humility, lies in the assurance that, left to ourselves, we shall certainly fall, but upheld by Him we need never fall.

Let Us Work While it is Day

Brethren, the time is short.—1 COR. 7: 29.

ACCORDING to the Bible there is an urgency in life. This is not to be confused with busyness or fuss, but with direction and purpose. The warning is given to save us from drifting aimlessly along, from wasting life's precious opportunities. Many of us already regret the mistakes of the past in this connection; we are reminded again of the need of girding up our loins so that our future may not be also spoiled.

It is first of all pressed upon us by Scripture insisting on the brevity of life. Our days are too few to be wasted. Some things and pursuits are merely temporal, while others concern eternity. As our days have eternal consequences, our interests and activities must be governed with the things which endure.

The urgency of life is also based on "the last things". The coming of our Lord Jesus Christ and the judgments. When He returns He will introduce the day of God, when our life, with its motives and service, will be examined. Everything dark and which will not bear the light of that day is therefore to be rejected, and this calls for constant self-scrutiny and self-control. How perfectly our Lord Jesus Christ lived such a life! He it was Who in youth said, "Wist ye not that I must be about my Father's business?" Later He insisted, "I must work the works of Him that sent Me while it is day." This did not produce haste or panic in His life. He had still leisure to enjoy the flowers and to spend time watching the farmers. He steadily pursued His appointed path, but He did not fail to use each day.

Such an attitude towards life will invest our time with a sacred sense of its value. We shall not be "killing time" but using it. It will demand that we cast off any works of darkness, that is, anything which is sinful or shady; and live in the light a life of open frankness and transparency. Moreover, it will mean living prayerfully, seeking wisdom from God as to how each day is to be spent, and He will not hurry nor drive us, but gently lead us into fruitfulness and peace.

Worthy is the Lamb that was Slain

Then said I, Lo, I come . . . to do thy will, O God.—HEB. 10: 7.

"GOD will provide Himself a lamb," said Abraham as with Isaac he toiled up Mount Moriah and the lamb they found caught in a thicket was both a sacrifice and a substitute.

Generations of trustful Israelites have travelled the same way. They had sinned and realized it, so in accordance with the word of the God Whom they had offended by their sin, they provided a lamb to die on their behalf, and in so doing trod the way of faith and pardon.

But here is God's Lamb, that is, God's sacrifice. He is unique in that He is not only guileless like the sacrificial lamb, but sinless; and not only sinless but holy. Moreover, in His Person He joins the nature of offending man and the offended God and is thus uniquely fitted to reconcile. His life is therefore unique and when it is given in sacrifice is precious. The blood of Old Testament sacrifices only covered the sin until in the fullness of time this one sacrifice for sins for ever, should be slain and the sins cleansed away and their guilt removed

Such a Sacrifice and Substitute has come into the world, and, in an obedience which was complete, has done God's will and borne God's wrath. Faith rests upon this perfect Sacrifice and upon this finished work and finds it the ground of hope in God. But the Saviour is also the Sovereign, and to the Lamb of God Who bore away the sin of the world is committed the judgment of the world. He alone is fit and worthy to receive power and riches, and wisdom, and strength, and honour, and glory, and blessing—and all.

He is Too Wise to Err, Too Good to be Unkind

Consider how great things He hath done for you.—1 SAM. 12: 24.

THE effect of sin upon our memory is to cause us to remember much more easily the failures and hardships of the past, and to forget the mercies. We are here commanded to sit down and think back, and to remember what God has done for us. If we do count our past blessings, we shall certainly find them both great and innumerable, and they will be positive proof of God's personal care for "He hath done" them "for you".

Past experiences also need to be rightly interpreted if we are to receive their full blessing. They were sent to prove us and to help to show our manner of spirit. We should have been humbled by those undeserved mercies, just in the same way as we should have been corrected by His chastisements.

Of this we can be confident that infinite love and Wisdom is working for us. The Lord's dealings with His children are right, and we may be sure that it was and is good for us that we were corrected in order to learn the better way, otherwise we should have continued going astray.

Three humbling and heartening facts make us to fall down and worship. Firstly, we have been dealt with in mercy and not in judgment; secondly, in all God's dealings His mercy is high above the earth, and is wise beyond question; and thirdly, He never forgets our frailty nor puts upon us more than we can bear, nor expects from us that which we are unable to accomplish.

Obedient and Abiding

If a man love Me, he will keep my words.—JOHN 14: 23.

TODAY we consider two apparently different and unrelated subjects; being perfected in the love of God, and being carefully obedient to the words and commandments of Scripture. The first would be considered spiritual and the second might be thought of by some as literal, legal and perhaps even mundane. The one may appeal more to the heart, but the other appeals directly to mind and conscience.

But the two are intimately related and must not be separated. To be concerned alone with the love of God may lead us to carelessness of conduct, while the whole page of selected Scriptures remind us that it is by seeking to express our love for and devotion to God by obeying His Word, by doing what He asks of us, that His love in us grows and matures. This all means that we must read Scripture with care and humility; with care because we need to mark its instructions, warnings and prohibitions; and with humility because we are to obey them.

To such as submit themselves and their conduct to the correction and guidance of the Word of God, there is a growing desire to please God, and the life is lived in a deepening fellowship with Him. Deep communion obtains and is preserved between the Lord and those who tremble at His Word. It is not therefore in the singing of devotional hymns, not in the meeting where deep emotions are stirred, but in the faithful keeping of the words of God and in pursuing submission of all life to His will, that the love of God is shed abroad in our hearts by the Holy Spirit. The commandments of God will be applied to all parts of our life, and walking in obedience to His truth, the Lord will draw us into an intimacy of fellowship with Him, which is life's most precious privilege.

Like a River Glorious is God's Perfect Peace

The fruit of the Spirit is peace.—GALATIANS 5: 22.

OF all the gifts and experiences which human beings seek, peace is surely the most coveted. That is because sin has introduced discord into the individual human heart, and also created disunity between man and his fellow, and man and God. The Gospel is good tidings that peace is possible.

It first of all announces the adjustment of the broken relations between man and God. The sin which has estranged and antagonized is removed. The God-man has intervened and given Himself as a Sacrifice; His blood means satisfaction both for God the offended and man the offender, there is "peace through the blood of His cross". Resting on that atoning work the mind is kept in perfect peace regarding sin and judgment.

Then there is peace in the heart which comes from the harmonizing of faculties which were in conflict. The heart has been longing for things which the conscience forbids, and the will has been torn between obeying the conscience or satisfying the desire. But when Christ is made Lord of all He takes the heart and conscience and will and makes them truly one. The will decides what the heart desires and the conscience approves; life is unified, and inward harmony prevails. This peace our Saviour knew and bequeathed to us, and as we love God's law, that is, seek to do God's will, we have a large bequest of this most necessary gift, peace which flows like a river and brings healing and help wherever it flows.

God's Promised Presence

Surely the Lord is in this place.—GENESIS 28: 16.

THE doctrine of the Omnipresence of God may appear to be merely a subject for academic consideration by the theologian and student, but like all the great Scripture doctrines it is also a subject for the most necessary and practical consideration of every Christian. It asserts that God is everywhere, and that in itself may seem academic, but it practically follows that if God is everywhere He is here now, and that there is no place where we can go but that He is there already. This doctrine rightly understood, and appreciated, adds both solemnity and joy to life and invests all places and all life with a peculiar sanctity so that we may say here and everywhere "Surely the Lord is in this place".

But unfortunately we live a large proportion of our lives forgetful of the fact; we are aware of His presence in the meeting but forget it in the market. Of course it is not possible to be thinking of God all the time, but yet, as Brother Lawrence would teach us, we can and should recollect God's presence whenever the opportunity occurs; such a practice soon encourages an attitude of living as in God's immediate presence, and will transform the ordinary life; for how can any place of duty be common if God is there?

And there is a special revealing of His presence when two or three gather in His name, as they are indwelt by His nature and moved by His Spirit. But most solemn and glad of all is the fact that this Holy God dwells in the believer as in a temple. This invests us with a divine power, for "greater is He that is in you than he that is in the world". The knowledge of His presence also humbles us to the dust. "Lo, God is in this place (indeed in me) and I knew it not."

Let Us go on to Perfection

I am the Almighty God; walk before Me, and be thou perfect.—GENESIS 17: 1.

PERFECT! the word may attract or repel. It may repel us by its distance and by the sense of impossibility of its achievement; or it may call us as an end which is worthy and below which anything else would be unworthy.

Perfect means whole, healthy, mature. And God is that, for with Him there is no incompleteness, no lack or excess which spoils His glorious nature or action, no failure due to ignorance or inexperience.

It is the Perfect God Who has called us with a holy calling and now commanded us to be perfect as He is perfect; that is, perfect in our humanity as He is perfect in His deity. His ideal for us is no incompleteness, no lack or excess to spoil our nature or action, and no failure due to ignorance or inexperience. It is because He is holy and perfect, because He has saved us by the Blood of His Son, and dwells in us by His Spirit, that He summons us to Christian perfection.

And the way He leads us on in this path is by showing us each flaw, each deficiency or excess, in the mirror of His word, which is the perfect law of liberty. If we take heed and receive the grace which assuredly accompanies the revealing, then, as a doer of the word, we shall be blessed in our way.

The calling is a high one, the flesh shrinks or rebels, but God will give us grace to ask for the searching, to follow the leading and to press toward the mark. It is better to have a high ideal than a low one, and may God save us from all vain excuses for continuing in error, failure and immaturity, when the river of God's grace is so full.

Strong in the Strength Which God Supplies

In the day when I cried, Thou . . . strengthenedst me.—PSALM 138: 3.

No one who truly believes in God has serious difficulty in believing in His almighty power. Every day thousands confess in the words of the Apostle's Creed, "I believe in God the Father Almighty, Maker of heaven and earth". If He were less than that, He could not be God, and would only be a superman. It is one thing, however, to confess His Almighty power in a creed, but quite another to really and practically believe the truth and to act upon it. It is one thing to say, He hath delivered us and will deliver us, but another to say, He doth deliver us now.

Today we are reminded of God's power and ability; let us think around our own circumstances and those of others and see if there is no challenge to our faith in God's almightiness. Is there no crippling circumstance in which we can triumph by His power, but in which at present we are defeated? Is there no sin holding us as a slave from which we ought to expect deliverance? The Lord has made heaven and earth and there is nothing too hard for Him; then what about this trait of character in me, which dishonours His name and brings me into shame?

While Daniel was yet speaking help came from God. The Psalmist was strengthened in the day he cried to God. Is there something in our lives which makes us cry to God? Is there some weakness which needs to be strengthened? Then why not expect some fresh experience of His power today? It is according to our faith and not our feelings that help and healing come. We are not to wait for feelings, then begin to believe, for faith deals with God and His promises, not with feelings which change from hour to hour. There is strength in God; it is intended for us; let us wait upon Him in expectancy for they that wait upon the Lord shall change their strength for God's.

Safe from Corroding Care

I would have you without carefulness.—1 COR. 7: 32.

How anxious the world is—anxious to obtain and then to conserve! Men are concerned about these very things, that is, what shall we eat and drink and that with which we shall be clothed. The daily necessities of food, drink and clothing give both individuals and nations their chief concern.

It should not be so, however, for our Heavenly Father knows our need of all these things, and has promised that there will be no want to His children. And what are the conditions enumerated on this page of Scripture?

1. Refuse to be anxious—"Take no anxious thought".
2. "Fear the Lord"—reverently trust Him.
3. "Seek the Lord"—regularly and earnestly ask Him.
4. "Have faith in God"—confidently expect of Him.

These exercises turn our confidence away from our own strenuous anxieties and anxious worries which may appear to bring our necessities, but certainly bring also a host of accompanying evils such as restlessness, irritability and often ill-health. That which the Lord provides will need our diligent gathering as the Israelites gathered the manna, and it may not be given so that we can lay up great stores, but as day by day the manna fell, so God's promises will be fulfilled to us.

And such a life of quiet trust brings joy to the God Whom we trust and affords a testimony in a world which is full of care. So God would have us full of prayerfulness and free from carefulness.

Harmony Effected

Mercy and truth . . . righteousness and peace have kissed each other.—PSALM 85: 10.

THE moral qualities or attributes of God have their expression and make their demands. Mercy is disposed to clemency and to pardon, truth to justice and to punishment. Righteousness must maintain the righteous and judge the unrighteous, while peace would rejoice in forgiveness. As being both made in the image of God and redeemed by Him, these qualities appear in us, and being opposite in their nature and expression, often create an inward tension by their demands. We long to forgive the offender but must maintain the rule of the house and the school. We would like to pass by the fault but to do so would be to countenance lawlessness and make for confusion; and there is the well-being of all concerned at stake.

All this tends to put all leaders whether in home, school, factory or land into the greatest difficulty and induces the greatest strain. Some err on one side and some on another—and few are able to maintain truth and shew mercy at the same time.

But there is no tension in the Godhead, for these qualities which in us appear to make contradictory demands, are met together, they are united. The redemptive love and act of God has united them and they have kissed each other. The righteousness that must punish has been satisfied and the mercy that would forgive has been expressed. All this has been accomplished because the righteous and merciful God has become incarnate and as the God-man has undertaken to represent both God and man, thus both declaring the chastisement and bearing it.

The height and depth of this great truth of Christ's reconciling work are beyond us. The wonders of redemption scale the heights of God's nature and plumb the depths of ours. The work of Calvary is finished and we may rest upon it and be justified, for God was in Christ reconciling the world unto Himself.

Unafraid and of Good Cheer

God is our refuge . . . a very present help in trouble.—PSALM 46: 1.

"IN trouble"—how common the experience and how varied also. Troubles of many kinds press upon us from every quarter and seek to distress us through the spirit, mind or body. But whatever their form we may find our refuge to flee from them or our strength to bear them in God. His name, that is His nature, is our strong tower into which we may run and be safe.

But there are trials of another kind and it is of these that the Scriptures of this morning speak. They are the troubles which affect others but the news of which may threaten us. Wars and rumours of wars in other places make evil tidings; the knowledge of calamities which are befalling others can be very disturbing to us. When will our turn come? When will God's punishment of the nations be poured out on our nation? Anticipated troubles are in themselves a serious threat to peace —how shall we meet them? What shall we do with the news which tells of deep distress in other lives or nations?

We must first of all make our refuge in the Shadow of His Wings. His promises of help and protection are meant to keep our faith steady and our spirit calm. Let us enter into His presence which is made so inviting here by being described as "Thy Chambers", "The Shadow of Thy Wings" and let us hide there.

But we are not to retreat there to forget the troubled world but rather to intreat for it. Our peace is not to be one of blissful ignorance but rather of confident trust and deepest sympathy.

If the children of God have trouble so do the children of the world and they know no secure chambers nor the Shadow of Eternal wings. In time of trouble ourselves or when reports of trouble for others reach us, let us refuse to be anxious but be careful not to fail in sympathy and intercession.

Deep Mystery

Therefore doth my Father love me, because I lay down my life . . .—JOHN 10: 17.

THERE are profound depths in the nature and ways of the Godhead which we can never fathom and indeed of which we can perceive only a little. There is, for instance, the mystery of the divine love which to us men appears to have made necessary the further mystery of the Holy Trinity. For love requires both object and response and may we not say that within the infinitely blessed Godhead, the Father found His Object in the Son, from Whom, in the Person of the Holy Spirit, He received His full and adequate response. Of this mystery of divine love we can only catch a gleam as we read such Scriptures as "My beloved Son, etc." "Mine elect in Whom My Soul delighteth." "I delight to do Thy will." "I do always those things that please Him."

But there is another and yet deeper mystery; the Father Who finds such an object of His love as His Son is also pleased to bruise Him, to put Him to grief. And the Son Who does always the things that please His Father finds His painful pleasure in suffering divine judgment. The Father gives the awful cup, the Son takes and drinks it. The Father plans the dreadful Cross, the Son accepts it.

But this is love indeed, for only love which is both divine and eternal in its quality can bear the strain and accomplish the redemption. And speaking after the manner of men is not the love deepened and extended thereby, deepened, as the Son could say "Therefore doth My Father love me", and extended in that once rebellious but now believing sinners are brought into its blessed enjoyment?

The Best is Waiting

Faith . . . the evidence of things not seen.—HEBREWS 11: 1.

THE Christian's path in this life is not usually easy; it was never promised to be so. Sometimes it appears harder and more difficult than the experience of the unconverted; and there may be good reasons why it must be so.

But the Christian has the promise of the life that now is, as well as that which is to come, and considering the sense of pardon and peace with God, and the deep fellowship with his brethren, the Christian life is far and away better than any other, despite the cross.

But this morning we are reminded of the fact that what we enjoy now is really on the earnest, the first part-payment of a full inheritance which baffles description and understanding. "Eye hath not seen . . . the things." The Spirit of God is given to us, however, and His presence in the heart assures us of all that which is in store.

Now the function of faith is to give us the anticipation of the life to come with all its glorious joys described as the completion of the salvation of our souls. The joys await us and the capacity to appreciate them will be fully given in due course, but even now we have the first fruits. Let us set our affection on things above, when things on the earth are difficult and disappointing. Let us look for and hasten unto the Coming of the day of God. The prize in front of us should quicken the pace and lighten the step and enable us to despise the treasures of Egypt; let us therefore not be overtaken with an unworthy love of this passing world and its toys, "Eternal glories gleam afar, to nerve our faint endeavour."

The Enemy Spoiled

Thanks be to God, which giveth us the victory . . .—1 Cor. 15: 57.

The Bible never minimises the power of our great enemy, Satan. He is a real person with great power, long experience, and apparent success; and he has at his disposal a great army of other fallen spirits—"the rulers of the darkness of this world"—which are well-organised and implicitly obedient. Let none underestimate his skill, nor forget that it is he, not men, with whom we wrestle in our spiritual conflict.

But this foe has been conquered at the Cross. His works have been exposed and cancelled; his strategy, cunning as it is, will ultimately come to nought. He was defeated in his own domain of death, and the Conqueror having risen from the dead has made an open show of his enemies.

The full triumph, however, is reserved for the future, and in the meantime the Devil is going about as a roaring lion seeking whom he may devour; or he is stealthily moving in and out amongst men as a serpent unnoticed; or he is making his appeal as an angel of light. We must watch and pray. But whatever may be the form or guise in which he appears and appeals, we may face each day, and therefore this day, with the assurance that the Victor will lead us in His triumph and share the victory and the spoils with us. We are weak but He is strong and we may "resist the devil and he will flee from us".

Alight and Alive

Awake to righteousness, and sin not.—1 Cor. 15: 34.

We are to shun both sin and sleep. With the former we must make no contract. We died to it in Christ on the Cross and our obligations to fulfil its demands are finished for ever. Moreover it is and always must be such a dreadful thing in God's pure eyes, such an antithesis of His pure nature, that our love of Him should make us flee from it.

Sin is always associated with darkness in the Scripture. The unregenerate sinner is in darkness, his works are works of darkness and he does not come to the light lest his deeds should be reproved. It is not strange that many of the most sinful things are planned or carried out in the dark hours of the night. But now we are children of light and of righteousness let us lay aside, let us cast off, everything which is dark and sinful and walk in the light.

It is, however, possible to be free from the works of darkness but asleep, that is, we may be negatively delivered from some things but not positively and actively walking and working in righteousness. In the General Confession we rightly confess our sins of omission first; they are the more numerous, for we leave undone many things which we ought to have done, and those omissions are sins. It is high time we awoke, for the day of the completion of our salvation is drawing nearer, and the world in its sin needs the Gospel we have received and know. What a tragic thing that with such a wonderful experience behind us as our first believing, and with such a bright prospect before us as the day of salvation, we should be asleep.

From sin and sleep, Save us Good Lord.

The Family Likeness

Beloved, let us love one another.—1 JOHN 4: 7.

GOD is love; this describes his very nature, though there are other descriptions necessary in order that we may be saved from thinking of God in such a way as to suggest He is sentimental. So the same apostle in the same epistle writes "God is light". But love is the essential character of God.

One of our great difficulties is to think aright of this divine quality. Our minds are human and like every other part of our nature affected by sin. There is therefore an almost inevitable tendency to selfishness in our love, that is, we seek to find a satisfaction for our own heart in showing love to another. But, God's love is self-giving and sacrificial; there is no joy or satisfaction which He needs, for love in its expression and reciprocation was eternally perfect with the blessed Trinity. God's love for man is therefore entirely unselfish. It is this unselfish love which is the nature of God.

But every true Christian is born of God. When we trusted Christ as Saviour, the Holy Spirit imparted the divine nature and we were born of His Spirit and became members of His family. Now the family bears the likeness of the Father, and as truth and love are the indisputable marks of God so they should be of the children of God. This means that, as God gave Himself for the redemption of the world, so are we to give ourselves to help God save others.

Further, in the family of God, amongst His children divine love is the family likeness; it is the hallmark and proof of our true conversion, and should be the attitude and atmosphere in which Christians live. "See how these Christians love one another" said the enemies of the early church. It is often not so now, but it is God's purpose and there is power; so let us ask that we may walk in love towards them that are within and towards them that are without.

Conditions of Prayer

When ye stand praying, forgive, if ye have ought against any.—MARK 11: 25.

WHILE God may in His great mercy hear the prayer of one of His children who is not walking before Him in truth, yet the normal conditions for receiving answers to our prayers are clearly set forth before us in these passages; and it is with the life of prayer where we regularly ask and receive that we are now concerned.

First of all there is to be maintained a right attitude to God and this is described as follows: without doubt, in faith, with no regard for iniquity in the heart. These call for a humble walk before God and a hearty renunciation of any kind of sin and unbelief, both of which, alas, too readily cling to us and spoil our motives.

Then we must be in right relations with our fellows. There must be no wrath but the offering of a full forgiveness. If this is not our state of heart when we come to God we are commanded to leave the altar and go and put things right with our brethren first.

But as we walk in the light and respond to the corrections and drawings of God we may come before Him with boldness, lifting up holy hands in prayer and waiting for His answers in expectation. To such, God offers to become a servant—"then thou shalt call and the Lord shall answer; thou shalt cry, and He shall say, Here am I." O wonderful and understanding Omnipotence which places Himself at our disposal thus!

Looking Unto Jesus

Who for the joy . . . set before Him endured the cross.—HEBREWS 12: 2.

IF any man is to be Christ's disciple he must follow Him. This means that from the first we are committed to a life which is in harmony with heaven but out of harmony with earth. Our standards and judgments must be God's and not man's, and our very testimony will therefore be a condemnation of the present passing world. Men will despise us as they despised Him because we are moved by the principles of another world.

And this must mean that we shall inevitably lose some of the apparent gains and privileges of this life. It may materially affect our income and possessions, our future prospects in business or profession, but it is enough for the disciple that he be as his Master, and in the doing of God's will we shall find our peace.

There will be times of loneliness, and lack of sympathy, but Jesus Christ our Lord knew such times more than we—and so did the Apostle Paul, but a life of devotion to God is after all a very great privilege. Therefore let us keep our objective clear and press on in the race. Heaven with all its unspeakable joy and with the Lord's sure recompenses is at the end, and in the meantime the Lord will stand with us and strengthen us. If we miss the company of others His company will just mean more.

Gone for Ever

No more . . . for the former things are passed away.—REV. 21: 4.

THE results of sin are terrible enough and all so well known to us. They come before us again in this page; death, tears, rebuke, mourning, weeping, sorrow and sighing. How close they all are, and how common! There seems more sighing than singing, more tears than triumph, and the whole world and the whole of history is affected.

But this morning we have the glad news that all the results of sin are to be banished for ever. The words describing this indicate the completeness of their destruction; let us gather them up. There is to be no more death, tears wiped away, rebuke taken away, days of mourning ended, no more weeping, sorrow flown away, and death destroyed. What a catalogue! And what a prospect!

The prospect is sure because of God's promise. This sad entail of sin will not end because of man's improvement, his social schemes or his more highly developed science, but because God will do it. The mouth of the Lord hath spoken it. And this glorious promise of a new heaven and a new earth wherein dwelleth righteousness is to be the last and eternal condition. The days of sorrow are numbered and will be accomplished, the nights of weeping are for a season and will be passed for ever. This is glad news to a sad world and many have not believed the report. But we, God's children by grace have, and so the glory of the coming day of joy even now lights up the night of sorrow, as we wait for the break of day.

Privileged Service

A servant of Jesus Christ.—ROMANS 1: 1.

WE were formerly in bondage, we had a tyrant for our master, and yet for a long time we did not know it. So subtle was this tyrannical ruler that we were even persuaded that we were free. But when the light of God's truth began to dawn upon us then the bonds became evident and the tyranny grew worse until in grace a new Master broke the bonds and set us free. Having been made free from the first master we became glad servants of our Liberator and found His service perfect freedom; we were at last servants of Jesus Christ.

Such new service involves implicit trust and continual obedience; we must follow Him, that is we must live and serve as He directs; we must learn of Him, that is we must remember that we do not ourselves know, and take our corrections and directions from Him, repudiating all else.

But this new service is love service for it springs out of loving appreciation of Jesus Christ Himself and the mercy He has shown us. On His part, also, it is marked with privilege and intimacy, for we are not only servants but friends. We sit at His table, hear His voice and share His victuals.

Only let us be careful not to turn again to the old life with its unworthy standards and spoil this blessed intimacy. It is not beyond a possibility that we who read may grow slack and careless, and fall and grieve Him; therefore let us serve with diligence, and watch and pray.

Walking Before God

Teach me, O Lord, the way of Thy statutes.—PSALM 119: 33.

THE strength of the claim and the authority of the command to be holy lie in the fact that they are given by the Lord our God. He is Himself holy and He desires our fellowship, therefore we are called to holiness in every part of our life.

This means that the commands and prohibitions of Scripture are to be taken seriously for they express the will of God for His people, and call for the continual setting aside of the will of man and the will of the flesh. To God's statutes then our attitude must be one of simple and implicit obedience. Much stress is laid on this throughout the whole Bible and it is not to be circumvented by any ritual or sacrifice such as is represented by the Jewish rite of circumcision.

For the living of such a life of obedience we are insufficient of ourselves, but there is adequate grace in God Who will not only teach us His laws for the spiritual life but Who will also supply us with the power, working in us both the disposition to obedience and the ability to live obediently.

To Him Who commands therefore we turn with our claim to be enabled and we are met by the promises which cover our need. He is able to make all grace abound to us that we having all sufficiency in all things may abound in every good work, and be made perfect in every good to do His will.

Ultimately the test of our discipleship is not the hymns we sing, but the life we live and our obedience to God's Word and will.

Life by the Son

I am the resurrection and the life.—JOHN 11: 25.

ST. John explains at the close of his gospel (20: 30–31) that he has written particularly that those who read the record may believe that Jesus is the Christ, the Son of God, and believing may have life. He also closes his first letter with a similar explanation, namely, that those who already believe may know for certain that they have eternal life (1 John 5).

What then is this wonderful gift which is offered to us and which the apostle is so concerned that we should be sure that we possess it? It is nothing other than the divine nature (1 Pet. 1) the life of God (Ephes. 4) the life also of Jesus (2 Cor. 4).

The life which is of God was brought to earth by the Son of God and in the Incarnation was united to the life of man, and then revealed and expressed in a human body in human life. After that, the Son died and rose again and the life and immortality became available for men. The Son hath life in Himself and giveth it to those who believe, so that the same life, divine and eternal, is our life and because He lives we live also.

But this new life in Christ is eternal. It will not only be our portion here but will be our privileged possession when the Call comes from heaven and we pass into the eternity from which Christ brought the life in the first instance. He liveth for ever and ever and so shall we because indwelt and possessed by the same everlasting life.

And all this is meant to have its own effect upon today, for we go out into the ordinary affairs of this day as the bearers of the life which is still the light of men.

From Sin's Guilt and Power

I will cleanse them from all their iniquity.—JEREMIAH 33: 8.

THE promise of the Gospel is both to pardon and to cleanse. Pardon concerns guilt and is for the conscience, while cleansing is from the power of sin and concerns the heart and mind. After his sad lapse into sin, and God's merciful restoration, the Psalmist prays that he may be thoroughly washed so that the conscience may be satisfied and the heart may be purified.

Here is an Israelite of old, he has sinned and is smitten with remorse. According to the divine institution the heifer has been brought before God, the sins of Israel have been confessed over it and it has been killed. Its blood has been caught and sprinkled seven times on the congregation; the carcase has been burnt without the camp and nothing but ashes remain. How are the accusations of his conscience to be met? The answer is by looking to the blood and the ashes, for they are the proof of the giving of an unblemished life, in the shedding of innocent blood on his behalf for his sin. God will not twice demand the punishment of the sin of the believer. Therefore as he trusts the word of promise regarding the substitute, his conscience is quiet and satisfied. Righteousness has been vindicated, judgment has been satisfied, sins are pardoned.

But he longs to be delivered from repeating the folly, so he prays for cleansing from his perverseness. Has God designs to do this? The promise is made in many forms. We are to be sprinkled with clean water and we shall be clean; we are to be saved from the power of sin so that God's mighty name may be honoured. Do we hesitate to ask Him to work deeply in us, to draw us that we may run after Him instead of turning to folly, to make sin exceedingly sinful that we shun it? Let us not fail through asking only for pardon, let us beseech Him to do for us much more

For His grace and power are such,
None can ever ask too much.

Self-Discipline

Take heed unto thyself.—1 TIM. 4: 16.

THE Bible is always confronting us with two opposite considerations and to give attention to one only would produce lack of balance. For instance in Phil. 2. v. 4, we are commanded not to look on our own affairs but also on those of others; this will be a blessing to them and help to make us unselfish. But the opposite counsel is also needed, for it is possible to give so much attention to others that our own life is not what it should be. Thus the command "Take heed to thyself".

This is a call to self-discipline, to keep our body and its needs under control, to lay aside weights which would easily beset us in the race, in order that we may obtain the prize.

It is a call to watchfulness against a subtle foe, and to see to it that we are clad in the whole armour of God. For we are up against a skilful enemy with well-organised forces both angelic and human, and with long experiences in conflict with men.

In order, therefore, to be spiritually fit and that we may be more than conquerors there are some things we do well to crucify. This is necessary that we may live in fellowship with the Holy Spirit and be guided by Him in things great and small.

Let us think these things over and we shall surely reap much benefit—a benefit which will be apparent to everybody.

Our Sufficiency is of God

Be strong in the Lord and in the power of His might.—Ephesians 6: 10.

The command is to "be strong" not to "feel strong". When we feel strong then we are liable to self-confidence and that is in itself real weakness; and when we feel weak then we lay hold on God and that is strength, for He is the Mighty God. It is thus that God's strength is exhibited in our conscious weakness, and we are able to prove that God's grace is sufficient for us.

The apostle had learned this lesson, following a time of urgent prayer for the removal of "a thorn". The Lord had spoken to him, not of relief from the trial, but of grace sufficient to bear it and triumph over it. Therefore he goes on to say that infirmities are really things in which to glory because they bring this sense of weakness which is in itself a claim for power.

So when we are feeling weak and insufficient then is the time for faith to triumph over feelings and say that we can do all things through Christ Who strengtheneth us and in that confidence, to assume the God-appointed task which is indeed beyond us, and to wrestle with the problem or the foe because He is with us.

It is God's wisdom that the treasure should be in weak earthen vessels, lest undue attention should be called to the vessel when the treasure is that which is important. So let us rejoice and be glad in spite of all human frailty, for strength comes in our joy, and the Lord's joy and the Lord's strength are sufficient to stand any strain which may be imposed or permitted by our understanding God.

Inward Peace

My peace I give unto you.—JOHN 14: 27.

OUR Lord Jesus Christ has given to us His own deep peace. This is the peace which kept Him so quiet and calm when He faced difficult situations and difficult men. It is the peace which enabled Him to be silent when misrepresented and to speak calmly whenever He did speak. He gives this peace to us gladly and generously and continuously, and not as the world gives.

But gifts must not only be given, they must also be received. Martha was apparently too busy to receive the gift and became fussy about details while Mary took time to learn and to take the Master's peace. And He would have us follow Mary in this respect.

We are intended to enjoy the peace, His peace, now in this world. We shall not be exempt from the trials and troubles of the world; indeed just because we are Christians and walking contrary to current views and fashions, we may be the more sure to have them. But with the tribulation we shall have the peace and this the world cannot hinder, it is the Lord Himself Who gives it.

This peace is not only His and His to give to His own, but it is enjoyed only in Himself. That is to say this blessed gift is not to be possessed apart from Himself. Only as we abide in Him shall we realise the peace which passeth understanding and which guards both the heart and mind. In this disturbed and fretful age it is above all things necessary that we know Christ's own peace; let us therefore take the gift and bless the Giver.

His Enduring Ministry

We have a great High Priest . . . Jesus, the Son of God.—HEBREWS 4: 14.

OUR Great High Priest, the Lord Jesus Christ, ministering after the fashion of Aaron, bears our names and needs before the Lord. And that is most necessary for it is not sufficient that we were once pardoned, there still remains the need for a ministry of holding us up and of restoring us when we fall. There He is in the heavens as our Representative and Advocate to maintain our cause, with our needs upon His Strong Shoulders.

And because He never ceases or fails in this heavenly ministry, and as a priest after the order of Melchizedec, never lays it down for another to take up, we may be saved to the uttermost. There is no sin which cannot be pardoned, no fetter which cannot be broken and no circumstance in which we may not be more than conqueror, if only we continue to come to Him for grace to help in time of need.

Let us not therefore fall because we fail to hold by faith the One Whom we love and to Whom we owe all our hopes of forgiveness or victory. Indeed let us come boldly and continually because of our great and continual need. So coming we shall dwell safely by Him and be protected and supported by His care.

There for me my Saviour stands,
 Shows His wounds and spreads His hands,
God is love; I know, I feel,
 Jesus lives, and loves me still.

Our Guest and Lord

Ye were sealed with that Holy Spirit of promise.—EPHESIANS 1: 13.

THE Holy Spirit of God—the name alone suggests much. He is first of all the Spirit of God "proceeding from the Father and the Son, and with the Father and the Son is worshipped and glorified". He is the Third Person of the Blessed Trinity; "the Father is God, the Son is God, and the Holy Ghost is God". Yet that same Spirit has by His Grace and power imparted new life to us, even "the life of God", and we are now children of God. Not only so but He still ministers to us of life, strength, comfort, wisdom and every virtue we possess, and He does this by uniting us moment by moment with the Father and the Son in a stream of life.

But the adjective used is also of the utmost importance. He is the "Holy" Spirit of God. Quite obviously He is holy for He is God, but in a way which is not done in the case of the Father and Son, He is very often called "Holy". This may be to remind us of the divine character and purity of the Person of the Trinity Who lives within us, and is intended to save us from viewing our gentle, awful Guest with less than deepest reverence.

The Holy Spirit of God is both Guest and Lord. To Him we should submit, and Him we must not grieve, for He is our Strengthener and Companion, our Monitor and Guide.

And every virtue we possess,
  And every victory won,
And every thought of holiness
  Are His alone.

Present and Eternal Mercies

How great is Thy goodness.—PSALM 31: 19.

It is not only true that God hath shown us mercy but that He showers upon us abundant mercies. His kindness is loving kindness and His goodness is great goodness. We can all testify of the fact that God has loaded us with benefits; this is according to His nature which is to give and to give again. Despite the disciplines and trials the true believer has the promise of life that now is.

But God's great mercies are only just beginning and they are in some measure limited by our capacity to receive and our ability to bear. In the life which is to come, more and greater mercies are laid up for us. The delights and pleasures are prepared by Infinite Goodness, they baffle description and they will abundantly satisfy.

Let us cultivate the view of God's goodness. Our actions, attitude and prayers, often tend to suggest that God is poor or niggardly, that we need to beg Him to part with His gifts. But that is not so. He has enough for each, enough for all and enough for evermore. Withholding doth not enrich Him nor does giving impoverish Him. What is our present need? If it is a real need it shall be met. But more than that the Lord loves to give His children extras, those tokens of a thoughtful love which come as glad surprises and enable us to say "How great is Thy goodness".

A Good Shepherd and Green Pastures

The Lord is my shepherd: I shall not want.—PSALM 23: 1.

THE relationship of the shepherd and his flock, so well-known to the people of the East, is used many times in Scripture to explain the relationship between Christ and His people, and a selection of such passages is before us today.

The picture of foolish sheep going astray is the first in the sequence of thought. Head down and concerned only with the food, or attracted by some inviting pasture, the sheep takes the wrong path and follows a dangerous direction. But the good shepherd finding the sheep in difficulties of its own making rescues it, though it costs him his life, and brings it back to the fold, afterwards caring for it and choosing the best pasture and the purest water.

And we were as sheep going astray. Left to our own devices we would have destroyed ourselves but our Great and Good Shepherd delivered us and restored us to the flock. And what shall we say of Him afterwards? Is it not true that He has shewn us nothing but love and care as He called us by name and led us forth to pasture and to service? It is true that He has used the rod to correct as well as to guide but that was love as well.

Most satisfying it is to know that while here below we shall be fed with His provision, even when enemies surround, and be kept fresh with His supplies of grace; and safely brought to the fold which is safe and satisfying for evermore. Christ is indeed the Good Shepherd.

His True Nature

Praise the Lord of Hosts: for the Lord is good.—JEREMIAH 33: 11.

THE Lord is good, that is the all-important fact, and the rest follows. It is this which is fundamental in our knowledge of God. Psalm 118, which our Lord apparently sang with His disciples in the upper room during the night before the day of His crucifixion, begins and ends with this statement. It is a truth to sing about and to sing about in days of darkness, for though the light of God's countenance appears hidden for a moment, this quality in His nature remains for ever, God is good.

Because God is good certain things follow as we are reminded here. For instance, His mercy endureth for ever, He is our refuge and strength, a very present help in trouble. God's mercy is His goodness extended to us in our sin or need, and because God endureth His goodness and mercy likewise endure. Our failure does not make Him change His disposition towards us, though it may cause Him to change His dealings, and our need must ever be the occasion of His loving provision. If we hold fast to this "that God is never otherwise than good", then we shall find in Him a place of retreat and defence, whatever experiences we may pass through.

But the Lord not only loves us but He knows us, knows whether or not we are truly His, knows our ways most intimately. The psalmist (Ps. 139) says that He knows our downsitting and our uprising, and our thoughts afar off. No one, however, knowing God to be good would wish it to be otherwise. The result of realising God's goodness and His knowledge, is surely to make us long to walk before Him in holiness all our days.

That Blessed Hope

We look for the Saviour.—PHIL. 3: 20.

IT is the coming again of our Lord Jesus Christ which brings the redeeming work of God to its completion. Without such another advent much would be left unfinished —and much which all believers long to see and enjoy.

For instance our bodies are to be brought into the redemption. They are included as part of the whole man in the plan of God, but still they are bodies of our humiliation, vessels of clay. They suffer from every kind of disease and become the channel and means of many kinds of sin, and the bodies of those who have died in Christ rest as dust in the earth. But when He comes they will become the bodies of His glory like unto His most glorious body, and changed and perfected they will serve their purpose in the eternal glory.

Then there is the world of mankind with all its sin and confusion. Wicked monsters inflict their gross misrule upon suffering subjects, wars disturb the life of quiet home-loving people, and peoples made of one blood to be brothers, live in suspicion and sometimes hatred. When Christ comes He will judge the wicked and release the oppressed, and man, so long misruled by every form of human government, will taste the rule of the Son of God.

It is true that the promise of His Coming is not a bright promise for the wicked for it will inaugurate their judgment. But for the Christian it is a blessed hope. We shall see Him, Whom having not seen we now love. We shall enter into His immediate presence, and into His higher service in the new heavens and earth. "When by His grace we shall look on His face, that will be glory for us"—and this anticipation makes the prospect bright and shortens the distance home. In the meantime let us "live looking for such an One".

The Precious Blood

It is the blood that maketh an atonement for the soul.—LEV. 17: 11.

THE teaching of the Scriptures on redemption by blood is all here in embryo in this Old Testament Scripture. Notice, first of all, that the life is in the blood. This means that it was the life, innocent in the case of the Old Testament sacrifice, but holy and righteous in the New Testament Sacrifice, which is in view. And what a life our Substitute's was!—Holy, harmless, separate from sinners, doing always those things which pleased God, utterly devoid of selfishness, self-seeking, self-advertisement and every other form of sin which doth so seriously infect us. His was a life not merely free from sin but filled with every virtue, and He was both God and man. Was ever life like this? The answer is "No".

But notice, in the second place, that the teaching of the blood includes that it is given to us upon the altar, that is, it is not the life lived and possessed which redeems, but the life laid down for sin. While the life of the sacrifice was in the blood in the veins it had no atoning efficacy, but once it was yielded up in sacrifice then, and only then, was pardon possible for the guilty. And so Jesus Christ could never save by His example or teaching, it must be when His full spotless life was given for us, and sin's judgment was borne that He became a Saviour.

The Christian is he who relies for his acceptance with God on that One life lived and sacrificed. The Son of God had in His incarnation identified Himself with man, and in His cross with man's sin. Now we by faith identify ourselves with Him. As the Israelite laid his hands on the lamb, expressing his trust in its acceptance on his behalf, so we lay the hand of faith on the Lamb of God and trust His death and blood for our pardon and acceptance, with His God and ours.

The precious blood of Christ; let us linger on the theme.

Worthwhile Striving

Let us labour to enter into that rest.—HEB. 4: 11.

THE Bible clearly sets before us many, most desirable blessings. There is heart rest, life, the Kingdom of God, the meat which endureth, the assurance of our calling and election, an incorruptible crown. All these are for all Christians but not all Christians will receive them all.

While we are saved by grace, discipline and endeavour are needed for their full realisation, hence the call to labour, to give diligence, and to self-control.

Must one then labour to enter into rest? Yes, indeed we must labour lest we miss the blessing. Many never know what it is to cease from struggling because they have never really struggled. There is too little earnestness and urgency. The blessings of God are received by faith, but we are usually and only prepared for such an act by renouncing and giving everything for its possession.

Let us take rest as one example, and in Hebrews 4 the word is used in several connections. There is the rest of pardon, the rest of the Sabbath and the rest of heaven, and all of them follow after labour and diligent search. Pardon is not given to the unconvicted and undisturbed. It is to the man who is most seriously awakened and desirous, to whom it is offered as a gift, and who is enabled to take it by faith. Only he who has laboured six days knows the joy of Sabbath rest, and they will know best the rest of heaven above who have known most of conflict below.

But of heart-rest, inward rest, which is to be our daily portion whatever the weather or the strain, this comes when after struggling to obtain it, and being bent on its possession, we enter into its enjoyment by sweetly resting in the divine governance and enabling. Thereafter all God's will is sweet and all our enemies He destroys. Let us labour to enter into that rest.

The Way of Prayer and Faith

All things are possible to him that believeth.—Mark 9: 23.

How utterly different from earthly power is the power that moves in spiritual things. The one is manifest in the strong physical frame, or in the possession of military advantage or material; it may consist in mental superiority, in social rank, or in skilful strategy. By means of sheer weight of force, of numbers, of resources, there is a pressure which moves and pushes aside its obstacle or crushes it beneath its weight.

But the power which moves to spiritual ends is not so. It operates when the knees are bent in prayer, through the foolishness of preaching, when no resistance is offered to wrong; the meek inherit the earth.

One of our perils is that we seek to accomplish spiritual ends without spiritual means, that is by trusting the arm of flesh. We fall into the error of assuming that by more advertising power, greater numbers, more influential supporters, the work of God will necessarily prosper—and yet it may not please God to bless us when we have all these. It is the Spirit of God Who convicts, converts and sanctifies. He alone can move the hearts of men to real repentance and faith. So to Him alone we must look that all our expectations may come from Him.

This emphasises once again the fact that God has ordained this simple way of fulfilling His designs for man's blessing, namely, the way of prayer and faith. Truly it sets aside many of the things in which we men most naturally trust. It takes the glory and the praise from man and gives it all to God to Whom it is due. But this is God's way, the best way, the only way. Let us therefore give ourselves to prayer, and as we see God work, our faith will grow, and we shall most reverently and naturally expect more.

A Divine Disposition

The fruit of the Spirit is longsuffering, gentleness.—GALATIANS 5: 22.

LONGSUFFERING and gentleness are marks of a disposition which is Godlike and rare. They are the gentle qualities and fragrant fruit which only come from a full enduement of the Spirit of grace.

They are not to be confused with their natural substitutes which are weak and superficial. The godly character of which these graces form a part is strong and discriminating. Longsuffering does not fail to see the fault, but it also appreciates the difficulties, and extenuates the other by a full understanding of the frailty of human nature. Gentleness is not weakness but strength which is held in control and which works with sympathy.

These qualities, and the other graces, make courteous Christians, God's ladies and gentlemen. They make one approachable and helpful, and it is to the longsuffering and gentle that bruised and wounded souls turn for help and counsel. These fruits of the Spirit are palatable and fragrant and by their sheer goodness lead men to our Father which is in heaven, for they are recognised as coming from Him.

But they and all other virtues are the fruits of the Spirit. They grow in the life which is yielded and trustful; they flourish where faith and obedience to God and His Word are at the root of the spiritual life. Such a disposition forgives for Christ's sake, is a proof of Christ's wisdom, waits patiently for Christ's returning, and is indeed found in the walk which is worthy of Christ, because it is like His walk before us in this world.

Self-Discipline

Here . . . no continuing city, but we look for one to come.—Hebrews 13: 14.

We are pilgrims moving towards the Celestial City. We have been mercifully led out of the world and we began the journey with high hopes. It is a great journey with much involved all the way along, and with a judgment-seat and rewards awaiting at the end. This calls for a willingness to give ourselves wholly to the journey.

Our loins must be girded, that is we must "pull ourselves together" and refuse to be slack. This concerns, first of all and most of all, the habits of our mind, for they will determine the conduct of our lives.

We need discipline in the use of our time—"Ye shall eat it in haste". Time to the Christian is sacred. This does not mean we must be always busy. There are times for rest apart, time for health-giving holidays and games; but it does mean that we must watch against becoming triflers who let the hours and days slip away with no purpose.

Discipline is needed that our lights may be kept burning. As with lamps of old the wick becomes encrusted and the flame dies down. It is necessary therefore to judge and correct ourselves that the light may burn brightly and we may live in the expectation of His appearing.

This will remind us of an abundance of Scripture teaching which calls for us to lay aside any weight which will hinder in the race. We began with high hopes. Let us continue in the same, and may the testimony to His faithfulness of our last days be the brightest of all.

It May Be Today

Watch . . . for the Son of Man cometh.—MATT. 25: 13.

ALMOST two thousand years have passed since the Lord first taught His disciples to expect Him back again, and since the apostles emphasised the teaching, it is easy to grow hopeless after so long a watch and the morning still tarries.

But He will come again, and we are to be ready, on the tiptoe of expectancy, perchance it should be today. Cares of home and business, or unrestrained pleasure and indulgence, may dim our hope and we are therefore to avoid both. Corroding care and unnecessary indulgence must be shunned. The former is perhaps the temptation of the anxious temperament and the latter is the danger of the phlegmatic and sanguine, but both are enemies of that preparedness for the day of His appearing which He Himself commands and expects.

It may be today, for we do not know the day or the hour, that is we do not know the time either approximately or exactly. When He is least expected He will come, and the last prayer of the Bible is, "Even so Come, Lord Jesus."

This attitude to the Second Coming of our Lord Jesus is a good test of our spiritual condition. If we treasure our own plans rather than God's, we shall hope for a delay until our schemes are realised. If we are not very busy about the Master's business, then how can we look for His return? What is our state this morning? Is the prospect of His coming full of thrilling joy? If we really love Him "more than these" then there is nothing more desirable than just Himself, Whom we shall then behold.

But Lord, 'tis for Thee, for Thy Coming we wait!

From Glory to Glory

We beheld His glory . . . as of the only begotten of the Father.—JOHN 1: 14.

THE ways of God are always from one glory to another and to a greater glory. This is so in reality even when the process seems to be in reverse. If our plan is thwarted, or, what was shewn to us years ago to be the plan, is now passing through a change, it is because God has provided some better thing for us.

So it was in the case of God's tabernacle among men. At first it was made of wood overlaid with gold, of fine-twined linen interwoven with symbolic colours. In this God dwelt during the wilderness journey and here the pillar of cloud and fire rested. But later the tabernacle was displaced by the Temple with its more glorious structure and furniture. In this case instead of one layer there was a molten sea ten cubits across; in the place of a floor of sand, reminding of the desert through which they were passing, there was a floor of cypress wood, and in every way the house was more magnifical.

But in the fullness of time the Word became flesh and tabernacled among us. "Will God in very deed dwell with men," asked Solomon. Yes, the Second Person of the Blessed Trinity was incarnate by the Holy Ghost, of the Virgin Mary and dwelt amongst men, living their life in obscurity at Nazareth.

But men with whom He dwelt destroyed this temple of His body on a hill outside the city wall. Even then and there the glory was revealed, the glory of His self-sacrificing love, and in dying He made peace between God and men.

All of Grace

Where is boasting then? It is excluded.—ROMANS 3: 27.

THERE is not the smallest ground on which we can boast, for our salvation, position and service, is all of grace.

As touching our salvation, the New Testament is always stressing this fact. It is taught negatively, "not of works", "not by works which we have done"; and it is taught positively "by grace are ye saved", "according to His mercy He saved us". When we look out upon the ungodly in their ungodliness and when we consider their latter end, which is terrible indeed, we can say "there go we but for the grace of God".

And if it was the God of grace Who in the beginning pardoned and justified us, and set us in His presence in the righteousness of His Son accepted in the Beloved, it is still the same grace which keeps and calls to service. The little that we do for Him is possible because He moves us and helps us. There is no ground for self-congratulation.

Boasting excluded, pride I abase,
I'm only a sinner, saved by grace.

All this we know in our minds but so easily forget to appreciate. Hence we become unsympathetic with the lost, and critical of them in their sins. Or we pride ourselves on our service, when the very pride itself taints the service and spoils it. Did we really believe that our standing and service were all of grace, then the two gracious fruits, humility and thanksgiving, would flourish.

The Delight of His Love

We love Him, because He first loved us.—1 JOHN 4: 19.

GOD is love; love is the very essence of His nature. And love must find an object. Within the Godhead the activity of divine love is reciprocal; the Father loveth the Son and the Son loveth the Father.

But God's love has been manifested; it extends to His creatures and is manifest in all its glory to us undeserving sinners, to whom God commends Himself by giving His Son to die for us. God has focussed His love upon us without finding any other cause than that He loves us. It is not because we who are His children are better or greater than others, but perhaps even the reverse. Yet the unworthiness of the object magnifies the disposition of the One Who so loved the world.

But there is a special and particular love of God which rests upon His own dear Son manifest in the flesh and atoning for sin. In Him as the God-man, renouncing His privilege of self-determination and choosing to do the will of His Father in heaven, God finds a perfect object, and in Him His love is satisfied. But that dear Son of God is also the Representative and Head of His people and all the favour of the Head is shared by every member of the family. "We are complete in Him." We are accepted in the Beloved, and we may live in the joy of God's unclouded favour.

So near, so very near to God,
Nearer we cannot be;
For in the Person of His Son,
We are as near as He.

Importunate in Prayer

Men ought always to pray, and not to faint.—LUKE 18: 1.

FOR reasons, some of which are readily understandable and others less so, God does not quickly respond to our prayers; we are kept waiting. The discipline of waiting is good; it sifts out mere impulses in distinction from desires; the delay develops patience and other virtues. Moreover there may be reasons and principles in the spiritual world of which we have some hint in the word of the angelic messenger to Daniel: "Fear not, Daniel: for from the first day thou didst set thine heart to understand . . . thy words were heard and I am come for thy words. But the prince of Persia withstood me one and twenty days." Here is Daniel praying on for three weeks and doubtless wondering if he were heard. Indeed he was from the beginning, but some resistance by a fallen angel prolonged the battle for three weeks. But Daniel did not faint and so the answer arrived. He prayed always and did not faint.

In the same way all the saints of the Bible and of subsequent Church history have found it both necessary and blessed to "pray through", holding on in prayer and faith, refusing to be discouraged and to faint, until God sent His answer. Such men are princes with God and, having first prevailed with God, go out to prevail with men.

To learn this lesson well let us climb the mountain of Olives where Jesus is wont to pray. All night He stays upon His knees, or stretches Himself upon the ground. But did He not say at the tomb of Lazarus: "I know that thou hearest me always"? Yes indeed, but even for the Son of God there were delays and He understands and strengthens us now when we have to continue long in prayer before the answer comes.

Mutual Delight

. . . *and He shall give thee the desires of thine heart.*—PSALM 37: 4.

ALL through the Bible there is described and illustrated an attitude to God of heart and mind which ensures His blessing. Here such a disposition is described in the following terms, "feareth the Lord", "trusting in the Lord", "delighting in the Lord", seeking "first the Kingdom of God", "sought the Lord". Such phrases describe the heart which is frank yet willing for correction, earnest and yet humble; in short, and to quote another Scripture phrase, it is a heart which is perfect before the Lord. Such a heart God loves; there is no cloud between Him and the soul, and communion is unbroken; and it is for communion God longs so much.

Now where God finds such a person He loves to show special favours. He makes the life to prosper, it is happy and things go well, He is with His child and adds many luxuries to the promised necessaries. The Lord loves to surprise His children who love Him; many unexpected mercies strew the path, and nothing seems too good for the godly.

But should the Lord appoint the painful and difficult for His servant, as sometimes He does, even for those most anxious to please Him, still He does well, and it only means that in such cases our Heavenly Father is shewing us favour in the blessings of heaven and not of earth, in spiritual and not temporal ways. God is covenanted to bless those who seek His face and are concerned for His glory.

Open Thou Our Lips

Never man spake like this man.—JOHN 7: 46.

IF, as Scripture teaches, we are condemned or justified by our words, then our Lord Jesus Christ is justified and we are condemned.

From all quarters testimony is borne to His fair speech. The Psalmist, by the Spirit of prophecy, speaks of the grace poured into His lips, the evangelist records the judgment of the officers sent to arrest Him, as "never man spake like this man". Who He was they knew not, no theological bias affected their thoughts, but the words of Christ convinced them of His superiority to all men. Words in season, words of help and encouragement, of correction and reproof, of life and salvation, all came from His lips, and all bare Him witness, and wondered.

But men cannot say this of us, and perhaps those who know us best know most of our failings. The fair speech is marred by criticism, unkind report, hasty and irritable speech and we can only confess with shame that our words condemn us.

But the glory of the Gospel is that we may be like our Lord, indeed we must be. If grace is poured into His lips, then it may be poured into ours, and the same words of truth may, through us, be quick and powerful, and healing and saving. For this God would be enquired of to do it for us. We are commanded to store our hearts and minds with His word and words. We are to pray daily, nay hourly, "Set a watch before my mouth, keep the door of our lips" and to ask Him to open our lips that our mouths may shew forth His praise. May it be so.

Looking to the Pit

We . . . were by nature the children of wrath.—EPHESIANS 2: 3.

IT is good for us to remember our condition when grace found us, or to use the words of the prophet, "to look to the pit from which we were digged". The Bible wisely reminds us that we were once children of wrath as others, with the wrath of God resting on us; we were dead in sins and unable to make ourselves alive unto God; we were in the far country far from God, alienated and enemies in our minds by wicked works; we were like others and could never make ourselves to differ from them. But the grace of God reached us and translated us out of the kingdom of darkness into the Kingdom of God's dear Son. The change was all of God and all of grace. The impartation of new life was the work of God's Spirit as the removal of the wrath was all the work of God's Son.

The remembrance of our natural condition will surely make us sympathetic with others who are still in the place where we were. We shall not judge them but love them and seek to tell them of the love of God, of the Cross of Christ and of the wonderful offer of the Gospel. When we see men and women in their sin we shall each of us say to ourselves "there go I but for the grace of God", and instead of thanking God that we are not as other men are, we shall seek to turn them to the Saviour by prayer and persuasion.

Just as the memory of our past sinful condition will keep us humble and sympathetic with those who are still in sin, so the remembrance of God's first visiting our soul in mercy will quicken our love to the Lord. It is good that we should never cease to marvel at the grace of God which saves us.

" 'Tis mercy all immense and free
For, O my God, it found out me."

Welcomed and Reinstated

His father saw him, and ran . . . and kissed him.—LUKE 15: 20.

IT has been said that the only occasion when it is suggested in the Bible that God is in a hurry is when He is receiving a repentant prodigal. It may be doubtful exposition to take a word from a parable and from that alone suggest something so unusual about God, but the basic thought is appreciated, namely that God is overjoyed when men turn to Him. And is it not encouraging to remember that every day more are converted than on the day of Pentecost just in order to maintain His holy Church throughout all the world, let alone to ensure its increase.

It is the Lord's nature to forgive and to do it joyfully. It is His prerogative to pardon and to pardon abundantly. All this is possible because sin has been dealt with and God can restore without question of His righteousness.

But pardon is only the threshold (wonderful threshold though it be!) of the new life. It introduces us into a position of favour which is altogether gracious. Not only are our sins removed from us an immeasurable distance, but we are made children and heirs by the adoption of grace; we are brought near to God and made friends of the saints. All the children of God, both past and present, small and great, are made my brethren for we are washed in the same blood, adopted into the same family, love the same Lord Jesus Christ, and are travelling to the same heavenly home.

> 'Tis mercy all! Let earth adore
> Let angel minds enquire no more.

Tried by Fire

The Lord your God proveth you.—DEUT. 13: 3.

EVERYTHING which concerns the Kingdom of God must be proved, for God is concerned with quality rather than quantity, with character rather than appearances, and He is working for Eternity. So the people of God, the children of Israel were tried as no other nation and the saints all down the ages have been tried as none other, because the Lord was seeking a people to worship Him and to shew forth His glory to others.

Testing is like a fire, it is both hot and consuming. The very same experience which is to burn up the dross and purify the character is at the same time hard to bear and painful to experience. This makes the Christian life a most solemn, while at the same time a most glorious, adventure. There will be things permissible to others which are not permissible to us, because of the high purpose of our lives. Kings and priests must live to purpose, and conduct themselves in a way which is in keeping with their station.

So all along the pilgrimage we are being tested as by fire, and both our character and our service is being purified. But it is not the flame in which God delights, but the object which is in view. He seeks a character of pure gold and service which will bear lasting fruit. We may be sure that as we pass through the fire it is only our dross to consume and our gold to refine; and He is with us all the time. When the work is done we shall come forth as gold; and without question in the glory which baffles all description, and is beyond our best thoughts, we shall bless the hand that guided and the heart that planned not only the end, but the way which led there.

United to Christ

I live: yet not I, but Christ liveth in me.—GALATIANS 2: 20.

HERE is the secret of Christianity, namely, that each believer is united with Christ in His death and resurrection. This is all of the grace of God, Who took the initiative first in coming to earth and taking to Himself our nature, then in carrying both our sinful nature and our sinful acts to the Cross for the judgment of God, and finally in rising again. All this He did as our Representative and Substitute. So that it is true that not only did He die and rise again, but that we died and rose with Him. All this became personally and effectively true when we were united to Him from our side by saving faith.

Life now is to be lived as being dead to sin and alive to God. It is not to be by cultivating and correcting the flesh, but by trusting and obeying the Son of God. We are able to abide in Him by simple active faith, that is, we are to count on His life in us and draw upon His grace. And this will mean also a definite refusal to live in the flesh, seeking one's own pleasure or glory. Our sinful selves are to be renounced and Christ is to be chosen in each test.

It is possible by the grace of God so to choose Christ and to refuse self that we remain in living communion with Him so that His life is evidently in control of ours, and we walk, in some measure, as He walked, in glad expectation of His coming again.

Suffering and Glory

If . . . we suffer with Him, that we may be glorified together.—ROMANS 8: 17.

THE cross and the crown are intimately related. No cross, no crown; a little cross, a little crown; a heavy cross, a heavy crown. And this is not merely so on the principle of compensation or reward; it is not only that God will give a crown to the one who has carried the cross, but that with the crown in view He appoints the cross. It needs the sufferings to prepare and enable us to receive a crown.

It is quite natural for us to shrink from suffering, to think more of the crown than the cross. But God, in His wisdom, knows how fruitful and valuable tribulation can be, and therefore He permits it. The discipline of the uncomfortable, moulds the character and matures the soul and, in some way not now understood, is preparing us for the privileges and responsibilities in glory for which we should otherwise be unfitted.

While, therefore, we are passing through our keen disappointments, sorrows and pain, the Lord has mercifully sent us words of comfort telling us of Christ's present consolations and of our future glory, when we shall rejoice with exceeding joy. If death is working in us now then life will be full then.

The end of God's purposes are glorious and beyond description, though the way to it may be painful. Let us therefore be persuaded by the teaching and take hold of the promises, so that we may not only be kept from failing but be enabled to triumph.

Secrets Revealed

There is a God in heaven that revealeth secrets.—DANIEL 2: 28.

How little man knows of God, or ever can know apart from revelation. Even that which is plainly revealed in nature of His eternal power and Godhead is often missed and man worships either the creature instead of the Creator or fails to worship at all.

But there is a spirit of humility and teachability to which God responds by unveiling Himself and His truth. The things we could never discover by searching out become known to us, so that we should pray not to be haughty nor have lofty eyes.

All this is true when we first come to the Lord and are first received by Him in Christ, but it is increasingly true as we continue in the Christian life. The secret of the Lord is shared with them that walk humbly with Him. He looks for those to whom he can trust His private affairs. "Shall I hide from Abraham the thing which I am about to do?" Alas, there are too few who are introduced into His intimate counsels.

Our Lord Jesus reminded us of all this when He spoke to His disciples informing them that they were not just servants, that is, not only His to do as they were told, but also friends to be acquainted with the counsel and reason of His commands. It is the ministry of the Holy Spirit first to make us teachable and then to lead us into the secrets of the Lord. Some secrets God reserves to Himself, we cannot bear them now, but many more would be revealed were we sufficiently aware to listen and to learn.

Without Sin and Without Suspicion

See that ye walk circumspectly.—EPHESIANS 5: 15.

THE Christian is never "off duty" as regards his conduct; he is everywhere to live and speak as becometh the Gospel. How easy it is to fail the Lord in hours of relaxation or on occasions of free social intercourse. There is a necessary slackening of discipline and in an unguarded moment something is said or done which disappoints and hinders someone who is looking to us for an example, or what is more important we grieve the gentle Spirit of God.

We are reminded today of the necessity of both acting carefully and of making the most of our fleeting years. This calls for purpose and demands all our heart and all our soul. There must be no slackening if the Lord's coming again appears to be delayed, for He will certainly come and it may be just when we are careless in our conduct.

So let us gird up the loins of our minds and be like men who are on trial, to whom others are looking and for whom Christ is coming. Those who live thus are blessed now, for there is present gain and happiness in such a manner of life, and when He does return, there will be a full recognition of our intention to walk wisely and live nobly.

Pleading as Suppliants

Praying always with all prayer and supplication.—EPHESIANS 6: 18.

PRAYER has many forms and varies greatly in its exercise. It includes silent adoration of which we know so little in our busy western world; it includes confession and praise, but here we are concerned with supplication, the humble approach to God to seek His favour on others and upon ourselves.

In supplication the petitioner is on his knees, other positions seem incongruous for such an attitude of spirit. He is pleading for mercy and not claiming his rights. There is a sense of deep need and urgency that words are often inadequate and set forms, of great value in other and ordinary circumstances, do not adequately express the soul's deep longing. The Spirit must help our infirmities; in His mercy He shares our concern—indeed He is the author of it—and prays in us and through us with longings which are beyond expressing in words.

If God has given us burdens and put us, or others, in places of need so that we can only supplicate His throne, then let us be thankful for He will appear for us. It may be others will be given to share the same concern with us; but whether this is so or not, let us continue to lift up our hands and wait God's time and answer. "It shall be done" and once again we shall be able to say "I love the Lord because He hath heard my voice and my supplications!"

And Glory Crowns the Mercy Seat

Let us draw near with a true heart.—HEBREWS 10: 22.

THE long patient lesson which God has been ever teaching mankind is how to draw near to Him. This He could only teach as men were able to bear, hence the lesson was line upon line, here a little and there a little; but without God teaching us we should never have found it and man would either have fled from God like Adam or come to Him in the wrong way like Cain.

But the way into the holiest has been not only taught but made and we may now draw near. It is a way which honours both God's righteousness and His mercy, for it is by the blood of Jesus and coming by that way we are accepted. There, that is, in Jesus Christ and through His shed blood, God meets man in grace and man meets God in faith.

In our approach to God we must draw near with a true heart, earnestly desiring to seek Him and putting away anything which is unfitted for His holy Presence. All pretence and hypocrisy must be shunned for He is a God of truth and must be sought with a true heart. But so coming we may do so in full assurance of faith; there is no need for us to be in doubt as to our acceptance.

But let us draw near, let us come boldly. How often we are satisfied to remain in the outer courtyard of activity, the place where men move to and fro, and traffic in news and business. Less frequently we pass into the holy place for service; but let us draw near to God in the holiest of all by the blood of Jesus. We may be silent there and worship, but God is still seeking worshippers.

Be Ye . . . For I Am

Holiness, without which no man shall see the Lord.—HEBREWS 12: 14.

MANY and varied reasons are given why we, who are God's children and servants should be holy. If we are to be usable by God we must be holy; as the surgeon uses only the aseptic instrument, so God can use only those who are clean. If we are to reveal God in Christ to men, not only in the words we speak but the character we bear, then we must be holy. If we are to witness personally, and seek to draw others to Christ, then it must be necessary, first of all, to be holy.

But the highest and chiefest reason of all is given in these scriptures. We are to be holy as God is holy, we are to be holy in every department of life because He is holy. What does this imply? Just this, that the chief call to and motive for holiness is not service or influence with man, but fellowship with God. Our moral likeness to Him is the measure of our fellowship with Him. Only as we hate sin, can we draw near to the Sinless One; only as we love righteousness can we dwell with the righteous God. And God is not only seeking those who will serve Him but He is seeking worshippers and those who love His presence and seek his face. This alone is a sufficient reason why we should be holy.

To that end let us put off that which is corrupt and let us put on the Lord Jesus Christ. This will call for deliberate decision and definite action, but as we desire and decide to be holy, the Spirit Who has been given to dwell in us and Whose name is the Holy Spirit will make us increasingly holy before God and man.

Wages for the Unworthy

Whosoever shall give . . . in My Name . . . shall not lose his reward.—MARK 9: 41.

IN view of God's unmerited love so freely bestowed upon us who were rebels, must we not all say that we are unprofitable servants and have at best done what it was our duty to do. Indeed we should all have to confess that we fell far short of even doing our duty. Our merit would all be demerit, and did we really receive wages at all we should certainly receive death, which is the wages of sin. But God not only saves us by grace. He also rewards us for our service, which we should surely wish to render in any case.

The opportunities of pleasing God are as numerous as the days of our life, and as varied. Whether therefore we are training children, giving cups of cold water to strangers, waiting upon God's aged servants, or whatever it may be, we shall not lose our reward. This will be proportionate to our labour, in keeping with our sacrifice and will be for many as great a surprise as those to whom the Lord gave a reward for feeding and clothing Himself and taking Him in when a stranger.

To view life, however, as an opportunity of pleasing God and of serving Him as He desires and deserves, is to lift it far above the drab and commonplace. Every turn of the road and every new face raises the question of whether or not there is some service to be done which will be a blessed occasion of loving someone for Christ's sake. And nothing so done will miss its wages, which pierced Hands will give, and make the reward so much more precious.

A Worthy Example

The Son of Man came not to be ministered unto, but to minister.—MARK 10: 45.

It is certainly true that, whereas many who are trusting in their own righteousness are more concerned with following Christ's example than with resting on His finished work, at the same time most who have accepted the truth "Christ suffered for us", have failed in giving adequate attention to the accompanying truth, "leaving us an example that ye should follow His steps". Let us consider, then, this life of discipleship; though it is costly it is commanded, and it is worthy.

Our Lord Jesus Christ, we are first reminded, trod the path of selfless service. He was not looking for what He could get, but what He could give; He asked not that others should serve Him but that He, the Son of God, might serve others. So He washed His disciples' feet and shewed us that being servant of all is being chiefest of all.

And he went about doing good, just doing good. This suggests that He was not always considering what spiritual results would follow, but was happy to do good as a worthy end in itself. The spiritual results did follow as we know, and will.

All this springs from a right disposition, the meekness and gentleness of Spirit, which in the sight of God is of such great price. Such a spirit makes it comparatively easy to forgive others, to be kind and tender-hearted.

If we are Christ's by trusting in His atoning death, let us remember that though we cannot die as He did—and there is no need—yet we must of necessity seek to live as He did. If this should be a life of self-sacrifice and loss, unpopular and unappreciated, the fact that there is the joy set before us, the joy of seeing Him, will help us also to despise the shame.

Believing God's Word

Nevertheless I live; yet not I, but Christ liveth in me.—GALATIANS 2: 20.

THE wonderful statements of the Bible set before us are true because in God's mercy Christ united Himself with us in the incarnation, and then became our Substitute and Representative in His death and resurrection.

At first sight they seem untrue and unreal and unrelated to the facts of life. Unbelief would reason thus, "the Bible says I have died, but my sinful self is very much alive as both others and I know; it is stated that all things are become new but in fact much remains of the old". Now this is the argument of unbelief but the argument of faith is otherwise. Faith says: "Christ has died in my place, therefore I died at the same time. God has told me that it is so and I believe it even though it is not always easy to do so."

Does all this seem artificial and unreal? Indeed it is the way we turn God's promises into facts and experience. We did it at our conversion when we accepted God's word about His Son bearing our sins. Let us now believe what is further written concerning our sinful nature. And as faith stands on God's word, rather than on past experience, God will make the experience agree with the word.

We are in Him, that is, we are vitally united to Him by grace through faith; His death to sin is ours and His resurrection to life is ours also. Let us therefore reckon ourselves alive unto God through Him to-day and thus walk in newness of life.

The Indwelling Presence

If I depart, I will send Him unto you.—JOHN 16: 7.

WE can easily enter into the sorrow of the disciples when they learned that their Master was to leave them. He had been with them for three years and His friendship had been so wonderful. How will they fare without Him? It is always the personal and immediate which threaten to endanger the blessing which is universal and abiding. So He says to them "it is expedient for you that I go away". In the long run it will be better for them and for all.

The change is to be from a visible Friend to an invisible One, from the Second Person of the Blessed Trinity to the Third Person, but it is all so wise and loving, for since Pentecost God has not only been with His disciples but in them, not only their example and guide but their life and power.

And the exchange has worked for the good of the whole Church throughout all the centuries. The Blessed Spirit is as near to us as He was to James and John because He dwelleth within. This indwelling unites all God's children, gives to all who believe the assurance of their acceptance before God, fills them with praise as they think of their Father. Moreover He enables us to pray, for He is the Spirit of prayer and fills us with joy and peace as we abound in hope, through His power.

All God's exchanges are for blessing. It is always the replacement of the good with the better, or of the better with the best; never otherwise.

Why Should We be Anxious?

My times are in Thy Hand.—PSALM 31: 15.

THE Christian's simple purpose should be to be in God's will. The intricate application of that will, as to times and circumstances, is God's responsibility and He will not fail. He will choose out for us both our places of service and of rest; He will mark out both our steps and our stops. And if our intention to follow is pure He will not suffer us to be led astray; we shall hear a clear voice behind us at the time of need or danger.

We may therefore quietly commit ourselves and our future to Him and rest assured that all will be well. Our best desires will be fulfilled, our noblest ambitions realised.

How satisfying is the Bible revelation of God! He is the Holy One, the Mighty God Who sustains all things and maintains His holiness in all His sovereign power. All this makes us to bow down and worship. But He is revealed to us also as our Shepherd, Who leads us and cares for us like an eastern shepherd, going before us in search of the best pastures and the coolest waters. Moreover He is also our Father, our Heavenly Father, Who pities us as His children and Who, desiring our fullest development, educates in the best school, and apprentices in the best place, that we may grow in grace and develop such character as will fit us for service above and bring glory to Him here below. Let us go out into this day resting on these four words of all-embracing promise—

HE careth for YOU.

Every Longing Satisfied

When He shall appear, we shall be like Him.—1 JOHN 3: 2.

WHATEVER sufferings of the body or disappointments of the mind we suffer in this life, nothing gives us such sorrow as our ignorance and failure, our little likeness to the Lord.

During our earthly life we only see through a glass darkly. The glory of God, the glories of Christ, the joys of heaven we only just begin to appreciate. How little we know of these great spiritual truths! It may be that it is impossible for us to understand much. Time, sense and the world of material things in which we live, all press in upon us and act as a darkened glass to dim the glory.

And our body is a body of humiliation often dragging us down by its frailty and too often becoming a means of temptation. It necessarily demands much care and attention, so that most hours of the day are required for its sustenance and most hours of the night for its refreshment.

But it will not always be so. The Lord is coming again to take us to be with Himself and to make us like Himself. Our bodies of humiliation are to be made like His body of glory, our vision is to be full, intimate and satisfying. To that end we have been already made sons of God and become partakers of His life. But the full glory which awaits us, none can comprehend or describe. Heaven holds out many promises, such as freedom from sickness, weariness and sin, but the greatest joy will be to see Him as He is and be like Him.

That will be glory, be glory for me.

Prayer that Enricheth

Oh that Thou wouldest bless me indeed.—1 CHRON. 4: 10.

THERE is something about the word "bless" which baffles definition. It means "to favour, enrich, make happy", and so much more. We all know how vain is the attempt to explain the meaning, but we all know also how desirable the experience. It is the prayer of Jabez that God would shew Him this mercy and do it "indeed", that is, "really, beyond doubt".

For God's favour makes rich with the true riches, with that increase which is of the heart, of mind, and of Spirit. The increase of material riches often brings care and sorrow, but with such enrichment as Jabez asked there is no sorrow added. No man-made trouble can lessen the blessing and for it there is no compensation or substitute.

Jabez also prays, however, to be kept from evil, a word which in the Old Testament may mean either sin or trouble. Let us assume both and make the same request. Nothing is of greater importance than being kept from sin. It is of much less importance that we be kept from poverty or sickness. From displeasing God in heart and life, O God deliver us! For with sin comes broken communion and sorrow, and a whole train of unhappy consequences.

The Bible states promptly that God answered the request of Jabez. The petitions were according to God's will and were heard. Many things we ask may not be wholly or even in part in keeping with the loving and wise plans of God; but when we ask to be blessed and kept from sin we may be sure that God will answer. Let us therefore make the prayer of Jabez our very own.

The Ground of our Hope

. . . *who shall stand, when He appeareth.*—MALACHI 3: 2.

HIS coming is both a cheer and a challenge. It is a cheer because we shall then see Him and be like Him; we shall be for ever beyond that which has caused us sin and sorrow. But the truth of His appearing is also meant to challenge us. His coming, or His presence as the word usually is, will bring us face to face with Him Whose holiness is so bright that the seraphim veil their faces, and in Whose presence all evil is shewn in its true character.

It is wise, therefore, that we should make sure that the ground of our hope is sure and adequate, for there is only one ground of acceptance, that is Christ's own Person and Atoning work, "all other ground is sinking sand".

But for such as trust in the Blood of the Lamb there is no condemnation, neither now nor then. The believer is justified by the righteousness of His Saviour received by faith alone, and because of that and that only, he will join the countless multitude of those who stand before the throne of God and before the Lamb of God, singing and praising Him to Whom they owe everything.

His coming is as certain as the dawn and when He comes He will introduce us to the Father's House, the Saviour's judgment seat, and the glories of an eternity which cannot be described.

Because He Lives

I know that my Redeemer liveth.—JOB 19: 25.

IT is a fact that Jesus Christ was dead, is alive again and alive for evermore. The wonder of this simple fact grips few of us. We acknowledge that it is a fact, we accept it as historically and doctrinally true, but the startling implications of the truth seem to be rarely apprehended. We do not go everywhere preaching Christ risen from the dead nor do we live as if He were.

If Christ died and is alive again then obviously death has been spoiled for it found its conqueror in Him. And sin is purged for He went into death bearing its curse. Sin within and the world around have no more power over us because, while He acted alone yet He represented us, and we may repeat that " Sin shall not have dominion over us". If by dying, Christ reconciled us to God, now by living again He imparts His own victorious life to His people by the ministry of the Holy Ghost, the Lord and the Giver of life. He is therefore able to save us to the uttermost and sanctify every part of our intricate beings.

All this we accept intellectually but do I know that my Redeemer liveth? Am I living in the power of His resurrection life? The results of such personal and experimental knowledge is that this world loses its hold upon us, the physical is made subservient to the spiritual and the temporal is held in the light of eternity. Death becomes a junction instead of a terminus, a place where we exchange the poor tent of our earthly tabernacle for a building not made with hands eternal in the heavens.

Because He lives we shall also and not merely after death, but even now we taste the power of the age to come and triumph over sin and death.

Life Without Friction

My yoke is easy, and My burden is light.—MATTHEW 11: 30.

ULTIMATELY everything in the Christian life depends on our right relationship with God. In saying that, reference is not only made to that adjustment which is made between God and the sinner, in the work of justification when the sinner's standing is made right, but also to that continual maintenance of fellowship which is made possible by the ministry of Christ as our Advocate on high, and the Holy Spirit as our Advocate within.

The maintenance of close fellowship with God calls for both faith and obedience, both for listening to His voice in the Word and to speaking to Him in the quiet place of prayer. But the blessing and value of such a walk with God is beyond description. Life may be set in very hard and uncongenial surroundings, but there is inward peace. The daily round may appear trivial but it is lifted into high service. His yoke is comfortable for He and we walk together keeping step, and His will, whether it takes the form of commands or prohibitions, of gifts or denials, is good and acceptable and perfect.

Happy is the man who learns this wisdom and lives this life. It is like a dynamo I saw recently in the Alps which is floating on oil. Its tremendous weight, its constant revolutions, its production of high electric power is all without friction so that both the engine and its surroundings remain cool and silent. For we should remember that no one liveth to himself. If our hearts are in peace we diffuse peace, but if we become anxious and burdened we introduce the anxiety into other lives.

Let us walk humbly and closely with God; there is a price to pay but the result is not only worth while, but of all things most blessed and most desirable.

Chastened but not Willingly

For whom the Lord loveth He chasteneth.—HEBREWS 12: 6.

LOVE is kind but it is strong and wise. It is not indulgent seeking its own pleasure, but is ever concerned with the highest interests of the loved one. True parents' love is of this quality and accepts the responsibility of correcting and guiding the growing life. This may sometimes involve chastising the child, and though the process is unwelcome it is carried through for the good of the one chastised.

The God of love must similarly chasten us; such chastening is a proof of His love and not otherwise. It is for our comfort to remember that He never punishes one of His children because His patience is exhausted, for that can never be, but always because the chastisement is needed and the correction is worth while, and with what love He Who has wounded binds up the wound.

It is necessary that we rightly understand the chastening of the Lord, and this can only be as we appreciate His loving and wise character. He is like a father, but only the very best father is an illustration of Him, and that a very feeble illustration. Such knowledge of God will help us receive our correction in a right spirit and profit thereby. Indeed as we walk with God and come to know Him better and how infinitely loving and trustworthy He is, we shall find it not too difficult to submit to Him and to kiss the hand which holds the rod. His pity assures us that the chastisement is not only good but necessary and limited to what we can bear.

A Grace without Alloy

The Lord is good to all.—PSALM 145: 9.

GOODNESS is a quality of spirit which greatly affects both our inner disposition and our outward conduct. It makes us well disposed to others, enabling us to interpret their actions with kindness and charity of judgment; it also gently compels us to act towards them as God would, not on the ground of their conduct but rather because of their need and the opportunity. Goodness is a positive quality; it is not so much the absence of evil but the presence of grace.

When Peter wanted to sum up the external and general impression of the life of our Lord Jesus he said, "He went about doing good and healing all that were oppressed of the devil; for God was with Him." We shall do the same if we are good; we shall not consider the evil that men have done to others or to us, but we shall seek an opportunity to meet their need and to shew them the mercy of God. This will affect our attitude to our enemies and those who despitefully use us and persecute us.

This grace of disposition is manifestly like God, Who makes His sun to shine on all alike. It is not a natural grace, for we would naturally shew favours to those who shewed them to us and restrict our helpfulness to those who appealed to us in some way. But goodness only needs the opportunity to act. If therefore this grace is a godly quality and we are here reminded that it is itself a fruit of the Spirit of God Who dwells in the lives of believers, is not our need that His Spirit should be more abundantly shed abroad in our hearts? And may we not ask for this—and receive Him in fulness?

No More Strangers

Now . . . no more strangers . . . but fellow citizens with the saints.—EPHESIANS 2: 19.

SIN not only brings with a sense of guilt the knowledge that the evil which has been done must bring its own punishment, but sin also produces a sense of estrangement. The sinner knows that his sin separates him from his God. In many cases it would appear that men are willing to remain far off from God, and many devices are invented to occupy the mind lest they should think too much about God and their guilt. On the other hand numberless attempts have been made to reduce or eliminate the distance and approach God.

But there is only one way back to God and to the recovery of His favour. It is the way foreshadowed by the passover and realised in the cross of Calvary. We are only made nigh by the blood of Christ; there is no other way.

We, therefore, who have been brought nigh owe it all to God, and this should fill our hearts with humble thanksgiving. We are now no longer estranged but made nigh; we have peace with God; and we eat the memorial supper not in order to be saved, but because we are already born again into the family of God. As such we are also fellow-citizens with the saints; all the redeemed are our colleagues and brothers. What an honour is ours to be in the same historic succession as Paul and Luther, Bunyan and Wesley. We are no more strangers to God, we are sons of God; we are no more strangers to the saints but their fellow-citizens; we are of the true and heavenly aristocracy.

Heirs According to Promise

Heirs of God, and joint-heirs with Christ.—ROMANS 8: 17.

"IF children"—that is the first and most important consideration and concerning this we must needs be perfectly clear. For we are not all born into the world as children of God, much as popular theology may teach us so; we only become children by grace and faith, and it is one of the glories of the Gospel that any sinner receiving Christ as God's appointed Saviour is instantly born again into God's family and becomes a child of God. "Behold what manner of love the Father hath bestowed upon us that we should be called the sons of God."

"If children then heirs." Surely it is sufficiently wonderful to be made children of God, but to become heirs also is altogether beyond description. But it is just like God to treat us thus and make us not merely servants but sons and heirs according to the good pleasure of His will; He delights to do it.

"And joint-heirs with Christ." This makes our inheritance all the more acceptable because we are partners with Him Who has made it all ours. Apart from Christ we should still be in sin, beggars, condemned; now in Him we are accepted, promoted and later to be exalted, for we are to sit down with Him in His throne and rule over nations.

Heaven must be a breath-taking place; and just to think of who we were by nature and of what we have been made by grace, will surely fill our mouths with singing throughout all eternity.

Holy, holy is what the angels sing,
And I expect to help them make the courts of heaven ring.
But when I sing redemption's story they will fold their wings,
For angels never felt the joys that our salvation brings.

The Gentleness that is Great

They brought young children to Him . . . and He . . . blessed them.—MARK 10: 13, 16.

GOD is gentle. Only infinite might can be gentle, for gentleness is strength under perfect control. There is a strength which is crude and which rides roughshod over others but gentleness is the strength which lifts and protects and does it with delicacy and perfect understanding. Such is the gentleness of Jesus, God's Son, and it was seen in His contact with the weak and the fallen and particularly with women and children.

It is to such an One that the lonely and comfortless naturally turn for understanding. John did at the Passover, and the women did when they sought a blessing for their children. His tender understanding was expressed in His concern for the hungry multitude and in His multiplying the few loaves and fishes. To make this vivid and warm the Scriptures suggest that God is like a mother as well as like a father, and as such He cannot forget those who lean on Him in their dependency and need.

But should not the same character and grace be manifest in us? In this cold, hard competitive world, has not the Christian to watch and pray lest he become cold and hard? Should not the weak and undefended, the widow and the orphan turn for help to us? Would that not be a mark of our likeness to our Lord? One can only pray that if in one's own sphere some widow should be in need, some brother require advice, that they would think of us, as John and the mothers thought of Christ. It would be an honour indeed, and greater than being the chairman of this society, or the president of that.

How He Loves

God so loved the world that He gave . . . —John 3: 16.

God is love. It is not only that He loves us but that He is love. This means that the cause of His loving us is found in Himself and not in us, and for that reason His love is changeless. Think for contrast of a human love. This is not wholly a matter of the nature of the one who loves. Love has been begotten in the human heart by seeing or meeting some other human being; it may have been that the second person had desirable and admirable qualities which attracted, or on the other hand that there was a condition of frailty or need which appealed, but in either case love sprang up because there was an object capable of response or appealing by its need.

It is not so with God's love; for God is love, and He loves us apart from our response so that His love does not fluctuate with our fickle nature.

His heart is disposed to us in love; He is rich in mercy; He first loved us. The result is that He commended His love to us, in that when we were rebellious He gave His own Son for us, and planned our restoration, our acceptance, our enthronement. A God Who loves and gives like that will surely provide all things which we need, and there is only one thing we can do in return, namely to love Him.

Words which Help and Heal

A word fitly spoken is like apples of gold in pictures of silver.—PROVERBS 25: 11.

OUR speech reveals our spirit; it is out of the abundance of the heart that the mouth speaks. If the heart be filled with grace the speech is likely to be marked with grace. Like the gauge of a boiler, which gives an external reading of internal conditions, so the lips reveal the mind and the conversation declare the heart. All this should make us pray with the Psalmist, "Set a watch before my mouth, keep the door of my lips", for by our words we are judged.

But right speech, the word in season, the message which is kind and uplifting, has a value without computation. It blesses those who listen; indeed the Lord listens and notes and treasures what is said. Would that our table talk might be worthy of record as was Martin Luther's and Charles Simeon's. And the free conversation of the social hour, spontaneous and happy, will leave no regrets either to us who spoke or to those who listened, if the speech be with grace.

There must be some harmony and correspondence between our speech to men and our prayers to God. The same mouth must not pour forth at one time blessing and another cursing. There is a condition of the heart and a wholesome discipline of mind which ensures that the member which blesses God blesses man also, that the lips which sing His praises do not bring continual need for sorrow and repentance.

Of our Lord Jesus it is said, "Never man spake like this man", "and they wondered at the gracious words which proceeded out of His mouth". Let us abound in this grace also by the power of the Holy Ghost.

He Understands and He will Help

My grace is sufficient for thee.—2 COR. 12: 9.

"LET no man say when he is tempted, I am tempted of God: for God cannot be tempted with evil, neither tempteth He any man" (Jas. 1: 13); but at the same time we know from both Scripture and experience that God permits us to be tempted. And so He did His own beloved Son when He led Him into the wilderness.

It was necessary for our Lord Jesus to be tested that we might see the Second Adam was different from the first, and that He Who was to become our high priest should be able to sympathise and succour. Indeed we should think not only of the keen introductory experience of temptation in the wilderness recorded in two of the Gospels, but remember that assault after assault was made upon His faith and obedience. At one time it was an open attack directly from Satan, at other times subtle suggestions to leave the path of dependence and obedience, made by intimate friends and disciples. Sometimes the temptation came through His earthly relations, at other times through the trying and persistent criticism of religious leaders whose hearts were bent on discrediting Him.

But He came through all triumphantly and offers Himself to us as our Friend and Guide for our temptations. On every plane He has met the same foe, contesting the same issues so that now He offers us both sympathy and succour. The succour comes in two ways, sometimes in giving us a way out, at other times grace sufficient to stand up under the test. Jesus understands.

Forgiveness and Cleansing

If we confess our sins, He is faithful . . . to forgive . . . and to cleanse.—1 JOHN 1: 9.

IT is true for most of us that when we first come to Christ we come with a sense of guilt as our chief concern. We have been made aware of judgment which awaits us and of a doom which is to be dreaded and yet which is certain. If we have thus come seeking pardon through the blood of Jesus then we already know the joy of forgiveness of sins, the sweet sense of pardon and acceptance. The distance between God and us is gone and fellowship is restored.

But later no doubt we become aware of sin's defilement and our need of cleansing. When we believed and were united by faith to Christ all the blessings of the Gospel became ours potentially, but we realised that time and knowledge and further appropriating acts of faith were needed to enjoy those blessings experimentally. So as we are made aware of need, the corresponding blessing is made clear; and here to meet the need of defilement we are reminded of the blessing or ministry of cleansing.

Our pardon is only really known by us, though the fruits of it in joy may be seen by others; but our cleansing is appreciated by all because it affects our thought and habits and our daily life. By God's grace sins are laid aside, as we realise their sinfulness, and we press on in the Christian life experiencing the increasing power of the blood of Christ and the power of His Spirit.

Be of sin the double cure,
Save me from its guilt and power.

A New Clean Garment

Bring forth the best robe, and put it on him.—LUKE 15: 22.

"ALL our righteousnesses are as filthy rags"—that is God's description of our sinful condition through Isaiah. It is a humbling thing to learn that even our best endeavours, our righteousnesses are no better than that. Yet men make various attempts to self-improvement with a view to finding favour with God. It is as it were either patching up the filthy rags or stripping them one by one.

But the Father's treatment of his prodigal son is the best illustration of God's way for saving those who repent and return to Him; He brings forth the best robe and puts it on him. We may assume that the old rags of the far country were first removed and a bath washed away the dirt that clung to him, but now he is in the best robe and reinstated in the father's home.

But we who have believed have repudiated our own righteousness which is by works, and received the righteousness of God which is by faith. Our new robe is Christ, Whose righteousness becomes ours by grace and so fits us to stand before the infinitely righteous God. Our transgression is forgiven, our sin is covered, and we begin to be merry because God hath clothed us with garments of His own providing, the garments of salvation.

What a blessed exchange! Rags for a robe, filthy rags for a robe which is as of clean linen, pure and white. And now we are called to live in a way befitting our robe and our station. We are the children of God, called saints, destined to high service and already the subjects of angelic enquiry.

Vouchsafe to keep us this day without sin.

As He Is, So are We

It is enough for the disciple that he be as His Master.—MATT. 10: 25.

MASTER and servant, this is a relationship between Christ and the Christian frequently taught in the New Testament. It is of course by no means the only one, for there is the relationship of friends (John 15: 14), of Head and member, and many others, each one full of meaning and power. But the subjection of the disciple to his Lord is one which is kept before us all through the Scriptures.

It reminds us of our responsibilities and obligations. As the eyes of a servant are to the hand of his master, so our eyes are to be on the Lord waiting to see what next He requires us to do.

It calls our attention, as in these passages, to the fact that we must never expect better treatment in the world than He received here—and yet most of us receive much better. If they persecuted Him we must expect some similar handling, and our too-easy path may rightly raise questions in our mind as to whether we are really servants of such a Master.

But the noblest feature of this relationship is the privilege rather than the obligation. Is it not too wonderful that while others serve tyrants, Satan, the world and self, we have been called out to act as messenger and servant and courtier to none other than the Lord of lords, and the King of kings. We are to stand before Him today as clad in royal livery, as commissioners to royal service. Our most menial tasks are actually fulfilled as in the royal palace. So we face the day to do service not with eye-service as men pleasers, but with singleness of heart, knowing that we serve the Lord Christ.

From Beginning to End

The steps of a good man are ordered by the Lord.—PSALM 37: 23.

IT is God alone Who saves. He began the work in us when He broke the tyrannical rule of sin, and snatched us as brands from the burning. Before this we were led captive by Satan at His will with no prospect of release, but He released us, our chains fell off, our hearts were free.

But He did not leave us there, for having taken us from the control of our one time despotic master, sin, He now is with us to strengthen, help and uphold us. Were He to leave us for a moment we should be in direst difficulty. It is not so much that God has given us salvation as that God in Christ has become our Saviour. Salvation is not just a gift but God the Giver.

And in Christ we are as much assured of a sympathetic and understanding Master as we are of an adequate and real Saviour. For He became man and has been tempted; now He can enter into all our trials with perfect understanding and sympathy. His help therefore is guaranteed at every step and in every emergency.

Now, lest we should at any time be tempted to think of our salvation only in terms of past mercies and experience, we are reminded that our present steps are directed by the Lord Who takes the deepest interest in our life. If we fall through carelessness or even through temporary wilfulness, He will not cast us off but will lift us up again. He Who began the good work is under promise to perfect it until the day of Jesus Christ.

God's Presence and God's Peace

He hath said, I will never leave thee.—HEBREWS 13: 5.

OUR enjoyment of God's presence may be a very fluctuating thing. He may be consciously present in some high moments or even hours, in corporate worship or in silent prayer. But again there are large stretches of time in each day when we have no such consciousness. But does God's presence fluctuate with our conscious awareness of it? Indeed not, for His presence is promised and assured for every day and every part of each day.

This reminds us of the basic necessity of being more affected by the promise than the feeling. " Because He hath said, I will never leave thee nor forsake thee, so that we may boldly say, The Lord is my helper, etc." Faith affirms what God promises, and so, resting on the fact, enjoys the promise.

Such an attitude of resting in God's promise and daring to assume God's presence at all times enables God to give us rest. His presence accepted and enjoyed means His peace. It is also the way to courage, for it is only in the measure in which we are more aware of the presence of man than of God that we are tempted to fear. "Because He hath said, He will never leave us we may therefore boldly say . . . I will not fear what man can do unto me."

Let us face each day, and therefore today, with the fresh acceptance of the fact that God has promised to be with us, that He is therefore with us according to His promise, and as we walk with Him He will guide us in the way, time the events of our history and keep us from evil.

He is Interested in Me

I am my Beloved's, and His desire is toward me.—S. of S. 7: 10.

"I am my Beloved's"—that is the basis of what follows. The Lord Jesus and I are one. It is personal relationship with Him which really matters. We may be persuaded that the creeds and Bible doctrines as held by the believing Church throughout the ages are correct, but we may not be able to say, "I am His". That includes some appreciation of the fact that He has redeemed us with His blood and that we have acknowledged His claim and bowed our hearts to Him in faith.

But if we are sure of His ownership of us and of our part in Him, then the other things follow. His desire and interests are all toward us. He is planning for us, working for us and working in us as though we were the only ones for whom He had concern. From that practical love we are persuaded that we shall never be separated.

But while this is relatively easy to believe in moments of quiet and when life is undisturbed, it is not easy to understand and appreciate it when the baby dies, the health is poor, the money gone; and it is at such times that Satan hurls his sharpest arrows of doubt suggesting that the Lord doesn't care for us, and that we are forgotten if not forsaken.

Let us meet all such temptations with the confession of the facts of God's unchanging love in Christ which are before us today. Let us turn each one into a personal confession of confidence in the written words of Scripture before us today.

An Overflowing Heart

Out of the abundance of the heart the mouth speaketh.—Matt. 12: 34.

These words of Scripture before us re-emphasise a truth which we all know mentally but are in danger of forgetting practically, namely, that the secret of both our influence and our testimony is in a right condition of heart. By this is meant not merely that there must be no sin permitted or even doubtful things allowed; that is true but is only negative. What is meant is that the heart is full and overflowing.

Therefore it is above all things necessary that the word of Christ dwell in us in abundant measure. Its words, its truth, its promises, its warnings, should be continually controlling and directing our lives. This will not only be a means of keeping us in the King's highway of holiness, but if our Bibles are rightly read and our eyes are daily opened, we shall be seeing Christ in the Scriptures and His glory will make our hearts to overflow. It is such an overflow which makes a testimony and produces such blessing.

This will remind us of the danger of thinking that these words only, or even principally, apply to the pulpit and the platform. The believer's, every believer's, life is one long sermon and we cannot easily dissociate our pulpit message from our common conversation. It is in the latter where most of us fail.

So let us guard our heart, seek its continual cleansing and filling. Let us fill our mind and heart with God's word and let us meditate on God's Son. This will mean a holy walk and a helpful conversation.

Something Like Heaven

Thy will be done in earth, as it is in Heaven.—MATT. 6: 10.

EYE hath not seen, nor ear heard, neither hath it entered into the heart of man to conceive the things which God hath laid up for us who love Him but God hath revealed them unto us, only in so far as we can understand them. The joys of heaven are spiritual and they belong to eternity; the description of heaven must be in vivid picture, but the reality is indescribable in human words. But this we may clearly understand that in heaven all God's creatures, the angelic hosts and the spirits of just men made perfect, do always all that God the Father wills. This makes heaven what it is.

When therefore the Lord Jesus came down to earth He came to live a heavenly life here among men, and that meant supremely doing the will of God from the heart; and we who follow Him are called to the same high objective. Our business as disciples and Christians is not to do this piece of work or suffer this hardness or loss, but our one concern is to do the will of God.

This wonderfully simplifies life for it reduces the principles of conduct and behaviour to a single principle, and though it may not always be easy either to discover or do God's will, yet if our eye be single we shall know it, and if our intention be pure we shall be helped in fulfilling it. So let us take for our motto today and every day "The will of God, nothing less and nothing else".

The Race of God's Anointed Priests

Ye are a chosen generation, a royal priesthood.—1 PETER 2: 9.

ONE of the results of our Lord's passion and death is that we who are redeemed have been called into the holy ministry of priesthood. As Peter reminds us, we are royal priests that we might show forth His glory, and we are holy priests that we might offer to God spiritual worship. Let us consider our appointment.

We are, all of us if we are truly converted, members of a Kingdom of priests. This ministry of spiritual worship and intercession is not reserved for the few but is the privilege of all. The Bible teaches the priesthood of all believers, as it also teaches that some are called and gifted by God for the ministry of His Word among His people. But it is one thing to defend the great Bible and Protestant doctrine of our priesthood, and quite another to exercise it.

To fulfil the ministry of a priest we must first of all be holy. That does not mean that we must merely recognise that we have been set apart by God from the world, but also that our lives must be marked by godly piety and righteous conduct. Those who bear the sacred vessels of the Lord are to be clean, and we must therefore shun all that is false and dark and unbecoming for a saint of God. The Christian Church is a holy nation, a holy priesthood.

The ministry of praise and prayer and intercession which is our priestly service also calls for diligence and discipline. It is not easy to enter our secret place and shut the door and pray to our Father in secret. But this is surely our duty and privilege, and of all engagements the most precious to God as well as the most blessed by Him.

As we go into this day's duties whether in office, workshop or kitchen, shall we repeat the words occurring in today's portions—"Priests of God and of Christ".

Amazing Love! How Can it Be?

Thou art a gracious God . . . merciful . . . and of great kindness.—JONAH 4: 2.

THE love of God has been put to many tests; it has been strained throughout the whole history of man. But the tests have only proved its divinity and the strain has only demonstrated its strength. Many waters cannot quench love, and God's love remains unchanged and undiminished even though man fell, and fallen man has rebuffed Him, rebelled against Him and often trampled His mercy under impious feet.

It is in this fact of God's unchanging mercy that our hopes of salvation lie. Were we to rely on anything we can be or do, even on our repentance or faith, we might well tremble and wonder whether the repentance is genuine or the faith unfeigned. But instead of unduly considering ourselves we look away to Jesus Christ, God Incarnate, God Suffering, God still loving the sinner while He bears his sin, and in such a Saviour we may rest implicitly. He is the final revelation of the gracious God, Who is long-suffering and abundant in mercy and truth.

But, and this we must also remember, He will by no means clear the guilty. Sinners who despise His mercy are exposed to His wrath, and professing Christians who trifle with sin must needs re-examine themselves to see whether they are in the faith or not.

If, however, the Lord has saved us and given us a hatred of sin and a longing for holiness, let us glory in His mercy and extol Him, Who has not dealt with us after our sins, nor rewarded us according to our iniquities. The Lord is gracious and the saint's appreciation of this divine quality of grace, that is God's unmerited favour to us, is the best test of our evangelical conversion and of our understanding of God, ourselves and our sins.

He Knows, He Loves, He Cares

The Lord knoweth them that are His.—2 TIM. 2: 19.

IN many portions of Scripture the people of God are regarded corporately as a body, a bride, a flock; but today's portions remind us of that other aspect, namely, that the Lord is personally concerned with every single one of His children, and with all that affects their lives. So we read of His calling each one by name. He did it with the men and women of the Bible. Listen as He speaks to them. To some He speaks in correction. "What doest thou here Elijah?"; to others in warning, "Simon, Simon, Satan hath desired to have thee", while in the garden He said "Mary" with such loving concern that the hearer could only say "Master".

Then He knoweth not only who are His, but also all about them. No temptation comes without His permitting and tempering the test; no loss of goods or friends leaves Him unmoved or unaware of what it means to us. We have a merciful and faithful High Priest Who is touched with the feelings of our infirmities.

Moreover, He is leading us on—and home. Each step is planned, each stretch of the road is under His watchful eye. Days of trouble will be permitted because they are necessary for our training and our development. In such periods we are weaned from earth and prepared for heaven. We learn to turn from man and trust in God. And there is glory in front of us, a glory which cannot be conceived by human minds, nor indeed revealed in human words. The Good Shepherd Who died to make us the sheep of His pasture is leading us, and we will walk with Him.

Holy, Holy, Holy, Merciful and Mighty

He that is mighty hath done to me great things.—LUKE 1: 49.

THERE were days when God was so regarded, when men stood in awe of God's holiness and trembled at His Word. But for most Christians those days are past and we live in a time marked with superficial and unworthy views of God.

Let us remember again His might. Concerning the creation of this vast unmeasured universe we read, "He spake and it was done, He commanded and it stood fast." When He said, "Let there be light, there was light." There is none like Him Who works miracles daily and to Whom nothing (except things contrary to His nature) is impossible.

This same Almighty God is also merciful. He hath delivered us with a strong hand and redeemed us with precious blood. With worlds dependent on His power He bends low to listen to the feeble and confused cry of one of His neediest children, and immediately moves heaven and earth to answer the prayer and supply the need. His might co-operates with His mercy in blessing His people.

And finally He is holy. This leads us to the highest consideration of God in His perfections and freedom from all moral taint. For His holiness consists not merely in the absence of sin, but in the presence of every moral quality in perfection. If a consideration of His might makes us feel weak, then the contemplation of His holiness will make us say with Isaiah "Woe is me for I am undone", and we shall all the more thank God for His mercy which endureth for ever.

Stranger and Benefactor

Jesus of Nazareth . . . went about doing good.—ACTS 10: 38.

OUR Lord Jesus Christ was certainly in the world and yet not of it. He lived a truly human life in close proximity with men and sin, and yet all the while His holy character was untarnished by His contact. The world's standards and judgments, the world's approval or its blame, never affected Him as He steadily pursued His course from Bethlehem to Calvary.

It was at the latter place that He completely conquered the world. In His early ministry the glories of the Kingdoms of the world were offered to Him on certain easy terms, but He refused them, choosing rather to redeem the world of men, and pass His final judgment of the world as the system of mankind organizing itself without God.

And so He lived as the Light in the world's darkness, throwing light into darkened cells of human life. All this He did as He went about doing good, His unselfish devotion to the will of God leaving man condemned in his own selfishness.

Now by the mercy of God we have passed from darkness to light, and we, too, are to shine as lights in the world. Living amongst men we are to be separated from them, and yet ministering unto them. Our great service to the world will not be rendered by voluntarily entering into its associations and societies, not by living with Lot in the midst of its evil, but by living in separation unto God, and by interceding, as Abraham did, for those who, though gay, are under a judgment about to be administered.

Put Off the Flesh

Put off the old man . . . put on the new man.—EPHESIANS 4: 22, 24.

THE teaching of spiritual lessons and the producing of Godly character has been accomplished by God in various and sometimes strange ways. In the case of the Bible we see the Lord using the gentlest and wisest methods of teaching line upon line as men were able to learn, and by object lessons which men might learn most quickly; hence the types and sacrifices of the Old Testament.

When God, therefore, would teach the children of Israel to be governed by spiritual principles rather than fleshly or earthly considerations, one of the rites instituted was that of circumcision. It tended to become, as so many other rites, not only an outward and visible sign of an inward and spiritual grace, but a mark of merit or of favour in itself.

To us upon whom the ends of the ages are come, these things happened for our learning and we are most certainly to put away whatever ministers to our old and fallen natures and to live our lives following the example of our Lord Jesus Christ, seeking His grace to live according to His word and Spirit.

The Lord hath given us His own nature, imparting to us His own life. Though this is supernatural in its origin and power, it is to be expressed in daily conduct by choosing the things of the Spirit and refusing all that makes for self-indulgence, self-pity and self-advancement.

Living Unto God

He died unto sin once . . . He liveth unto God.—ROMANS 6: 10.

THE death of Christ is the central point of history and it is the central fact of eternity. In heaven we shall be reminded of Calvary by the Lamb in the midst of the throne; on earth we are to remember His death until He come.

Its ultimate interpretation must baffle the human intellect because it is divine as well as human, and concerns eternity and infinity as well as time. But we know that He died for sinners, that is, He received a judgment which was theirs and in this we glory. But here we are reminded of another aspect of that many-sided death, namely, that He died unto sin. In dying he repudiated sin once for ever and passed out of its sphere and power.

Now in all and every aspect of His death Christ is one with the Christian and so we are enjoined in Scripture to remember that we have died unto sin in Him and thus we are to repudiate sin for ever, and continually reaffirm that in Christ we are dead to it in every form. So dying we shall have the same mind as He with regard to God and ourselves, and, deliberately refusing to live after the principles of self-government we shall give ourselves to doing only the will of God from the heart. There is nothing but sorrow and frustration in seeking our own will, whether it appear noble and justifiable or otherwise; in the doing of God's will there is rest, sweet rest.

The End of All Things

The coming of the Lord draweth nigh.—JAMES 5: 8.

EVENTS are moving towards the end; there is abundant evidence of a quickening of the pace. This end will be inaugurated when the Lord Jesus returns, and of His coming we learn that the time is unknown, though the event is certain, for the Lord is not slack concerning His promise. This should make us watchful and prayerful and add a note of urgency to our life.

But the end to which we move is an end of things temporal. Houses, land and all possessions, as well as all positions and earthly honours, will come to a full stop and only what is spiritual will remain. The money we have saved will be lost, that which we have used for God will be saved. There are great changes impending when the last shall be first and the first shall be last.

This calls for loins girt and for full preparation for the journey. We must quickly gird up the loins of our mind and think correctly about time and eternity, about false and real wealth, about the passing world and the coming glory. For the end of all things is the beginning of new things. "Behold I make all things new." Glory will begin and the things of earth will disappear. Will there be any sense of loss because down here we saved so many goods but saved so few souls?

Under His Chastening Hand

Let Him do what seemeth Him good.—1 SAM. 3: 18.

THE Lord is good, His tender mercies are over all His works. All that He does is good and therefore His works of chastening and judgment for His children are good. When He gives it is good, what He gives is equally good; when He takes away it is good, and what He takes away is also good. So that we may say with Job, the Lord hath given, the Lord hath taken away, blessed be the name of the Lord.

This does not exempt us from sorrow, indeed it may be the very reason why sorrow is sent or permitted to us. We may still weep but the weeping will only endure for a night, even if a long one, and joy cometh in the morning.

This morning's meditation is a call for patience under the chastening hand of God. We are enjoined to accept His correction in the right spirit. If we fail to do so we shall fail to reap the blessing and betray a flaw in our character. The peaceable fruit is for them who are exercised thereby; that is, who are jealous to understand the meaning and reap the harvest of the sorrow. If our hearts be set to do this, then we shall be strengthened to endure and will be surprised at the peace and patience which grace ministers.

It will most help us, however, if we remember that God is good and that all He does or sends is done or sent in a love which is completely wise.

Let us kiss the hand which holds the rod.

Dead and Alive Again

We know we have passed from death unto life.—1 JOHN 3: 14.

WE have passed from death, so great a death. The condition in which mercy found us is described in many ways. Concerning the matter of everlasting life we were dead, for we did not possess it, we were alienated from the life of God through our ignorance and sin. We were, as the Psalmist described our condition, sinking in a horrible pit and miry clay. We were lost and awaiting judgment.

But God, who is rich in mercy, for His great love wherewith He loved us, hath made us alive together with the risen Christ. He has imparted divine life to us by uniting us with His Son. We have the Son and so we have His life, and the Spirit of life in Christ Jesus is operating in us where death formerly worked.

We are thus God's children by a new birth. Our hearts are assured and we have confidence toward God. Of all men and women we are the most privileged because, having been accepted in the Beloved, we are and ever shall be the object of the Father's love and care. No good thing will be withheld from us because with Christ He has freely given us all things. But it is all of grace, so pride is impossible and unthinkable; instead humility and praise must fill our hearts and minds.

Led by God, Following by Faith

I am the Lord . . . which leadeth thee by the way that thou shouldest go.—Isaiah 48: 17.

The life of the believer is a conducted tour—the skilful guide is Abraham's God and ours. He knows the end of the journey which is in view, and He knows the best way to arrive there.

It is good of the Lord to consider us personally and to choose our inheritance for us. Who is better able to do it? Certainly not we ourselves who can only see the immediate surroundings and not the distant scene. To that twofold end God is leading us; not only to the heavenly city, but also to the goal of a Christlike character.

He also chooses the way, with great wisdom. It may not be the shortest or the easiest way. Israel was led round-about so that they might not meet certain foes before they were ready, and also that they might learn certain lessons and be put through valuable discipline. Wherever He leads let us follow.

But the Lord who so skilfully guides us has planned that, all along the way, our lives shall bring blessing to others, whether through our service or our suffering. It is a walk by faith; as with Abraham, "not knowing whither". And we have not yet arrived, here have we no settling down. But we know our Guide, so we do not need to know either the way or the end.

He knows the way He taketh
And I will walk with Him.

God Revealed

Christ, Who is the image of God.—2 Cor. 4: 4.

No man hath seen God at any time. No searching can discover Him. He dwells in infinite light which we cannot behold.

> The Spirits that surround the throne
> May bear the burning bliss,
> But that is surely theirs alone.

And yet the infinite love of God must be expressed, His character must be revealed, and so from the beginning, as soon as man had fallen, He began to prepare for the display of His nature. So He became flesh, took upon Him our human nature, and tempered the brightness of His glory by revealing Himself as both God and Man in One Person. The Eternal is revealed in Time, the Infinite God is " contracted to a span, incomprehensibly made man", and in the Lord Jesus Christ we see God manifest in the flesh.

But wonder of wonders, the self-revealing is not only in a divine-human life, in a Person Who lives and serves among men, for God reveals Himself in a divine-human death, when Jesus deals with sin and bears it away. Now He is able to forgive and begin the glorious work of making men like Himself. Having first imparted to us His divine life in our regeneration, He is now concerned with conforming us to the image of His Son. The process has begun; it will end when we see Christ face to face, and we are with Him and like Him for ever.

Love's Achievements

Love one another, as I have loved you.—JOHN 13: 34.

THERE was no exaggeration when St. Paul wrote in 1 Cor. 13 that if he had gifts of eloquence, prophecy and knowledge and yet was lacking love, all the other gifts went for nothing. Indeed divine love shed abroad in the heart is of all gifts the one that most eloquently interprets and understands the Divine Mind. Our greatest need does not concern the externals of a public ministry but rather the condition of a loving Spirit. Before this, prejudices dissolve and barriers fall.

We must needs, therefore, live our life in love, under the sweet restraint of God's active love for others. This will please God and make possible a continuance of Christ's own personal ministry to His disciples, as through us He again washes their feet, and listens to their triumphs and their failures.

Such a spirit will also bear its witness to those who are enemies of our Lord and of His Christ. What our arguments and discourses cannot do, a loving Spirit will be used to accomplish as we yield our rights and do not resist or return evil for evil. Living on a higher level may be used of God to convict them of their need of a Saviour from sin.

Let us therefore ask of God today a loving spirit which is kind and generous in its judgments, warm in its appreciations, and let us ask that it may be genuine and active.

That Blessed Hope

The glorious appearing of the great God and our Saviour Jesus Christ.—TITUS 2: 13.

ALMOST two thousand years have rolled along since our Lord Jesus Christ promised that He would come again, and He has not arrived even yet. The reason is given in 2 Peter 3 where the delay is explained as due to the long-suffering of God, for He is loth to close the door of Salvation. But come again He will, for He has spoken, and shall He not do it?

In the meantime the whole creation groans, for discord has entered; man and man, nation and nation live in suspicion, while the whole of the animate creation suggests that sin has created disharmony. And we who are redeemed also groan within ourselves. There is the problem of sin around—and, alas, within; there is suffering everywhere, and while we are here in the world we are in sympathy with its groans of sorrow.

But He Who testifieth these things saith, Surely I come quickly. When we least expect Him and without special warnings the heavens will be rent, and God's Son and Sovereign will come to receive His own and to reign over all in righteousness. All our hearts will then be glad and we shall say "This is our God; we have waited for Him and He has come at last".

The promise of His coming again is the ground of a hope which is called a blessed hope. It is meant to make us glad, to keep us from fainting in the battle. The prospect of coming victory and glory should give us a happy spirit when we are most pressed. So we look longingly to see Him Whom we love.

Amen. Even so, Come, Lord Jesus.

Heavenly Wisdom

Seek those things which are above.—COL. 3:1.

THE choice, which is continually before us, is that which is between the higher and the lower, between the heavenly and the earthly. It must even be so while we are in the world, because we belong to both spheres. We are citizens of earth by virtue of our first birth and we are citizens of heaven by virtue of our second birth; we are sons of men as well as sons of God.

Now the danger is that we live an earthly life and are more influenced by earth than heaven and that we betray the fact that we are sons of men more than that we are sons of God. We need, therefore, definitely and purposefully to seek the things that are above. Our hearts, like the Psalmist's, cleave to the dust and we need to lift them up unto the Lord.

The wisdom which is to guide us is not worldly wisdom but the wisdom which is from above, which is first of all pure, then peaceable. The motives which are to prompt us are to be those which belong to Christ and the new life which He has given us; for we have died with Christ to the old life and we live in Him unto God.

This calls for the renunciation of everything which is sinful or doubtful, and which would therefore hinder us in running our race. Instead, stripping ourselves of much that is permissible to others, we are to fix our eyes on the heavenly country where dwells the Lord our Righteousness, and move with deliberation towards it.

Run the straight race through God's good grace,
Lift up thine eyes and seek His face.

Determined Effort

Endure hardness as a good soldier of Jesus Christ.—2 TIM. 2: 3.

THE Christian life is not a picnic but a strenuous battle, and we are called to be soldiers, good soldiers. Christ never softened His appeal or minimised the hardships; He told the men of His day that following Him meant a cross and the continual denial of self-indulgence and selfish pleasure. It had been better if we had done the same when we have presented the Gospel.

Our foes are powerful, desperate and cunning, with long experience in fighting both by fair means and foul. At one time the attack is open and courageous, at another it is subtile and cowardly; no principles are regarded, the object is to get the Christian warrior down and beaten.

This calls for us to gird our heavenly armour on, each piece of it, and then to stand for the battle. Even as we work for God it must be with sword and trowel as in Nehemiah's day, with one hand building Zion's wall and with the other holding our sword. We must watch and pray. But our eye must not be on the enemy alone, but on the Captain of our Salvation Who leads us; for His wisdom is wakeful and He will direct us in the conflict. He is Leader and Commander to the people of God.

We shall overcome if we follow Him, but we shall certainly bear in our bodies the scars of battle. But who among us wishes it otherwise? The battle may be longer or shorter but it will end in joyous song. Then the shout of victory and the march of triumph, and the Captain's own "Well done", and the eternal rest. Now is the time for conflict, not for resting.

From silken self, O Captain, free
  Thy soldier Who would follow Thee.

I Live by Faith

Lord, I believe; help Thou mine unbelief.—MARK 9: 24.

IN life there are some qualities which we can afford to be without, but without faith it is impossible either to begin or continue the Christian life, or to please God. Faith is essential. It is necessary for salvation; for though we are saved by grace, it is through faith. It is necessary for holiness; for though this is by the Holy Spirit, it is through faith. And so we could continue enumerating the blessings and privileges of the Christian life and shewing they are all through faith; that is, that while God provides and offers them as gifts of His love they must be received by us.

What then is this faith which is so necessary? It is the attitude of soul which believes God's word and acts upon it. It is not merely intellectual in the sense of mentally accepting a statement, but it also includes the whole man and especially the decision of the will to live on the truth or the promise. If pardon is offered on condition of repentance, then I must believe that God means what He says and commit myself to thanking Him for the blessed gift and rejoicing in forgiveness as a present mercy. If peace is offered, I must take the gift and refuse to be anxious. Faith is the soul resting in and acting on the word or promise of God. Unless it works—that means is active—it is dead and not a living, saving faith.

Now as the Christian life is begun by faith, so it continues by taking God at His word and living to prove it is true. This involves not only the glad acceptance of God's gifts of pardon, peace, purity and power, but of the corresponding renunciation of guilt, worry, impurity and weakness. Faith not only puts on the Lord Jesus as a daily garment but puts off the things which are contrary to Him.

> Faith, mighty faith, the promise sees
> And looks to that alone.

So we no longer live as governed by things seen.

Worthy is the Lamb

Christ our passover is sacrificed for us.—1 Cor. 5: 7.

Of all the many titles of our Lord this one, the Lamb, is among the most precious to sinners. To those who have no sense of personal sin and trust in their own righteousness, and to those who have no sense of the holiness of God, the name has no charm. But "to sinners in the hands of an angry God", to quote the title of Jonathan Edward's famous book, nothing can be a substitute for that which is taught by this singular title "The Lamb of God".

In the first place it links together the Testaments. "In the Old the New lies hid, while in the New the Old lies open" wrote St. Augustine. This title of Christ reveals the unity. Here is the One Who offered Himself as a full, perfect and sufficient sacrifice, oblation and satisfaction, and of Whom all the paschal lambs and sacrifices of Old Testament times were the type. For sinners of both dispensations are in the hands of the same God and face the same judgment and need the same atoning sacrifice.

But principally do we love this title because it speaks peace to our own guilty conscience, by assuring us, first of all, that the Lamb which bore our sins was not only of God's providing but God Himself, and, secondly, that He has suffered adequately and been accepted on our behalf. When Satan accuses and conscience arises, then the blood of the Lamb is the answer, and the enemy is silenced and conscience satisfied.

And the sacrifice of this Lamb is eternal in its effects and benefits. For the Lamb was slain from the foundation of the world, though manifest in these last times for us. That is, the atoning principle was ever present in the heart of God, though the atoning act in history is focussed on Calvary.

We who have been bought at such a price are to walk in the same path of self-sacrifice and love.

Thus Prostrate, I Shall Learn of Thee

His mercy is on them that fear Him.—LUKE 1: 50.

THE fear of the Lord is the beginning of wisdom. It may not be the beginning of knowledge, though it would surely set knowledge on a right course, and for a right purpose, but it is certainly the beginning of true wisdom. The fear of the Lord is the attitude of reverent trust and worship. The man who fears the Lord bows low before God's holy majesty, yet loves Him because of His mercy. Rightly to fear God we must needs know something both of His holiness and His love.

If we are thus disposed to God two things will result. First of all it will affect our conduct, the way we pass our time of sojourning. We shall be zealous to please God, we shall live with eternity and the judgment of God in view. We shall treat the children of men as though we are to give account of our opportunities and stewardship. All life will be affected.

Then, secondly, God Himself will shew us mercy as He cannot do to the proud and arrogant. His great goodness is stored up for the meek in spirit and they will be kept safe in the secret of His presence; that is, God will be so near as to put Himself between the one who fears Him and all his foes. Moreover He will hear their cry and answer their prayers. God looks for such as fear Him and when He finds them looks after them, delighting to shew them favours and enrich their lives with spiritual blessings.

They that know His name put their trust in Him, for everything about God makes Him trustworthy; and they that know His nature fear Him also, for all that is revealed of God in His Son and in His Word conspire to make us bow low in reverence in His presence.

O Come, let us worship and bow down;
Let us kneel before the Lord our maker.

Jesus Paid it All

But this Man, after He had offered one sacrifice . . . sat down.—HEBREWS 10: 12.

IN one word of triumph shouted by a dying Man, the greatest achievement of history, the most far-reaching act of all time, was effected. It was when Jesus Christ cried "Finished" (one word in the original language).

What was finished? Doubtless several answers can be given to the question—such as His life of humiliation, or the long line of divinely-approved animal sacrifices; but the supremely important answer is that the Lord Jesus Christ had undertaken and now completed the work of reconciling man to God, a work we normally describe by one word: atonement.

Here then is the greatest need of God and man met, and met completely. For not only does man need more than anything else an atonement for his sin, but God needs that such a work be done, or else how can His redeeming plan be effected? The work is completed, eternal justice is satisfied, divine love revealed.

That the work is complete is proved by the fact that when Christ returned to heaven He sat down on the right hand of God. This is unlike any earthly priest who ever ministered in an earthly tabernacle and offered animal sacrifices. His work must necessarily continue because the sacrifices could never finally deal with sin; but this sacrifice, once offered for all time, has paid sin's penalty and no more sacrifice is needed or possible.

Here is the surest ground for peace for the guilty conscience. The God Who must punish sin and maintain the moral character of the universe has Himself borne it in the person of His Son made man. Sinless Himself, He took the sin of mankind upon His soul and suffered vicariously. Now His presence at God's right hand proves that His Sacrifice is accepted and we may go free. Because He is accepted, so are all those who trust Him. So let faith lay its hand on Christ's head and rest in His finished work. For if it is finished there is nothing left to do but to glorify Him both by lip and by life.

Walking in Holiness

If any man be in Christ, he is a new creature.—2 COR. 5: 17.

IN the days of our sin and self-management our wills decided to yield our faculties to serve sin. This does not only refer to the gross sins of the flesh such as yielding our bodies to indulgence but also our lips to speaking evil or bitterness. We sinned, however, because our wills decided to sin even though the reason may have been weakness and inability to resist temptation.

As ye have yielded . . . even so now yield. A great change has come through grace and the will is now able to decide to use our faculties in acts of righteousness and with a view to holiness. We are deliberately to present our body and its members to God, and henceforth to remember they are His living holy and acceptable possessions which must not be used for any purpose other than He will approve.

The change is great; it is to be thorough, covering all departments of life, for it is nothing less than a new creation. And if we live this transformed life we shall be blessed with peace while those who walk after the vain principles of the world will be unhappy and unhelpful.

Let us then deliberately and once for all renounce the old nature, the old life, with all its practices, and let us, with equal deliberation, decide to live according to Christ and our divinely implanted new life. This will mean both putting off and putting on—both discipline and devotion. Holiness is by faith, as we yield to His leading and drawing; it is by action also, as we put off and put on.

Accepting Correction

No chastening for the present . . . joyous . . . nevertheless afterward.—HEBREWS 12:11

GOD'S love is no sentimental thing; it is not indulgent as parental love may easily be. The Heavenly Father has no spoilt children, He loves them too much to allow that. When, therefore, occasion demands God chastens and corrects His sons. It may well be that He has first sought by His Spirit and His Word to correct the heart and conscience, but now something harder and more painful is necessary and thus the body, family, business or Christian service is touched.

But it is touched by a Father's loving hand, and therein lies our comfort. It is done in faithfulness by Him Who does not willingly afflict the children of men. It is needed, greater things are involved, so with pity He chastens us.

Only good can come when our Heavenly Father corrects us. He has thoughts of peace and not of evil; He is working for an expected and desirable end, and this is the only way to it. His thoughts and ways are beyond our comprehension but at least we know they are wise and good.

Everything depends, however, on our reaction to His correction. If we resent and resist it, then in faithfulness He will need to continue until the lesson is learned and the correction made. If on the other hand we humble ourselves under His mighty sovereign hand, then He will lift us up again. We may be sure that the affliction will not continue a moment longer than necessary, and when we have learnt the lesson, He will speak comfortably to us, for not only does God correct as a father does, but like as a father pitieth His children, so the Lord pitieth them that fear Him, for He knoweth our frame, He remembereth that we are dust.

Holy, Heavenly Guest

When He the Spirit of truth is come, He will guide you.—JOHN 16: 13.

"IF thou knewest the gift of God"—how truly this might be said of all God's gifts! We know so little of the greatness of His gifts so there is little wonder and worship in our hearts. Think for instance of God's initial gift of pardon, of what it cost, of what it is, of how deep and thorough it is! It is illustrated in Scripture by an object being cast into the depths of the sea, a cloud being wiped away, and the separation between sinner and sins "as far as the east is from the west", which is an immeasurable distance. So we might continue with Scriptural definitions of God's pardon, and so we might continue thinking of His other gifts, "if thou knewest". Is this not a call to study? Would not more knowledge of God and His gifts make for our increasing love and devotion?

But the gift under consideration this morning is the Third Person of the Blessed Trinity, the Lord, the Giver of Life, here called the Comforter, the Enabler, and Strengthener. He is a Gift. He is first given when we trust the Saviour but we are to know Him in increasing fullness. Some have conscientious scruples against asking for Him, and if this meant to suggest that He was not already dwelling in the believer, well they might. But the asking is for His dwelling in us to be in power and grace, filling and controlling, and this is according to faith and in answer to prayer. "Ask and receive that your joy may be full."

The measure of God's Spirit indwelling our lives is not to be judged by feelings of fullness or by the power to sway the crowd with eloquent speech. "When He is come He will convict"—and here is the test. His presence in our lives will make us a challenge to all sin.

But let us not vex or grieve this Gentle Mighty Guest and Lord with self-indulgence or selfish plans, or we may find that His working in righteousness is contrary to our wishes and designs.

Progress in Holiness

Then shall we know, if we follow on to know the Lord.—Hos. 6: 3.

We are called to holiness; we have been transferred from darkness to light and are called to walk in the light. As we do this we find ourselves in a path which grows brighter as it proceeds. This means that the whole of life must be lived increasingly in the light of God; things which were once permitted must be disallowed.

Whatever critical experiences we have had, whatever progress we have made, there is much land ahead to be possessed. The oldest and saintliest have only just begun to scale the heights or plumb the depths of the knowledge of God. We have not yet already attained, or as one modern translation has it, "not as though I had already arrived". We are in the way. Grace has put our feet there; let us seek to press on beholding the glory of God in the face of Christ and being gradually changed ourselves into the same image.

But the promise is that one day this somewhat slow progress will be complete. We shall see our Saviour face to face and be like Him. All the old idiosyncrasies which made us difficult to live with, all the failures in character and temper which made us unlike Christ, will be for ever gone. Now we only see through a glass and the view is confused. Now we wrestle against evil foes without and against sin within, but then, oh glorious day, we shall be satisfied, for we shall be like Him.

And the hope of His return and our gathering together unto Him should hasten the process of our purification. "Even so, Come, Lord Jesus."

Perfect in Christ

The King's daughter is all glorious within.—PSALM 45: 13.

TWO wholly different descriptions may be given of a Christian; he may be described as what he is in himself by nature or what he is in Christ by grace. The former is the true and humbling picture of such passages as are collated in the first paragraph of today's portion. The whole being is spiritually sick and unclean and there is nothing good to be found. This is true of all, which should make us all humble before God and understanding towards every other human being.

But God in His mercy has worked in those who are His children, they have been washed and made holy, they are all fair and without spot. How comes this wonderful transformation, and is it true? The answer is that the believer is so united to Christ that his sins have been judged when Christ, our Substitute, was judged, and his sinful nature carried to its death when Christ our Representative died.

We are now seen by God only as in union with Him Whose righteousness is ours and Who is daily made unto us true holiness. We are complete in Him, the perfection being through His own worth and moral beauty, which are shared with us.

Therefore we must give all the glory to the Lord Who has saved us and Who keeps us, and while rejoicing in our perfection in Christ, we are to live daily as those whom God has so graced. To us, therefore, everything which is sinful is abhorrent and unworthy as we look to the day when we shall be presented, not only without spot, but even without wrinkle or any such flaw.

Kept from Sinning

Now unto Him that is able to keep . . . be glory.—JUDE 24, 25.

THERE is one thing worse than pain and more to be shunned than poverty: it is sin. If, as saintly Brainerd said, "nothing matters but holiness of heart and the salvation of souls", then the converse is true, namely, that of all things to be avoided sin and carelessness of souls are the most important. For this our great High Priest in heaven is praying, that we who are Christians may act as light in a dark world, and as salt in a corrupt human society.

Our Risen Lord's ministry is first of all preventive; He is engaged in keeping us from sin. Were we sufficiently watchful and sensitive, were we sufficiently near to hear the warnings of the still small voice, then we should be saved from many temptations into which we fall, but even as it is, we are kept from countless snares about which we know nothing because He ever liveth to make intercession for us, asking that His Father should keep us from evil.

He is able to keep us from evil, from falling, and there is no inability on His part. Let us dwell on that today. Let us take some promise from the page with us into the life and service of the ensuing hours. What better word than the benediction from Jude's epistle which closes the page of texts? "Unto Him that is able to keep you from falling and to present you faultless before the presence of His glory with exceeding joy, etc." Learn it, believe it, trust Him Who gave it to fulfil it, and our feet will be kept from many a snare today.

Death is Conquered

O grave, where is thy victory?—1 COR. 15: 55.

DEATH is not only the last enemy but it is also one of the first and most enduring. In every age men have feared it, and sought to postpone it. In every land means have been sought or invented in an endeavour to take away its sting. Attempts have been made to appease evil spirits, paper money has been burned and food offered so that there may be no lack on the part of the dying and the dead, but yet wailing and sorrow have wrung the heart when death has snatched away a loved one.

But now in the Gospel of Christ all is changed for the Christian. Death, though real, is for loved ones just a temporary separation, while for the one who has gone it means to be with Christ, which is far better. Thinking of our loved ones taken from us we rejoice in their joy and find our tears are sweetened.

Death itself, however, is to be abolished one day when redemption's work is all complete and the number of God's elect is accomplished. Then the believer will challenge death and hell to shew their sting and victory. What is more, our Lord Jesus Christ by His dying has made Satan, who has the power of death, impotent. This evil prince is not all-powerful, his might is strictly limited and made subservient to a higher power.

We should therefore walk through life and even through days when death is at work, with no fear of evil, for we know Him Who has conquered death and we know that death is but the gate of life.

For a Time and for a Purpose

Though He cause grief, yet will He have compassion.—JEREMIAH 3: 32.

NOT all days are sunny days for the Christian. Such would only make superficial character. There are lessons about God to be learned in the dark which can never be learned in the light.

Moreover we are so imperfect that the Lord Who loves us must needs correct us, and this He does by various means—by blowing upon our programmes so that they do not work out, or by withdrawing the sense of His presence, as the sun is hidden behind the clouds. We appear cast off and forsaken and our work which may have been too absorbing then shews up for what it is, while we realise with sorrow the sense of loneliness and forsakenness, or have time to review our life and acknowledge our sins.

But the appearance of being forsaken, the feeling of being cast off, will only be for a season. It is sent for the purpose of correction and of drawing us away from our sins or selfish interests; when that is done and there is heart repentance the sun will shine again, the Lord will lift upon us the light of His Countenance. We shall be brought forth purged and profited. The trial is only for a purpose and therefore only for a time. And with what enthusiasm God restores our former joy; "For a small moment I have forsaken thee, but with great mercies will I gather thee"; "in a little wrath . . . but with everlasting kindness".

While the darkness is upon us for our good, let us remember that we are not forsaken nor ever could be. The sense of His presence only, and not His presence, has been removed that we may learn to trust and obey; and the latter end will be better than the former.

A Glorious Expectation

If I go and prepare a place for you, I will come again.—JOHN 14: 3.

HIS coming again in glory is just as certain as His first coming in humiliation; the history of the latter is no more certain than the prophecy of the former, for God spoke concerning them both. To a church groaning under oppression or to the people of God living in a particularly ungodly age, the returning Lord seems to be tarrying, but we encourage our hearts not only by the promise, but by the form of it. "He that shall come will come and will not tarry", not even for a day beyond the appointed time.

Then what a change will be ours! For many of God's saints it will be from poverty to an inheritance, for all it will be from a scene of corruption to an inheritance which is incorruptible and undefiled. We shall leave behind everything which now drags us down and wears us out; the sights and sounds which chafe the redeemed soul set upon the way of holiness will be seen and heard no more.

> Sin, our worst enemy before,
> Shall vex our souls no more.

Instead of the moral foetidness of many a camp, factory and office we shall breathe the pure air of heaven.

The hope of His coming and expectation of His presence in glory is to nerve us to endure. He Himself endured the Cross for the hope set before Him, and as we fix our eyes and hearts on the coming glory we shall be able to endure.

> O Lord Jesus, how long, how long,
> Ere we hear the glad song?

Partakers of God's Joy

The joy of the Lord is your strength.—NEH. 8: 10.

WE sometimes miss much on account of the archaic language of our Bible, beautiful as it is. Here, for instance, reading the older form of the possessive case "the joy of the Lord" we may fail to realise that it is "the Lord's joy", which surely means not only the joy the Lord gives but the joy He enjoys. He is the ever-blessed God Who rejoices when sinners repent and on many other occasions and for many other causes.

Now as the Lord loves to share His life and gifts, giving His own peace to His servants, so with His joy. When He imparts His own joy to His own people it becomes their strength even as sorrow tends to weaken us. And the Lord calls on us to rejoice with Him; the things which gladden Him are to gladden us. The Shepherd having found His lost sheep calls His friends and neighbours to rejoice with Him.

Of course the chief cause for sharing the Lord's own joy is when we share His salvation. Our burden of sin gone, our conscience free, our mind at peace, how can we but rejoice with Him. As a bride is dressed for her wedding we are adorned in Christ's righteousness, and therefore we share Christ's joy. We have received the atonement, therefore we receive the gladness.

But the last text this morning reminds us of the need on our part to be determined to rejoice. An enemy would rob us of our joy by making us think overmuch on our problems. Our minds tend to focus on our losses rather than our gains as Christians; on our disappointments rather than our blessings. Let us therefore purpose to rejoice in the God of our salvation, for there is abundant cause; and as we share God's own joy we shall be made strong for the walk or the warfare.

With Every Grace Endued

The God of peace . . . make you perfect.—HEBREWS 13: 20, 21.

As Christians we are to be perfect in every good work, furnished unto all good works, bearing all the fruits of the Spirit. Ours is to be a life which is balanced and full, not one which specialises in one grace yet lacking others; we are called to be perfect, that is, whole and mature.

For such a life we are heavily handicapped by nature. We have a sinful nature and a particular temperament. The former produces evil fruit and the latter predisposes to unbalance. Our temperaments tend to make us either hasty and impatient or slow and lacking initiative; we are hopeful or pessimistic, cheerful or depressed.

But the God of peace is at work in us. His work only began when He convicted us of sin and we were born again; since then He has been working in us, both towards a willingness and afterwards an ability, to perform that which gives Him both honour and pleasure. This work He continues by shewing us the graces we lack, either as they are revealed in Christ or another Christian; then after we have received the desire to shew forth these particular virtues, by imparting them to us. They are the fruit of the Spirit and so the Spirit reproduces them in us. By this means impatient and unreliable Simon becomes the gentle, rock-like Peter, and Saul the bigot becomes Paul the missionary with the heart of a mother and a nurse (1 Thess. 2: 7–9).

What is the lack of which God is making us specially conscious and which at this moment seems so far away from us? As we wait upon Him and seek His glory alone, it shall be given us. We are meant to bear all the fruit of the Spirit, and to represent to the Father and angels above and the Church and world around, the beautiful balance of character which is really "Christ in us".

A Magnificent Temple

Know ye not that ye are the temple of God?—1 COR. 3: 16.

THE Bible is from one point of view the story of a series of temples, of God's dwelling-places. First there was the tabernacle in the wilderness, portable yet wonderful with its gold and silver, scarlet, blue, purple, and fine twined linen, and with its three compartments, the outer court-yard, the holy place and the holiest of all. This was followed by a more permanent structure when Israel was settled in the land of Canaan and Solomon was enabled to fulfil his father David's desires to build a temple on Mount Zion. This temple, later destroyed under Nebuchadnezzar, was replaced by Zerubbabel, under Cyrus, and this in turn was again replaced by what was called Herod's temple. The same was in Jerusalem when Christ was here, and was razed to the ground, so that one stone was not left upon another, in the year A.D. 70 by Roman soldiers.

But there was a deep change in God's dwelling-place when Christ came, for of Him John wrote (1: 14): "The Word was made flesh and tabernacled (lit.) among us, and we beheld His glory." Here then was God's new dwelling-place among men, His own Son, the God-Man, Who could say "the Father dwelleth in me" (John 14: 10). But He in course was raised again and ascended into Heaven and now the temple of God is the church of Jesus Christ of which we, by grace, are living stones. It is indeed exceeding magnifical, its stones have been quarried in strange places but they have been gathered and are still being gathered out of every people, kindred, tribe and tongue and builded together for a dwelling of God through the Spirit. This makes the Christian a most favoured being and calls for a most holy life. We must needs then remember that bought by Blood and being prepared by His infinite skill, we are to be free from that which defiles, for the temple of God is holy, which temple ye are.

Praying for Others

The . . . fervent prayer of a righteous man availeth much.—JAMES 5: 16.

THE message of today's portion may be summed up by saying that there is given us an injunction to intercession followed by three conspicuous examples of those whose intercessions availed, namely, Abraham, the Lord Jesus and Elijah.

The injunction is to intercession, that is, prayer for others. It is obviously a higher exercise than praying for one's self, though that is most necessary. Prayer for ourselves may become selfish, but intercession for others not so easily. When our thoughts are filled with the needs of others and our Spirit is lifted up to God for them, our mind cannot be on ourselves; so the very exercise is good for us. But its chief concern and blessing is for others.

In the Church of Christ intercession is meant to be mutual, that is while I intercede for another, he, or someone else, will be interceding for me. This reminds us that we all stand in need of the prayers of others, and a ministry of intercession does not make us less in need or give ground for pride.

The examples are given for our encouragement. Abraham's pleading for the cities of the plain did not appear to be answered. One wonders if he had pressed the matter what would have happened. In any case the heart of God Who hears our prayers is revealed. Our Lord Jesus is, of course, the perfect example. He interceded even for His murderers. But it cost Him much time and toil; see Him on the mount alone all night. Elijah, a man like us, prevailed in prayer, and so may we if we pray earnestly and continue.

We are to pray for one another that we may be healed in spirit, mind and body. When the church is really quickened mighty answers to prayer will be seen.

There is None Like God

O Lord God of hosts, who is . . . like unto Thee?—PSALM 89: 8.

GOD is absolutely alone in His being, wisdom, love and power. The ever-blessed Trinity, Father, Son and Holy Spirit, ever one God, is sovereign and supreme.

All other beings are creatures whom He has made to serve His purposes. The angelic hosts serve Him in one sphere, human hosts are within His plan and even the hosts of darkness must somehow serve His ends and must sometime bow the knee. They are all the work of His hands, dependent upon Him for the continuance of their existence, and none can therefore compare with Him.

This means that the children of God who live in His fear need not be afraid of any other being or thing. God is supreme and God is our Father, therefore what have we to fear?

It means also that, dark as the present may seem to be, the world which God hath made and still sustains is moving towards its appointed end. To see God ruling in His power, even though things perplex us, is to find quiet strength in an age of confusion, and to go forth with real confidence to our service of winning the sons of men to faith in God.

Much that God is now doing is beyond our ken. It must be so God being Who He is, and us being who we are. But the end of His ways and purposes baffles human thought and words. Eye hath not seen, nor ear heard, nor has the human mind the ability to understand; the glory which awaits God's children is eternal in duration and majesty and character. So much of it could not be revealed to us while we live in the body and in time and while our thoughts are all conditioned by things seen. But what little is revealed, whether in statement of fact, or in vivid picture, is such as to shew that God is incomparable and His glory is like Himself.

The Witness of a Holy Life

. . . *walk worthy of God, Who hath called you* . . .—1 THESS. 2: 12.

EVERY Christian is called to holiness of life in both its aspects, those of a separation from sin in every form, and a positive dedication unto God. This is not for the few but for all who are redeemed by Christ's most precious blood. The death of Christ which saves us from sin also purchases us for God. And because God is holy we are called to holiness. The chief reason why we should live holily is not that we may be effective soul winners or workers, but because God is holy and He desires fellowship with us. Our conversation therefore is to be worthy of God.

Our holy walk is also to be a witness to others. We were, as they still are, children of darkness, unsaved, and governed by the world, the flesh and the devil, even though their life is seemingly upright. But now a great change has taken place in our lives; grace has saved us. And all we are, and have, and do is to be a witness of this change and to Him to Whom we now belong. This means sometimes giving offence to the world because its deeds are evil and we can have no fellowship with them, but as we are filled with the fruits of righteousness we shall bring glory and praise to God and testify to others.

Such a life must be transparent and whole-hearted. Our light is not to be hidden by doubtful or dark practices. All our common ways, including eating and drinking, are to be sanctified and to the glory of God. Such a life is not, as it would seem on first consideration, difficult and unhappy; it is one of peace, for the government and the choices rest in the God and Father of our Lord Jesus Christ, and our Father. His choices are the best.

And who is sufficient for these things—for such a life of holiness? Our sufficiency is of God Who has given, and is still giving to us, His own Holy Spirit to make us holy.

God's Counsel Standeth

God . . . which keepeth truth for ever.—PSALM 146: 6.

CHANGE and decay in all around we see, helpers fail and comforts flee, but God changeth not. The years, the political or religious changes, the approach of old age, the rise of younger men, all these and all else do not affect the Lord though they very much affect us. With Him there is no shadow cast by His turning. He is the same yesterday, and today, and for ever. He has shewn this to us very plainly lest our unbelieving minds should doubt. His Word, which is in itself sufficient, has been confirmed by an oath. So that by two unchangeable things we might not doubt but trust Him.

This unchangeableness of God is ultimately the basis of our peace both as we think of ourselves and of the world. Were any change possible in the Godhead then we could never be sure that our sins were forgiven or that our standing before Him as righteous in Christ would not be revoked. Conscience would never really be at rest and the mind would be tormented with the possibility of God changing His mind.

The same concern would arise regarding the world of men. Six thousand years of human history have passed and human beings are still suffering from human beings, and from dread disease or famine. The world seems out of course and wicked men in the ascendancy. But God's counsel standeth fast, He is working out His purpose as year succeeds to year. It is not always easy to determine and appreciate what He is doing, but we know that in the end every knee will bow to His Son, and the Church elect from every nation will share the glory of her Head. All His ways are right. Happy is he who puts his confidence in God Who keepeth truth for ever, and in His Son Whose blood will never lose its power till all the ransomed Church of God is saved to sin no more.

What More Can I Need?

I will greatly rejoice in the Lord.—Isaiah 61: 10.

God's gifts to us are more than can be numbered, though that fact should not prevent us from counting them. They are of every kind and to meet every need. There are gifts for the spirit, the mind and the body; gifts which are sheer necessities and gifts which are just luxuries. Let us cultivate the habit of recognising them when they are given, and of acknowledging them as from above, from the Father.

But God's greatest gift is not something, not even pardon, peace, or purity; it is Himself. We receive Him when as sinners we come in our need and receive His Son as our Saviour. Then we are made partakers of the divine nature (2 Peter 1: 4) and we receive the life of God (Eph. 4: 18). Not only do we become His but He is ours for ever and for ever. Greater than all the gifts is the Giver and now He dwells in us who are His children.

This means that His righteousness and His holiness are ours; His peace and power may be enjoyed by us. Indeed all our need is met by God Who is the Source and Fount of everything. There is no reason we should want for that which is necessary for life and godliness, since He is the portion of our inheritance.

If God be ours what more can we need? We may have little of this world's goods but we have enough, and if there is a real need He would have us tell Him that He may meet it. There is no straitness with Him whatever the economic conditions of the world or country in which we live. But most of us are more conscious of our spiritual need, that is of more patience, more love, more likeness to Christ. All that we need is in Him; let us not fail to ask and receive that our joy may be full.

Living Only for God and Others

None of us liveth to himself.—ROMANS 14: 7.

TODAY we face the solemn fact that not even the least conspicuous of us lives an isolated life. This means that we are all of real significance even in the smallest sphere and the most trivial deed. It is also a most blessed fact, for like all truths it cuts both ways and brings this great encouragement, that the least known of God's children is exercising a ministry quite beyond his thoughts.

Though the modern study of psychology has been fraught with many perils, and its use, like that of the sciences, has not all been helpful, yet it has taught all who would learn the very great power of human influence—the effect for good or evil of one life upon another. All our thoughts and inward reactions, all our words and gestures, all our purposes and deeds, go to make us a centre for broadcasting waves of influence which are emanating all the time and touching all whom we meet. No man liveth to himself. We meet each other and instantly feel we have met a friend whom we can trust or one whom we must suspect.

This calls us to a life of singular devotion and simple piety. Our intention must be pure, we must purpose only to glorify God. Our love must needs to be without cloak or guile, that we may diffuse kindness to all without reserve. And this in turn is only possible as in Christ we are practically and purposefully dead to self-seeking and alive for Christ and others. If that be so then Christ will be glorified before men, either by our daily living or by our daily dying, and it will not matter much by which it is.

O fill me with Thy fullness, Lord,
Until my very heart o'erflow;
In kindling thought and glowing word
Thy love to tell, Thy praise to shew.

Because of His Love

With loving-kindness have I drawn thee.—JEREMIAH 31: 3.

GOD loved us because He is love: He loves us still for the same reason. It was not because our case was pitiable, though indeed it was, or that our end was desperate, though indeed it was; but He loves us because His nature is love. Our pitiable condition and our coming judgment afforded Him a supreme opportunity of displaying His love but was not its cause. The cause of our redemption and of all that flows from it is found alone in the nature of God.

This reminds us of something which many Christians foolishly despise—namely the theology of the Bible. Its doctrine of God, when it is arranged in an orderly fashion for the mind, becomes the queen of sciences. For, undergirding all our hopes for eternity and our possibilities of living a godly life in an ungodly world, must be the character of God. Here today we are reminded that God is love, a fact which cannot change, though it must needs be supplemented with other facts concerning the nature of Him Who is infinite and eternal in His being, wisdom, power and love.

Such a God loved us and loves us still. His love being eternal was operative before we were, and will remain so unto the eternity which is future to us. He did not love us because of anything He saw in us, for He loved us before we were born and took knowledge of us before ever our names were inscribed in an earthly register of births. And from our first beginnings He worked in our hearts, setting us apart for Himself, convicting us by His Spirit and drawing us to His Son and enabling us to receive His truth. Herein is love, not that we loved God but that He loved us, and took the initiative in giving His well-beloved Son while yet we were enemies. He drew us and we followed on—that is all.

He Knows, He Loves, He Cares

He knoweth the way that I take.—JOB 23: 10.

WHEN we read "We have not a high priest which cannot be touched with the feeling of our infirmities, etc.", we are being told negatively for strong emphasis that we have a high priest who is touched with our weaknesses. One of the great purposes of His earthly life, as distinct from His death, was to enable Him to understand as a Man and so sympathise as our High Priest. So we see Him in the Gospels weeping, wearied, misunderstood, lonely, and in that He hath been tempted and suffered, He is fitted and able to stand alongside His tempted and suffering servants today.

Then he knows the way He is taking with us. The events and experiences of our life are not determined by chance of circumstance or by the dictates of our foe. The Lord Himself is guiding us, and along that planned highway He has anticipated every need as well as arranged that blessing shall come from every difficulty and danger. He knows the way He takes and the end He purposes—not the end of arriving home in glory one day, blessed as that is, but the end in the development of our character and service. May it not be, in a far greater degree than we are sometimes tempted to think, that our life here is preparing us for the special service which is appointed us in heaven?

He cares. He that touches us touches Him. Saul was not only persecuting the Church but the Church's Head. That makes it a solemn thing for anyone to harm a child of God, and similarly a happy and worthy thing to help one of Christ's friends. In all our affliction He is afflicted; He is not unmoved or unsympathetic.

Jesus knows all about our troubles,
He will guide till the day is done.

Lest We Forget

God, Who is rich in mercy . . . hath quickened us.—EPHESIANS 2: 4, 5.

Two great considerations should save us from any pride; one is the state from which we have been brought by grace and the other the day of judgment to which we are hastening. These we are so apt to forget when that unholy weed, pride, springs up to stop the growth of heartsease and other lovely things.

And what a catalogue of Scriptures meets us here. We have been delivered from the rock, the pit, the miry clay. We have been taken from the corruption and guilt of our original iniquity when we were cast out as a subject of loathing. There is no ground for pride for it is all of grace. No struggle we ever had contributed to our deliverance. He brought us up out of the clay else we had been there still, and the new song He has put in our mouth must be sung to His praise. "Not unto us, not unto us, O Lord, but unto Thy name give glory."

But this condition and position in which we were, gave God the occasion for shewing forth His great love. Because we were sinners and deserving judgment God shewed His mercy and commended His love. The richness of His grace is shewn forth in its brightness against the dark background of our death in sin and He has taken the opportunity of quickening us together with Christ, of imparting to us eternal life which we could never otherwise have obtained.

Now, as with Paul, we are become ensamples of His mercy. If God could save us He can save our relatives, our fellow-travellers and workmen. None are too bad and we should despair of none. If we do, let us look again to the pit from which we have been digged, and both thank Him for His mercy to us and pray in hope for others.

Wholly Set Apart for God

Holiness, without which no man shall see the Lord.—HEBREWS 12: 14.

HOLINESS is both a position and a condition; we both belong to God and we are to be morally like Him. We are set apart by God for Himself and we are to set ourselves apart; which means both turning away from anything unholy and also turning to the Lord in an attitude of positive devotion to His pleasure.

In ourselves we are unclean and separated from God by our uncleanness; our best attempts at holiness are soiled by selfishness and sin. "Such were some of you but ye are washed." But God has looked upon us, has loved us and saved us by the work of His grace. Ye are sanctified. Now we are the Lord's own possession; His inheritance, a people for His possession. This means that we are called to be like Him in His hatred of sin and in His love of truth and holiness. We are to love the unlovely as He does. Only so shall we see God in the sense of understanding Him and tracing His ways, and only as we are longing to be like Him shall we be able to worship Him.

For this, two things are suggested as being of the greatest help in our daily life before God. The first is that as the High Priest of old wore upon his mitre a plate engraved "Holiness to the Lord" so we are to have ever engraven upon our minds that all we are, have and do, is wholly the Lord's. This means that every part of life comes under the sweet governance of Christ. We are not His in church alone, but in the office and the kitchen. This will affect the way we keep our ledgers or wash the dishes. These simplest duties are to be done as serving the Lord Christ. The second thing of which we are reminded is that the same Lord has passed into the heavens to make all this daily and practically possible, and He would be enquired of by us, to do it for us. Let us therefore come boldly unto our risen Lord Who sits on the throne of grace.

Bright Rays in a Dark World

Thy Word is a . . . light unto my path.—PSALM 119: 105.

WE are travelling through a dark world and our feet are often set in slippery places; foes lurk about us seeking to trip us up and keep us down; moreover there is the problem of our own failings and weakness. To meet these needs God has given us His written word and His indwelling Spirit.

His word is like a lamp to our feet. It gives its light but must be held near the path so as to shew the way and the pitfalls. Our use of Holy Scripture is not to be merely academic but personal and practical. It was written to guide men away from hell and towards heaven. Let us apply its light to our personal walk each day.

It is also a preventive of sin and for this purpose must be hid in the heart, treasured in the mind and be regarded as the final adjudicator of conduct. If the Scriptures command some attitude of forgiveness or some line of conduct then the believer must seek to obey its precepts and thus he will be kept from the paths of the destroyer, and prevented from many a fall.

The Bible is to us the sure word of prophecy unto which we do well to take careful heed. It shines in the dark places, it is God's instrument for directing us along the way and for maintaining us in holiness and righteousness all our days.

At present our apprehension of God and of His way for us can only be partial and imperfect; at present we see through a smoked glass. The light shines adequately but our mind is finite and we know only in part. But a day is coming—glad day!—when we shall see perfectly and know as we are known. No longer shall we be in a dark world and our feet be tempted to stray. No longer shall we see dimly for we shall be in a land of light and love which is lit by the glory of God and of the Lamb. In the meantime we need all the light of God's word and careful application to the study and obedience lest we miss the best which God had for us both on the journey and at the end.

More Than Conquerors

Thanks be to God, which giveth us the victory. . . .—I COR. 15: 57.

THE enemy, Satan, the Devil, the slanderer, the accuser of the brethren has been cast down, not yet into the abode of eternal darkness which is to be his final lot, but from a place of privilege and authority. It is not easy to believe this when his power in the earth and over men appears to be so great and widespread, but the fact remains that he is limited now, and doomed.

In proof of this God can say to us, weak as we are, "Resist the devil and he will flee from you" and we may be sure that his power over the children of God is usurped and unnecessary, and that it only continues with the permission of the saint. Satan's power over his own is not disputed except that even in their case it must be by their own willing submission.

The victory over Satan was accomplished by Christ in His death. At His Cross He rendered powerless him that hath the power of death, that is, the devil, and we are called to celebrate and experience the victory. We therefore are to overcome and to be led by our risen Lord in humble triumph as we follow and trust Him, bearing our simple witness to the power of His blood.

This means that we must be prepared by being fully armed. For this a complete armour is provided in which we may not only stand our ground and refuse to yield but actually take the initiative and advance. Let us prayerfully put on Christ as our salvation, who will protect our mind; as the truth which will make us strong; as our breastplate which will give us rest of heart and conscience; as our shoes which will enable us to walk in love and run in the way of His commandments. Christ is all we need but we desperately need Him in every contest and in every part of our life. So equipped, we shall then need to take His word of truth and by it hold back and push back the enemy, causing him to yield ground all around.

The victory is ours by grace; do we know it experimentally? If so we must thank Him Who always leadeth us in triumph.

Trust Means Happiness

Whoso trusteth in the Lord, happy is he.—PROVERBS 16: 20.

To trust the Lord is to rely upon His character and to be fully persuaded that what God has promised He is not only able to perform but will perform. Abraham is cited as an example. Everything was against the fulfilment of God's promise to give him a son, but Abraham trusted God to do what He said. Later when God asked Abraham to offer up the same son in whom all his hopes were centred, he hastened to obey, believing that God could even raise Isaac from the dead. Abraham relied upon God's promise and upon His character. There is no one but God and nothing but His word on Whom and on which we may so rely, and yet so often we are guilty of unbelief.

Such trust in God brings happy results. The life is marked by a quiet confidence; even if the world is all disturbed yet the believing heart is quiet from fear of evil knowing that

> The soul that on Jesus hath leaned for repose
> He will not, He will not desert to its foes.

Trusting we are assured of guidance step by step both in the daily details and in the major crises when big decisions have to be made. We know that if, through our weakness or ignorance, we fall we shall be lifted up again.

All this is the portion of the man who trusts God, who relies upon His faithful and unchangeable character. Whoso trusteth in the Lord happy is he and only he is happy. The life which is characterised by not trusting God must be guided by changing circumstances or human scheming. The mind must necessarily be busy endeavouring to discover what is the best way, and yet all the time unable to see ahead. But the man of quiet confidence learns God's will, accepts God's choice and is blessed.

The King's Court is Open

The King held out the golden sceptre, so Esther drew near.—ESTHER 5: 2.

WE who are Christians have been made nigh to God by the precious blood of Christ; this means that, not only is the estrangement between God and us removed for ever, but that we now have access into His presence in the interests of others. Those who are still exiled because of sin should have in us a friend at court, who can represent their need and plead their cause. It is of God's love that we are made so near.

Our access is not to be like that of Esther, who is in view this morning. She came tremblingly into the court of the king saying in effect, "It is dangerous for I have not been called, but I must come, because the situation is desperate, and if I perish, I perish." But we have our access with boldness (though we must ever come to God with reverence and Godly fear) and we are in no doubt about our welcome for He has bid us come. Neither is there to be doubt about our acceptance, for we are accepted in the beloved. Let us come humbly and boldly to the throne of grace that we may find mercy, grace and help both for ourselves and others whose need is greater than ours.

We do not have access to the courts of earth nor are we ever likely to have such. At times we long for such high privilege if only we could help to right the wrongs and make some contribution towards holding back the great tide of national sin. But we are more highly privileged in that we have access to the Court of heaven where every king and president must receive his appointment. Let us therefore draw near to God. He waits for us; He welcomes us for His Son's sake; and within the wide circle of His loving and wise plans there is large scope for our representation of others still in darkness, and for our brethren in the world who are in pressing need.

The Joyful News of Sins Forgiven

I have blotted out . . . thy transgressions.—ISAIAH 44: 22.

FOR men who are conscious of having sinned against a holy God, for all whose consciences are burdened with a load of guilt, there can never be a sweeter sound than that of pardon. To hear and to believe that the holy God Whom we have so grievously offended, has sent the message of a full and free forgiveness, is to make the heart glad. When Bunyan's Pilgrim came up to the Cross, the burden on his back, which is meant to illustrate the burden on his conscience, was loosed from off him and rolled down the hill, and, disappearing into a sepulchre, he saw it no more for ever. "Then Christian gave three leaps for joy and went on his way rejoicing," writes Bunyan with his intimate knowledge of human experience.

There is no sinner too vile to be pardoned and there is none so righteous as not to need it. We are all alike in need and there is mercy for all who will repent and believe. Though our sins be of the most heinous kind they can be completely forgiven and removed, because it is God who forgives, and He alone is also able to forget. The cloud between Himself and us He can remove and reinstate fellowship.

Now if we are Christians we have already experienced this great joy, but does the fact of our pardon still make us wonder and worship?

> That Thou should'st love a wretch like me
> And be the God Thou art,
> Is darkness to my intellect
> But sunshine to my heart!

And does the wonder of it still move us and make us witnesses to others who have never heard the glad news?

Blessed Are the Meek

The meek . . . shall increase their joy.—ISAIAH 29: 19.

MEEKNESS is not to be confused with weakness; it is strength, but held in check. It does not consist in thinking meanly about one's self, but in thinking soberly about both ourselves and others. Meekness is certainly not an inferiority complex, it is on the other hand a truly gracious quality which, wherever it is found, beautifies the character and adds an indefinable grace to every other trait and gift. If a man is "gifted" his very efficiency may be a snare and he may become cold and critical of others not so gifted, but if he is also meek he will be helpful to the less privileged and wonderfully understanding and sympathetic.

Such a grace is a fruit of the Spirit; it is not a mere efflorescence of the natural man but a product of the life of God in the soul. Where it is lacking, and in most of us it is, let us seek the Lord for the increase of His Spirit in our lives and meekness will be one of the results. We are certainly to follow after this grace which in the sight of God is of great price, and we shall follow it as we take up Christ's yoke and walk with Him Who is meek and lowly in heart.

If meekness itself is a fruit of the Spirit, then itself produces fruit. The meek increase their joy in the earth, they find rest to their souls. The proud are restless ever seeking more honour, the meek accept the Lord's appointments and delight to do His will.

But the way of the meek is the way of faith. It may often mean not defending or explaining ourselves; it will mean committing ourselves and our reputation to the Lord Who judges righteously. Our Lord had this experience.

> It is the way the Master went.
> Should not the servant tread it still?

But if this grace is, in the sight of God, of great price, then it must be of more importance to seek it than to become great in this world's judgment or rich in this world's goods.

Weakness Exchanged for Strength

Wait on the Lord . . . and He shall strengthen thine heart.—Psalm 27: 14.

There are few of God's children who are not made continually conscious of their own weakness. The strain of the days, the spiritual conflict of the hour, the demands made upon our wisdom and patience all make us aware of the frailty of our nature and the limitations of our humanity. Generally speaking there must be some obtuseness or unawareness of life's problems if there is no such sense of weakness.

Where such is found it is the first qualification for strength. As a sense of sickness causes one to repair to a doctor, as thirst drives one to water, so our weakness casts us upon God, the mighty God, Who fainteth not, neither is weary, and Whose understanding is infinite. It is Him we need and it is His own strength and wisdom He proposes to impart. "They that wait upon the Lord shall change their strength" the margin reads in Isaiah 40: 31. It is not a renewal of our human strength but a receiving of divine strength which is promised and needed. God's strength being adequate, all the infinite demands made upon Him must surely be adequate for the few small demands made upon us.

But his strength is to be sought, to be asked for and to be received. It is not given to the careless or the too-busy; we must wait for it. Time is required and quietness of spirit before God. The fever of haste must die down and in quietness and confidence we shall find God's strength. Many of us are putting forth more than we are receiving, the output of strength is greater than the intake. We have been adding machinery but not adequately increasing the power, hence our weariness and weakness. Let us seek the Lord and wait quietly before Him, asking that He himself will meet us and renew us. Our human strength has run out and we are weary and impatient; we need Him in all His fullness.

The Pure in Heart See God

The fear of the Lord is to hate evil.—PROVERBS 8: 13.

THE pure in heart are those who are pure or undivided in their intention; they desire to please God and to walk before Him in holiness. Where there is any intention of parleying with sin the heart remains divided and the vision is blurred for the pure in heart see God.

The question which is raised in today's passages of Scripture is whether or not we purpose to tolerate evil in our lives. We may often fall, we shall often fail, but do we intend to do so or do we fully intend that our lives shall be free from evil.

If we truly know God, the God of heaven and holiness who hates sin, and if by His grace we have begun to love Him, then surely we must hate and abhor that which is evil, and seek to abstain from its very appearance. This will mean that we must purge out the old leaven. The unregenerate man's ideas of truth and falsehood, of honesty and dishonesty must be put away that we may remember Christ our Passover Sacrifice, with sincerity and truth untainted with permitted evil. Let us examine ourselves and depart from every thing which is condemned by God and man.

This way of life may be a costly way but it is certainly a blessed way. The conscience is void of offence, the heart is undivided, the mind is enabled to think more truly and clearly. And whatever may be the cost on the one hand or the results on the other, it is the right way for the believer. It is certain that personal blessing is hindered by permitting the leaven of sin to remain in our lives, and it may be that the long-desired and very necessary revival throughout the whole church of Christ is delayed on account of this very matter. We shall never be sinless, but we can today, by the grace of God, begin to refuse any quarter to sin or to continue to know evil practices.

In Quietness, Strength

Sit still, my daughter.—RUTH 3: 18.

WE are living in a busy world; its pace has been greatly quickened during the last few decades. The radio and the motor-car, increased speed in travel and the rapid growth and pace of machinery have all made their contribution to disturb the quietness and serenity of a previous century. The Christian is called to live a quiet life in the midst of this disquiet and so witness to the peace of God which passeth understanding. If the rush of the age enters into our soul disturbing our peace and communion with God then serious results will follow to the spiritual life.

So the command comes to us today to sit still, to take care and be quiet. It will need care if we are to do this, and it will need time. We must have set periods when we retire from the busy world and cease to listen to its din that in the quietness we may hear the still small voice of God. Then let there be some time each day and, if possible, more than once a day, when we withdraw. To some, whose life is without privacy this may be difficult, and we all admire the busy mother who, finding it almost impossible, learned to throw her apron over her head for some minutes and so found her sanctuary.

The fruits which grow in stillness are manifold. We know God; we see His glory and He is exalted before us. We are saved from many snares and find our strength in God's presence. As we cease activity and wait for God we give Him a chance to work in us and for us, we are delivered from the fear of bad news. And not least we are saved from a hasty spirit which spoils both actions and words.

When we are the busiest, and the most tempted to be disquieted, then is the need to seek most a holy stillness before God. Martin Luther is reported at one time to have said that he was so busy that he could not get through his work with less than three hours of prayer. Alas we are so busy that prayer is crowded out. Be still and know.

Members of Christ's Spiritual Body

He is the Head of the body, the Church.—COL. 1: 18.

SPEAKING through David by the Spirit of prophecy the Son of God said "Lo, I come . . . a body hast Thou prepared me". A thousand years later this was first fulfilled when great David's Greater Son was born in Bethlehem. By a real and indisputable miracle the Son of God had become incarnate through the Virgin Mary, and had begun His life in a human body in which for more than thirty years He accepted restriction in space in order to reveal God to man and to accomplish man's redemption.

Then His body was broken for us and He died and rose again that He might impart the life of God to the souls of men, and God began to give His Son another body of which the apostle Paul wrote so much, the Spiritual body of Christ, the Church, of which Jesus Christ is Head and Lord.

In order to build this body the Holy Spirit was given to and by the Ascended Christ and began His special work in the world of giving to men repentance toward God and faith in our Lord Jesus Christ. Those who believed have been built together into a spiritual body and the process continues to the praise of God.

By God's infinite grace we who read this have doubtless been born of God and made to be a member of Christ's spiritual body. This is not necessarily the same as membership of a Church in the world, for, alas, there are many members of local churches who are not born again and therefore not members of the true Church of Christ and therefore not members of His body. But if we have been saved by God's grace then we are truly members of His body, and that being so we are to be careful to be healthy members, fulfilling our function and contributing to the health of the whole body. This is possible as we live in living touch with the Head, from Whom we receive both our life and our instruction, and being in right relation to Him we are adjusted in true fellowship with all others who are also members of His body.

God's Servant in the Sanctuary

Let us lift up our heart . . . unto God in the heavens.—LAM. 3: 41.

GOD dwelleth on high, His throne is exalted and His Kingdom ruleth over all. His sovereignty and His power over all creation is too easily forgotten by both vain man in the world and even by His servants. Let us think often of Him far above all.

We are to lift up our hearts to the Lord in worship and praise. His love to us is better than even His best gift of human life for it is expressed in the gift of His own Son and in Him includes eternal life. He is good and ready to forgive, which means that all that He does is good and His spiritual mercies, such as pardon, are meant to cause us to lift up our hearts in adoration and thanksgiving.

We are also to lift up our hearts in longing to know Him better. He has given us a thirst for Himself and for a closer walk with Him which should draw or drive us into His presence. There let us seek Him and ask Him to satisfy us yet more deeply with His life and His love.

We must also draw near to Him and lift up our hands in supplication and intercession. We need Him much; others need Him desperately. We are therefore to lift up holy hands in prayer, seeking His mercy and grace to help for God's saints who are being tried in many ways and in many parts of the world. We are also to carry the unsaved of the world upon our hearts as we draw nigh to God. Millions yet have never heard while millions more have not heard adequately or paid no heed. The whole world gropes in darkness while he light shines upon us; it groans in its pain and sorrow while we rejoice in God. Let us intercede for them encouraged by the promise that whatsoever ye shall ask in My Name, that will I do.

Think What is Before Us

The hope which is laid up for you in heaven.—COL. 1: 5.

To become hopeless is to become lifeless and powerless and unfitted for the duties which are appointed. We have all seen those whose bodily powers were greatly weakened kept alive by hope; they refused to despair and to give up. It is the same in the spiritual life, for we are saved from fainting and ceasing, by hope of a future for the work or for the salvation of the individual.

But this is all true also concerning hope for the more distant future and for eternity. Hope as a general quality becomes more specific and we often read in the New Testament of "the" hope, the blessed hope. Indeed it is this particular hope which is most evident—the hope of the coming of the Lord and our entry with Him into glory. To be held by such a hope will enable us to go through much discouragement and tribulation down here. Our Lord Jesus for the hope before Him endured the Cross and despised the shame; and as we look for and lay hold of the glories which await the children of God we shall be nerved to endure the conflict which is upon us and which may grow as the days go by.

One of the most certain results of hope in God and for the future is joy. We rejoice in hope just as we sorrow in despair. If our hope is bounded by this life we must be sad, for there is little here which gives good ground for hope. Misunderstanding between the nations grows and sin stalks unashamed, but our hope is in a Kingdom which is established and shall not pass away. Therefore we rejoice for we have been brought into such a Kingdom and we anticipate the glories and the triumph of eternity. We have a lively hope and we rejoice with a joy which defies expression. Let us look well to the hope before us and hold loosely to the transient things and plans of this world which must pass away.

Glory, glory dwelleth in Immanuel's land.

Weighed and Wanting

. . . a God of knowledge, and by Him actions are weighed.—1 SAM. 2: 3.

EVERY one of us shall give account of himself to God, to God Who searcheth the heart and knoweth all our ways. From Him nothing is hid and both thoughts, words and deeds are all open and justly appraised. Before such a God we are already found wanting, we have come short of His glory. Much which appears praiseworthy amongst men is found condemned in His pure eyes; what is a credit in human eyes is a debit in the divine reckoning. For God's standards and methods of judgment are true and righteous. He judges according to the true nature and value of character and action, and His judgments, rewards and punishments are all praiseworthy.

It is therefore a matter of highest wisdom that we first seek to know God and His standards. The ways and ideas of this passing, changeful world are not to be our ways and thoughts. Indeed if we are moved by divine and eternal considerations we shall find ourselves thinking and acting very differently from those who live for time and for the approval of others. It matters most that we have God's approval. "We labour to be accepted of Him", or as it has been translated "we are ambitious to be well pleasing unto Him". This is a true and commendable purpose which should govern all our ways.

But if we are left to ourselves we must always fall short of the standard and be found wanting. Our own righteousness, that is the very best we can do, is as filthy rags. Our poor attempts and attainments do not justify us before a holy God, but we have one Who has come to our help and represented us before God. It is God's Son Who bore our sins and offers us His own righteousness. The things therefore in which we placed our confidence in the hope of acceptance must be renounced as a ground of hope, and Christ alone received and trusted. Christ received is holiness begun and Christ trusted and obeyed is holiness continued and expressed.

The Hungry Satisfied

He hath filled the hungry with good things.—LUKE 1: 53.

ONE of the marks of a healthy spiritual state is a hunger and thirst after God, a deep longing for holiness of heart and life. And one of the most unhealthy and disquieting signs is the unconcern of a self-satisfaction which is described in the Bible as "at ease in Zion". It would at first seem that the satisfaction and heart-rest which is so often promised in Scripture excluded further hunger but this is not so. For the method of God appears to be to give a hunger and then meet it and further hunger met by further satisfaction. Is this not the same as with our bodies? We hunger and thirst, then we eat and drink; and some hours later the need is apparent again.

The hunger of the Christian is a most blessed thing if it is for the right satisfaction, namely for God and righteousness. When a child of God is longing for that which is worldly or merely material then the hunger may be dangerous, and unless it is satisfied by new discoveries and appropriation of God it may lead to serious backsliding. Then let us be assured that our deep longings, however they may appear to us, are really the longings of our deep spiritual life for more of God and His righteousness, and let us be aware when the mind and heart become set on other things.

To the hungry and thirsty God has given the most reassuring promises; they shall be filled, they shall never hunger and never thirst. This means that whenever we find our spiritual life conscious of its need, that is in other words hungry or thirsty, as we come and eat and drink of Christ we shall indeed be satisfied; and so we shall be not only sustained but we shall make progress in the Christian life. Moreover the promises go far beyond the meeting of our own needs, for we read that if we continue to drink, out of us will flow rivers of living water to refresh others.

Unity Though not Uniformity

I will give them one heart and one way.—JER. 32: 39.

THERE is a true unity of spirit which already exists between all believers. It is not something to be striven after, for it already obtains, but it is to be guarded most jealously; we are exhorted to do our best to maintain it.

This unity is not allied to uniformity of thought and practice in non-essential matters. There are, and will be, many different forms of worship and many different views of prophecy but there is at the same time one heart in the acknowledgment of God as Sovereign, of His Son as Saviour and of His Spirit as Regenerator and Sanctifier. It is the deep conviction of a few basic truths and a heart love to the Lord which forms the ground of the unity in spirit. Those who are participants possess the same life of God in their souls, since they are born of the same Spirit and they are moved by the same motive to please God. In prayer, in evangelistic meetings and conventions for the deepening of the spiritual life they are free and glad to meet as "all one in Christ Jesus".

This is the practice of a true unity which is most precious to God and which is most healthy for the Church of God. Moreover its prevalence is a witness to the world which often looks on with perplexity or even disgust at our deep divisions. For its development we need to be charitable in thought and restrained in word; not holding our doctrines with less conviction but remembering that some things such as method in worship, etc., are not outlined in Scripture and on some things of our faith we only see at present through a glass darkly.

Our Lord prayed for our unity. He has effected it by His giving to us His own risen life, and to us is committed the responsibility of maintaining it in the bond of peace. If we are meek, willing to be taught and corrected and to see another's viewpoint, we shall see a growth-of-heart union among true believers which may grow in its outward expression to the glory of God.

Beware of Lingering in Vanity Fair

... what communion hath light with darkness?—2 Cor. 6: 14.

We who are the Lord's belong to another world—the heavenly. We have been delivered from this present, passing world at infinite cost. Its methods and standards are unacceptable to God and must be so to us. For all that is in the world is the lust of the flesh, the lust of the eyes and the pride of life; in other words it is governed by the desire to indulge, the desire to possess, and the desire to impress. All this is contrary to the Spirit of Christ and to be eschewed by the Christian. To live in this fashion and governed by these motives is unworthy of the child of God.

Separation from the world which the Bible teaches, therefore, is first of all a matter of spirit. We do not love the world and its show. We are of another spirit and care for heavenly things. Meekness is to us preferable to the pride of this life, and the Christian's ornament is of a meek and quiet spirit rather than of jewels and dress.

To love the world, which is moved and conducted by principles so contrary to God's is to be at enmity with God. and we must choose whether we are to be friendly with one or the other. And seeing we are redeemed from the power of the world and have been made partakers of a world which will never pass away, surely we must live more and more for eternity.

There is an intimacy with Christ which is only known to the lowly in heart. To be highly esteemed among men may mean that we miss the high esteem of the Father, and the privilege of walking daily with our God. The world is passing away, all its concern and desires will soon fail, but doing God's will is eternal. Why do we enslave ourselves so much to this passing world and its ways? Our minds must needs be renewed and our vision cleared.

Diagnosis and Cure

I am the Lord that healeth thee.—EXODUS 15: 26.

THERE is no part of our lives hidden from God, and no act or thought which He does not mark. We are altogether known by Him. Such statements might well strike terror to the heart, and indeed to the sinner unrepentant and unforgiven, they should bring conviction of sin and need. But to the child of God the truth of God's omniscience is filled with comfort; we would not have it otherwise.

In the first place we know God in Christ, and all we know of Him causes us to trust and love Him. If this all-knowledge of us were possessed by some creatures or by some so called gods, then we would certainly fear, as the worshippers of false gods invariably do. But the God and Father of our Lord Jesus is worthy of all knowledge. In Him it must be used for good.

In the second place it is because He knows our spiritual sickness or weakness that there is hope of recovery. Sometimes we ourselves do not know that we are sick of soul. We may backslide without knowing it. While being careful about some things we may be seriously at fault of others, and yet unaware of the condition. Because God knows and cares He will surely bring it to our notice by one means or another. This may be the painful prelude to the cure but it is most necessary, for God does not heal the hurt of His people lightly nor cover up the festering spot.

It is the same understanding Lord who heals us. By His stripes we are healed. The healing is applied by His gentle spirit. No wound is too deep and festering, no weakness too great, no long-standing habit too difficult but that His strong and skilful hands can deal with it. The healing is half wrought when we know we are sick, for then we can come to our Great Physician. Let us give God time to search and cleanse us, that healed and happy we may be helpful to many in this sick, sad world. Is there trouble in our lives, hidden or open? His promise today is, "I have seen . . . and will heal".

From Thirsting to Overflowing

Ho, every one that thirsteth, come ye . . . —ISAIAH 55: 1.

"IF any man thirst"—this does not mean that some men do and some do not; it is not the "if" of probability but of logic. All human beings thirst for God, they are so constituted. Alas millions do not know the true God and millions more do not know for what or whom they are thirsting. They first seek their satisfaction in the worship of false gods, or it may be in degrading indulgences and the others, with mistaken notion, think their souls will be satisfied with money, pleasure, possessions, etc. But they remain thirsty still. Their soul is thirsting for the living God and they do not know it.

To such the word of the Gospel is "come ye to the waters". The Spirit and the bride say, "Come . . . take of the water of life freely". The assurance is given that whosoever drinketh of this water will never thirst again, and millions have drunk, that is they have trusted Christ and made Him their own, and have proved the promises true. The attraction of the world with its possessions and positions is gone. Indulgence of the flesh is not required or permitted.

O Christ, He is the fountain.

But the discovery of God in Christ which is the experience of every true child of God is so wonderful that it begets a new longing, yes a new thirst, to know God better, to experience more of His satisfying and sanctifying presence. So like the Psalmist we still long, yea even faint for the presence of the Lord as the pilgrim desires water in a dry and thirsty land. We too are passing through a wilderness; the world can offer us nothing to satisfy, and we must therefore come and come again to the Lord Jesus, and drink and drink again of His grace. For the one who keeps on coming and keeps on drinking is the one out of whose life streams of blessing keep on flowing.

Understanding and Strength

I, even I, am He that comforteth you.—ISAIAH 51: 12.

UNFORTUNATELY the word "comfort" as ordinarily used today does not truly represent the word which is written in Scripture. We use the word when we think of a mother calming the distress of a child, or of a friend trying to say helpful things to one who is bereaved. But while such a ministry of solace may be included in the original word it is by no means its most important meaning.

It has often been said that a Comforter in Scripture is "one called alongside to help". The thought includes that of an advocate who represents our cause and interests and the word is so translated in 1 John 2: 1. Understanding of our need, sympathy to represent it to another, strength to continue or recover; these are the qualities which a Comforter, in the Bible sense, brings to us.

Our God fully supplies all these. Some of our friends have deep sympathy but lack the ability to strengthen, others who can represent us, fail in human understanding or are pre-occupied. But the Lord is He who comforteth us, and while the comfort of another fellow-saint is most precious, the fullest comfort comes from God:

> There is no place where earth's sorrows
> Are more felt than up in heaven;
> There is no place where earth's failings
> Have such kindly judgment given.

—and with the understanding there is a help and strength imparted for present need. The Lord is like a father and full of all comfort or possessed of all the qualities of a true Comforter. He knows and understands our human frailty better than we ourselves and bids us cast our need and weakness upon Him.

But the texts wisely include the reminder of a day which is coming, when there will be no more need for sympathy or for the representation of our need, or the restoration of our souls.

Glorioulsy Free

Sin shall not have dominion over you.—ROMANS 6: 14.

THE longing for freedom is a basic human instinct. As the bird desires the open sky and a fish the broad stream or deep ocean, so the human heart longs for a condition which is free from bondage.

But there are strong fetters upon each soul; they come to us in birth, for the whole human family is bound, and they are strengthened when sinful tendencies develop into sinful habits. It is sin which binds us all. The form of the fetter differs greatly, but the nature of it is the same for all. This means that none of us can help ourselves and certainly none can help another. Someone, with another and a sinless nature, must come for our deliverance.

So in the purpose and providence of God Jesus came, born of a Virgin, sinless in His nature while truly human in His sympathy and experience. Having identified Himself with our human nature in His Incarnation, He then identified Himself with our sin on the Cross and suffered God's judgment on human rebellion, and took our sinful nature to its death.

And now is preached the good news, this Gospel to the believer, that sin shall not have dominion over us; its power is broken and the Spirit of life in Christ Jesus hath emancipated us from the tyranny of sin and death. Believe it, O my soul, believe it my brother and sister, then thou art free. Does the news seem too good to be true? But it is true and waits thy acceptance. God giveth us the victory and the freedom now. Take it from His hand and rejoice.

There will be many attempts made, however, both by Satan and by men to take the blessing away. There will be temptations to doubt the Saviour, His finished and His present work; temptations to doubt the good news and to become entangled with sin on the one hand or with the method of struggling on the other. So refuse both and stand fast in the liberty which is yours today in Christ.

God Both Knows and Understands

He that searcheth the hearts knoweth.—ROMANS 8: 27.

IT is one thing to accept the fact of God's all-knowledge but it is quite another to see its application to one's own life—and to welcome it. It is certain, however, that there is nothing hid from God's knowledge, for it is the nature of God to know everything.

First of all He knoweth us perfectly, the way we take, the deeds we perform, the thoughts we think and He most certainly knows who are His and who are not. It is His perfect and complete knowledge not only of deeds, but of motives also, which enables God to judge us impartially. Here on earth we punish the man who has fallen into sin and been caught, without giving any attention to the fact that he was tempted scores of times and refused to do wrong. Or we judge only the deed, without consideration of the desire. Some are born into the world with heavy chains around them, with a temperament which is awkward and a nature which is rancorous. Those of us who are naturally kind and generous find it difficult to put ourselves in the place of a person who has to struggle to be kind and who feels cross and cantankerous all the day long. But God knows and cares and judges righteously.

Then the omniscience of God is not only full of warning lest we think we can sin and escape, but it is also full of encouragement because He marks all our longings after holiness, and must often say to us when we have failed, "It was good that it was in thine heart." All our desire is before Him and our groanings and yearnings are not hid from Him.

But lest we should draw only comfort from these truths, let us also remember that there is challenge in them also. If we name His name we are to leave our evil ways. It matters greatly how we live if we are called Christians, and not only because of our testimony in the world but also because our Saviour is our Judge and we must needs give an account of the deeds done in the body.

Vouchsafe to keep us this day without sin.

The Kindest Shepherd

A bruised reed shall He not break.—MATT. 12: 20.

HOW gentle the Son of God is! His mighty power is under perfect control and so the smallest deed is skilfully performed, the simplest word is helpfully spoken. Among men we are often acquainted with two very different types of men. The one is strong but brusque, brutally strong; he is able to carry through his designs for he tramples on the opinions or feelings of others as he marches on to triumph. The other is the weak man; he is afraid of hurting anyone and so often therefore does nothing. We hesitate to commit ourselves to him for, though we admire his kindness, we have no confidence in his character and do not count on his decisions.

But our Lord Jesus Christ possesses the qualities of both, and possesses them to the full, while He is free from the inherent weaknesses of each. He is strong but He is understanding; He is able but He is also considerate. So His actions are marked with strong understanding or understanding strength, for the qualities are blended and never separate.

This means that there is no one like Him for raising the fallen and lifting up the discouraged. And alas the world is full of broken lives and bruised hearts. Many are needing not only new social schemes but new human sympathy, and our evangelistic concern would often be more successful if we had more loving sympathy with men and women in their sin.

The Lord dwelleth on high but He is meek and lowly in heart. He holds the stars in their courses but He lifts the burden from the oppressed. Widows and children are His special care, and those who have slipped and stumbled are sure to have His sympathy.

But to lift men and to lighten the burden of women and by all means to save some, the Lord needs human hands and feet. May He not have my feet to visit the widow, my hands to lift the burden from a brother or to bless the children?

Divinely Illuminated

Open Thou mine eyes, that I may behold wondrous things.—PSALM 119: 18.

TODAY'S portions began with a prayer for the opening of the eyes of the mind and heart. It is right that any consideration of the soul's illumination should so begin, for without the help of God none of us, not even the cleverest, can ever understand divine truth. And the prayer does really concern both heart and mind for the truth of God is apprehended by both. Some having divorced these two have sought, on the one hand, mere intellectual knowledge, or on the other hand, mere emotional stirring.

The request is that the eyes be opened to behold wondrous things out of God's law. We are turning then, first to God as the Source of light, and afterwards to the Bible as the medium through which it is to come. Well might we address ourselves to the Word of God which is God-breathed and which is the enduring record of His self-revealing and His will. The books of men may be good or bad, helpful or confusing, but the Word of God interpreted by the Spirit of God to the enquiring mind and heart of the believer, is God's means of teaching His children.

Concerning the two who journeyed to Emmaus we read that their heavenly Stranger did actually open their understanding that they might understand the Scriptures. The prayer of the Psalmist for the open-mind is answered in their case, as it will be answered in ours.

Those who learn from God can only testify that He freely communicates to us His truth, that the light is clear and increasing and that His discoveries of Himself to us are numberless. So that we are left to exclaim, "Oh, the depth of the riches both of the wisdom and knowledge of God."

It is the Lord Who made and understands the secrets of the universe; it is He that hath called us and is now sanctifying us through the truth; it is He Who is working to a glorious end.

Unfailing Supplies

The God of all grace.—1 Peter 5: 10.

GRACE is the infinite love of God adapting itself to our finite needs; it is God's nature. It is because of this that God is well-disposed to us for both His righteousness and His love are included and satisfied.

God is the Source of all the grace that any sinner or saint can ever need. There is sufficient to save or sanctify any one. The Source is perennial, the store is boundless, the flow is adequate. All grace is infinite grace; it is like a sea without a shore or a bottom. There is therefore no need for any one of us ever to be concerned as to whether our need now or in the future will be met. The Father's resources are more than sufficient even if our need be very great.

There must be a continual adapting of grace to meet the personal, present need, and there is grace of every kind for every need; grace for the leader with crushing responsibilities, grace for the follower with his humble contribution of help in the less conspicuous place; grace for the mother and grace for the father; grace for the one in whom physical life flows strong and in the one in whom life's resources are ebbing away. There is grace to save any sinner and grace to sanctify any saint; grace to meet the trial of any situation and to break the fetter of any sin.

And should the needs grow greater then the supply will match the need, for He giveth more grace; and should others be in need then we may be to them good stewards, that is, liberal dispensers of the infinitely-varied grace of God.

The Christian's life and privileges are wonderful. We are to be spiritually enriched ourselves with the added joy of introducing others to the same God of all grace, and whether they are saved or unsaved it is Him they need.

Grace there is my every debt to pay,
Blood to wash my every sin away;
Power to keep me spotless day by day,
In Christ for me.

Most Desirable Gifts

Counsel is mine, and sound wisdom.—PROVERBS 8: 14.

WISDOM is the practical application of knowledge, understanding is the appreciation of the true character of things. A wise and understanding man appreciates the true nature of a situation or an event and applies his knowledge to meet it. Happy and privileged is the person who possesses these qualities. But where, or by whom are these qualities dispensed?—and to whom?

The wealth of knowledge and the complete ability to apply the knowledge is in Christ, Who being the Eternal Son of God and becoming the true Son of man not only possesses these desirable gifts but has made them available to all who are united to Him by faith. If therefore we are in Christ we are in closest touch with wisdom and at the very centre of understanding.

But while all true believers are in Christ and these gifts are theirs in Him the question further arises, how are they actually applied to us and become effective in us?

"The fear of the Lord is the beginning of wisdom." An attitude on the one hand of self-distrust and, on the other, of reverent love of the Lord is the first requisite for receiving wisdom and understanding. And this attitude of soul and condition of spirit is not only the beginning of wisdom but the essential condition for its continuance.

No servant of God can therefore pride himself that he is able to assess the nature of things and apply his knowledge to present needs and problems. His trust must be in the only wise God Whose wisdom is available to him because, by grace, he is found in Christ Jesus. Let no one boast of his wisdom but only of his union with Christ; let no one become proud of his power but only that he has personally come to know the God of power.

God is to be Trusted Utterly

All things work together for good to them that love God.—ROMANS 8: 28.

WE are reminded today of two most important things which the child of God must ever remember: (1) that everything in every sphere is under the control of God, and (2) that being under that control must ultimately bring good to God's people.

"All things" means exactly what it says and must therefore include not only the things which appear beneficial but things which appear otherwise. Bad rulers as well as good, dull weather as well as bright, happy circumstances as well as sad are all included in the statement. Moreover, these all things "work together", that is to say they fit into a pattern and are not unrelated. As in a large machine the many parts, differing in shape, size and function, all work together to serve one end. So all things work together in the life of the world whether in its larger or narrower spheres. The temptation which comes to us when things are difficult is to think that the present circumstance is an exception to the rule. If that were so the text would have no meaning and the whole truth of God's Sovereignty over the affairs of men would break down, and the statement would be untrue and yield no comfort. All things work together.

"For good", which means that God has an end in view and that the end is such as to be worthy of Him, and to command our fullest approbation when, at last, we cease to know in part and to look through a glass darkly. At present we cannot easily or always see the end and certainly cannot judge if it is good; therefore the truth is meant to be received by faith and thus to minister courage and comfort when such are most needed. If therefore we are facing a display of the wrath of man we may be assured that it will ultimately praise God and that which cannot do so will be restrained. The evil which is purposed by wicked men is turned to our good, and all things become ours and work for us an enjoyment of the eternal glory of God.

It is Good to Think of Christ

My meditation of Him shall be sweet.—PSALM 104: 34.

OUR thoughts and consideration are necessarily and often concentrated on life's problems and our own concerns and failures. The daily round and common task take up much of our days and a thousand details of our lives make their exacting demands on time, thought and strength. How pleasant and welcome it is to turn our attention to the Lord Jesus Christ in Whom all glories and perfection dwell. Our lives are marred but He is perfect; human affairs are full of problems but He is full of power. To turn from earth to heaven, from thinking on business or household cares to meditating on Him is like passing from the dark clouds and a dull day to the glowing sun in a blue sky. It is pleasant and exhilarating, it makes us glad.

All our thoughts of Christ are gladdening. He stands alone in His divine-human glory. He is God united with our humanity. He is Man as man should be, with every desirable human virtue manifested in perfection and in complete union with every other virtue. None in heaven or earth can compare with the Lord, and His qualities baffle description.

His character, His dealings with us, His Word to us are all alike trustworthy and we cannot but be glad when we think of them. Sadness and weakness come upon us when we think of other things and second causes. Let us then think on Him and be glad. It requires that we determine to do so. Like the Psalmist we must often say "My heart cleaveth unto the dust" but let us deliberately lift up our heart and engage our thoughts with Christ crucified, risen and coming again.

It requires time set apart for this Godly exercise, and time must be "made" in these active days. But if today even in the busyness of our life we can turn our thoughts for a moment to the Man at God's right hand, a shaft of heavenly sunlight will lighten the hour and sweeten the mind.

Living by Faith not by Feelings

The Lord will not forsake His people.—1 Sam. 12: 22.

THERE is no more difficult thing to bear than the sense of being desolate and alone. It is difficult when we are forsaken by or cut off from our fellow human beings, but to feel forsaken by God is to touch the bottom of despair.

The pathos and desolation of it was experienced to the full by our Lord Jesus Christ when He hung on the Cross for those three dark hours. Cast off by the crowd, forsaken by the disciples. He failed to receive the human friendship for which He looked, but more than that He was at the same time estranged from God His Father, while He bore our sin away. The desolation of His cry, "My God! My God! Why hast Thou forsaken me?" rang out through the mid-day darkness near Jerusalem and rings still down the centuries to remind us of One Who was forsaken for our sins and for our sakes.

But while the Lord has promised never to leave us nor forsake us, yet He does permit us sometimes to feel forsaken. We must make a distinction there; it is one thing to feel alone but it is another to be alone; and when the heart feels alone it is then that we must rest on the promises and not allow the feelings to overwhelm us. We feel forsaken, but according to God's solemn word we are never forsaken, we can never be alone.

Out of those periods of felt desolation great blessing may come to us. In the first place we have the opportunity of shewing God that we trust Him and believe His word without any sense of His presence, and this is real advance in the Christian life. In the same way if the loneliness is not quickly ended we have the privilege of declaring to God that we can wait His time though our heart may be breaking. It is in the dark that the portrait of Christ is developed in our souls; it is in the dark that the deepest work is wrought in our character—and be assured that the Lord will once again shew us the light of His countenance.

In the Secret of His Presence

A day in Thy courts is better than a thousand.—PSALM 84: 10.

THE way into the presence of God has been opened. No longer need we hide from Him as our first parents did in the garden, for the very thing which made them shun the presence has been removed and sin need no longer keep us away. The blood of Jesus hath given us access and acceptance, and we are welcome as we come.

It is not only possible for us to draw near to God but it is needful. Life quickly tends to be lived entirely in the outer sanctuary, in the court of the Gentiles. Our hours of business and duty must be spent amongst men; this is God's arrangement but life will deteriorate if we do not make our way into the sanctuary, that is the nearer presence of God. This means withdrawing from the interests of time to think on eternity and prostrate our spirits before the Lord Who hath redeemed us.

It is also a blessed thing to seek God, it is good to draw near to Him. Subsequent benefits are beyond all estimate. The Lord is good to all who seek Him, He is waiting to bless such. His mercies are dispensed chiefly to those who take time to enter His courts. And the time spent in His intimate presence is, to the true believer, the most delightful.

In the secret of His presence, how my soul delights to hide. If we are in right relation with God through faith in Christ's blood and obedience to His will then we delight to be with Him.

But another consideration should move us to seek Him, namely His longing to have us alone with Himself. The Father seeketh spiritual worshippers. He longs for communion with His children. God desires to impart spiritual graces to us and enrich us, but we may be so busy here and there, that our hearts and hands are empty when they might be filled with good things. God is seeking our fellowship today. He is waiting for us, waiting to be gracious to us. Let Him not wait in vain. Having therefore boldness to enter . . . let us draw near.

A Sequence with an End in View

Let patience have her perfect work . . . —JAMES 1: 4.

"TRIBULATION worketh patience; and experience, hope: and hope maketh not ashamed." It is a sequence with this end in view, namely, that we be unashamed and with God's love filling our hearts.

The trials which are so unwelcome to our human nature, are not without a purpose. They offer us the only opportunities for the development of that rare and priceless quality of patience, the ability to bear with things and people, the ability to wait God's time for events. Then patience is God's means for producing hope, a bright expectation of a worthy end.

Now, for a season, we may be in various trials but God is working for our enrichment and His glory. The end is not that we are able to do more service but that we may be better in character, more hopeful and loving. Those who hope all things are usually they who have been through trials; they have learned patience and found that God sustained them. They expect Him to do the same for others and that hope makes them unashamed.

Therefore let tribulation have its valuable work and let patience do her completing work. The polishing of a piece of furniture is the last process in the producing of a work of art and usefulness. Patience serves a finishing work, toughening the steel, brightening the surface, smoothing off the harsh edges. We have need of it that we might enter into possession of the enduring qualities of character which are promised to us.

Our Lord Jesus Christ Himself, and God, even our Father are at work in us. They are choosing our circumstances and appointing our engagements with a view to bringing out the character of the Saviour in our lives. The sculptor labours to bring out features in his statue and our God is labouring to make visible the features of His Son. Let patience proceed with her finishing process; there is a worthy end in view.

Righteous and Trustworthy

A just God and a Saviour.—ISAIAH 45: 21.

WHEN we think of God we are only able to think of one quality of His nature at a time, and in order to think truly and adequately our thought must pass from the consideration of one attribute to another. With most of us there is the inevitable tendency to think of His love more than of His righteousness, of His mercy more than of His justice. For that reason it is necessary to be reminded of those qualities in God's nature which are less attractive to us than others.

Such features of God's character are His righteousness and justice, and while at first they may appear forbidding yet at the same time they are fundamental. Our hopes of a just settlement of the moral problems of the world rest on this fact that God is righteous. Any hopes we may cherish for the punishment of the wicked and the reward of the righteous is built on this divine attribute. He is a God of truth and without any iniquity or inequality; He is just and right; He judgeth righteously; everyone must be judged and receive a just pronouncement which will commend itself, and the God Who made it, to our conscience.

Thus God is made known as a just God and a Saviour. If He were known only as just we might well fear, if only as merciful we might reasonably be anxious. But for the maintenance of a moral universe and for the pardon of our sins God is both, now and always.

It is the appreciation of the whole of God's nature which makes for true worship and strong love. We could not truly worship God if we were in doubt about His character. Oh come let us adore Him.

Bending Low Means Lifted High

Humble yourselves . . . that He may exalt you . . . —1 PETER 5: 6.

PRIDE is the chief of sins and the root of many others. It is hateful to God, and the proud in heart God keeps at a distance and will ultimately judge. But how unseemly and uncalled for pride is in human beings; we are so dependent on God, we are so sinful before God that every sinner should bow down very low in His presence. On the contrary God loves the humble in spirit, and dwells with him who is of a lowly and contrite heart. The humble He fills with good things, while the self-satisfied and proud He sends empty away.

Here then is a test of our condition and character which faces us today, and the future will be exactly the reverse of today. If we are humble now we shall be exalted in due season, but if we are proud we shall be brought low.

Two persons are involved in the process of humiliation but one only in the exalting. In the humbling God is working, shewing us our pride, producing circumstances which afford us an opportunity of rejecting it. This means that we must make an overall decision to accept God's estimate of us and tread God's pathway for us. It calls also for the daily renouncing of ourselves and the choosing of the lowly place before God. It is the way of divine approval in which we receive the supply of divine grace, but it is also the way of moral decision when we repudiate high views of ourselves and instead deliberately put self under foot. We are being humbled by God but we must also humble ourselves.

We shall be helped in this way by the remembrance of our frailty and God's mighty hand. He is so strong and we are so weak; He so holy and we so sinful; there is only one place for us, that is, on our faces before Him.

> O Come let us bow down; let us
> Kneel before the Lord our Maker.

And the promise of His exalting of us in due time will also help us, as we bend our stiff necks and die to vain pride.

The Honour of His Name

The Name of the Lord is a strong tower.—PROVERBS 18: 10.

A MAN'S character is ultimately expressed in his name, the mention of which calls up before us what the man is; in other words his name is his reputation. It is so with God, although God's name means more than that.

Long ago God put His name upon the Israelites, that is He made them partners in His reputation. They were His people not only for the enjoyment of the privileges to be enjoyed but also to bear the responsibility it involved. Israel became God's representative people; if they lived worthily then God's name was had in honour, if they sinned and murmured then the name of the Lord was dishonoured. The Christian now bears that worthy name, and that fact invests our lives with a solemn responsibility and high privilege.

Thus our bearing the name of Christ (for we are called Christians) gives us a plea in prayer. As our failure means Christ's dishonour we may ask boldly for grace to help, and as a holy life of love will give the Lord Jesus an increased reputation we may seek from God a full supply of His Spirit for the honour of His Son. So of old the prayer was made, "Hearken and do; defer not, for thine own sake, O my God; for Thy city and Thy people are called by Thy name."

But the name of the Lord is also a strong tower for the righteous. God's character is ultimately our only and sufficient refuge. What God is must ever be the foundation of our hopes both for our own salvation and for the world. Ultimately we expect to reach heaven not because of anything we have done but because God has undertaken to bring us there and has both dealt with our sin, has called us to Himself and bound Himself by His promises to see us through. His character, His truth, are our guarantee; and similarly as we face the troubled world, where sin appears to be in the ascendancy and wrong on the throne—it cannot be really so for ever.

The Love Which Passeth Knowledge

Beloved, if God so loved us, we ought also to love one another.—1 JOHN 4: 11.

GOD's love was love in deed and truth. It was not some inward emotion which finds delight in itself but was expressed to us in a way which none of us can ever doubt. He loved us so much and so long that He gave His only Son; that is how it was expressed by the Father. He loved us so as to lay down His life for us; such is the Son's expression. And the Spirit loved us in following us up and tracking us down, and by opening our understanding so that we acknowledged God's love and responded to it. Was ever love like this?

Such a love as God's empties itself in giving and expresses itself in forgiving, delighting to impart both gifts and forgiveness to its object. With the passing days we discover how changeless and abiding the love is. Through dark days and bright, in age as well as youth, in times of failure as well as success, in sin as well as holiness, God loves us. On this solid rock we stand, in His strong arms we rest.

But the disposition of the Father is to be the disposition of the sons. As He is, so we are to be; as God does not deal with men according to their sins nor reward them according to their iniquity, so must we. The disposition of God rather than the disposition of our fellowmen is to be the guide of our judgments and actions towards all men, both saints and sinners. Is anyone waiting for our forgiveness? Let us give it freely today. If we have a misunderstanding, or a quarrel, let us take definite and immediate steps towards conciliation today. Ours is to be the initiative and if that means humiliation, we are following in the steps of Him Who came down to earth and stooped further to suffer. And if there is any opportunity. of ministry to others, let us seize it as a thing to be grasped with both hands for this is real Christianity.

All that is God-like is possible because in the case of the Christian he has become indwelt by the life of God. A new nature, the divine nature has been imparted and by the power of the Holy Spirit daily bestowed we may hope to follow His steps.

With Mercy and with Judgment

When He hath tried me, I shall come forth as gold.—JOB 23: 10.

THE Christian is a traveller; he is not here to live as if this life were all. As a stranger and pilgrim he is passing through this world to the heavenly city. But there is an end in view which is not only to be described in terms of a location, that is heaven, but also in terms of character. The pilgrim way is intended to produce a character which is suited to the place and to the service of that eternity in glory.

To produce such a character, as well as to bless others on the way, God has ordered our path. No step or stop is by chance; the urges forward and the frustrations are all part of His plan. The closed as well as the open doors serve us in the way. Many of the strange providences we can never understand down here; how can we poor finite and ignorant beings understand the mystery of the ways of the only wise God. But our very inability to understand affords us an opportunity of trusting God, of telling Him and shewing Him that we are assured that He knows what He is doing and that it must be good.

So as we travel on, holding lightly to worldly things and with eternity in view, we are being refined as to our character and trained for future service. When we are tempted to feel that we are doing nothing, let it comfort our hearts that we are being disciplined and prepared. Our days on earth are our apprenticeship days; we are not only doing but learning. We are being taught how to do things and how not to do them, how to grow and how to trust.

We are God's people. He knows our frailty and is strengthening us through the burdens we carry. He knows our failures and is training us through our mistakes to do better.

There is no question but that when we have reached Immanuel's land we shall be able to sing "with mercy and with judgment, my web of time He wove", but is it not the triumph of faith to sing it now in anticipation and really to believe that all His providences are mercies?

Spiritual Athletes in Training

If any man will come after Me, let him deny himself.—Matthew 16: 24.

No honest reader of the Bible is left in any doubt as to the nature of the Christian life. Its beginning is utterly simple and often easy; the empty hand of faith receives God's gift of His Son and with Him Eternal life. Sometimes this great transaction is costly and the first step is contested by Satan, though sometimes the light shines in without great disturbance of the emotions or great demand on the will. But once the life has begun then it is a life of contest and battle and of striving against sin.

This calls for a discipline which affects the whole life. We must learn to save time or there will be none left for those necessary exercises of prayer and Bible Study. We need to conserve our money, to restrict our interests lest we become shallow and purposeless. But above all we must learn to say "No" to the invitations of the world and the solicitations of the flesh. Temperance (or better still self-control) is most necessary.

Paul, who lived with eyes wide open to the age in which he lived, noticed how the athletes disciplined themselves to win the Greek races. Food was voluntarily rationed, and exercises were imposed in order to be fit and win the race. They did it, he wrote, to win a crown of laurels which faded soon, but the crown we strive to win will never fade, therefore should we be less disciplined? For himself he meant to keep his body under control being as a servant to the spirit, for the race was strenuous and the fight was real.

There are some things, therefore, which the Christian must refuse. It is not always a question of their use being right or wrong but sometimes it is a question of whether or not they are good for Spiritual Athletes in training. We must eschew what others may use, and that means saying "No" firmly with both feet down. We must keep food, drink, sleep and recreation all in their place as serving one purpose, namely, to fit us for the Christian race.

Oh, Blessed Release

Who is a God like unto Thee, that pardoneth iniquity?—MICAH 7: 18.

WHATEVER separate burdens individuals may carry there is an intolerable load which every single person born into the world bears and feels himself dragged down and fettered. All struggle for release from the burden of sin, though in many instances the nature of the load is unrecognised and the form of the struggle for release from it is not understood. In one instance the sinner struggles to be free while at the same time seeks to propitiate the anger of some god or evil spirit, in another the soul turns to asceticism or engages in some meritorious deeds. In reality these are attempts to find release from a power which wields despotic sway over mind and heart and will, or from an accusing conscience; but they are all vain attempts and offer no release.

To such burdened men and women the Gospel is sent by a God of righteousness and love. It satisfies the conscience because the sins which have defiled have been punished, and the accusations of conscience are answered by the blood of the divine Victim Who was worthy and able, and Who suffered in the place of the accused. To such as trust this Victim, the Son of God Himself, the iniquity is pardoned, the sin forgiven. It has been borne away into an unknown place and it cannot be found. The Lamb of God has been our Substitute, has carried our sins and borne our iniquities and they have been removed from the holy eye of God and from our own burdened spirit. We sinned and deserved to die eternally; He was without sin but took our place and died for us. But death could not hold Him so He arose and lives in heaven to give repentance and remission of sins to all who ask Him. Have we ever asked Him to blot out our sins and trusted Him to do it? Then why carry about an accusing conscience or a burdened mind? The burden is gone, the spirit is free from sin. When Bunyan's Christian lost his burden at the Cross he gave three leaps for joy, and went on his way rejoicing. Oh! blessed release.

Amazing Love, How Can It Be?

Many waters cannot quench love.—S. OF S. 8: 7.

THE Son of God has loved us—the statement appears so simple and the fact so well known, that its wonder is easily forgotten. God's Son is equal with the Father as touching His Godhead. He is heir of all things, by Him the worlds were made and by Him the whole creation with its whirling worlds without number are held in their courses. Yet He loved me. The giant spheres are dependent upon His word but He still has a place in His plans for me.

But the greatest expression of His care and love is that He gave Himself for us that He might wash us from our sins in His own blood. The Son of God was made flesh and died for sinners—and for me. That holy and unique life of the God-man was offered as a sacrifice for rebels, and for me. All the tests of His love, the rebuffs of sinners, sins against light, sins against love, could not quench His love. Love is strong as death and as tenacious as the grave.

He loves us still, blessed be His name! The failures and the sins committed since we believed have not quenched His love. The denial by Peter, by thousands since and, alas, by me, find Him loving us still. Our slowness to learn, our diffidence to follow and obey only shew the more how much He loves us. If our salvation rested upon our faithfulness we should have been cast away long ago and we would never feel secure; but we are loved and held by Him still.

> And round my heart still closely twine
> Those ties which naught can sever.

If this be true what more can we do but praise Him for ever, and seek to shew forth His praise not only with our lips but in our lives, by giving up ourselves to His service. Selfishness is to be abhorred, sin is hateful in view of such a love. Holiness, likeness to Him, love of His people, a care for His world of sinners, these things must result from an appreciation of His love—they are our reasonable service.

Unconscious Glory

Moses wist not that the skin of his face shone.—EXODUS 34: 29.

MANY Christians are perplexed with the growing sense of unworthiness and sin which almost always accompanies a growing likeness to Christ, and is almost an essential phase of developing maturity. The explanation of it is that the nearer we are to Christ the more glaring the least blemish of character becomes, but the purpose of such discovery is that we may never be aware of our Christlike character, and so become proud. Any idea of "holier than thou" or "holier than yesterday" would appear contrary to true holiness, though in actual fact we must be better than yesterday and more godly than others who do not earnestly seek His grace. The glory of the Christian life is unconscious and it is all the more glorious on that account.

The glory of the Christian is a reflected glory; it shines from the Source, the Lord of Glory—upon us and lightens our darkness, before it is scattered again to lighten the darkness around. It is unlike earth's glory which tends to pride; it is indeed associated with self-abasement, lowliness of mind, serving others; and, knowing our own hearts better than others, esteems others better than itself. To catch such light it is necessary to seek God in private and to walk with Him in public. We must behold the glory, that is, we must spend time in those cleansing, healing, illuminating rays of the glory of God which shines in the face of Jesus Christ. It takes time to do this and often means the restriction of other activities.

But there are results from such communion. Having caught the light we ourselves are lightened, then we reflect the light, and life becomes a powerful testimony to the grace of God. We become like cities set on a hill, lamps placed in lampstands. The same sovereign grace which lit the light, places it in a strategic position and it gives light around. Let your light so shine, in your small corner or important sphere; for that life is ablaze with glory which is lived in God's presence.

A Sharp Call and a Ready Reply

Call upon Me in the day of trouble.—Psalm 50: 15.

There are times for ordered prayer and painstaking devotion, and there are occasions when desperate need can only be expressed by a call. In the case of the latter the mind seeks no polished expression or orderly arrangement; the need is great, the matter is urgent and a short sharp cry most naturally and poignantly expresses the heart. It is a day of trouble and we call, and calling we are heard and answered. For the cry reaches God, as Jacob's did when he called upon God in the way, and afterwards built an altar to mark the place and the occasion. It was the same with Peter when sinking, who made no long petition but sent up his cry of distress, "Lord save me."

The Lord has bid us call upon Him, and encourages us to cast our burden upon Him. He has revealed Himself as a God at hand and not afar off—the near-at-hand Lord as St. Paul describes Him in Philippians 4: 5. The Spirit is the Comforter, the One Who is alongside to help. Oh, what peace we often forfeit, oh, what needless pain we bear, all because we attempt to carry the load or stifle the cry. If any reader is at present under a crushing load let him send up to heaven a short petition in simplest form—a telegram—where words are economised but need is urgently expressed.

To such cries God listens and sends an answer. In the darkness the Psalmist is comforted and light begins to break as he realises this and says, "For I shall yet praise Him." He knows the answer is coming because men everywhere have found that the Lord is good and ready to forgive and full of mercy when they call.

Because of our experience of God's immediate help we learn to love Him. Every fresh deliverance deepens our trust and increases our love. Answers to prayer and deliverances from distress, bind us to the Lord Who bends low to hear us when we cry and Who stretches out His hand to deliver.

The Lord Jehovah Reigns

Abba, Father, all things are possible unto Thee.—MARK 14: 36.

THE Lord God—what strength the name suggests, and how reassuring it is. His name God, brings to our mind His eternal nature and power. In the beginning God created, at His Word darkness gave place to light, chaos to order, and nature came to birth in all its diversity and grandeur. By His skilful hands our first parents were made, and by His word of power the whole universe exists. The Lord—this name suggests His love and His activity on behalf of man, and reminds us of His care for and guidance of Israel and of the Church. The Lord God assures us of the harmony of God's grace and power, of His intimate love as well as of His infinite power. Such a God we can trust and worship.

We are next reminded of His almightiness, that He can do everything; the things which are impossible with men are possible with God, and the things which are difficult are easy to Him. When He works His will none can offer ultimate resistance or stop the progress of His Kingdom. As we, therefore, face the present difficulty He is challenging us to see if we believe that He is able to do this very thing. The only reasonable answer is, "If Thou wilt, Thou canst."

Now all this which at first seems very much theoretical and theological is intensely practical as indeed all true theology is. It is meant to apply to us, to me, and to me now. Let me pause a moment to reflect on my own personal pressing problem. Does it concern myself alone? Is it concerned with personal relations? Is the heart heavy for another who is lost or straying? Then the Lord is asking, Believe ye that I am able to do this?

Some are turning in one direction and some in another for the solving of their problems, but we are determined to call to mind the name and character of God. He is the Lord God omnipotent, and we commit to Him this present difficulty saying, Lord I believe.

A Guide in the Way

Cause me to know the way wherein I should walk.—PSALM 143: 8.

THERE is unspeakable comfort in the knowledge that the direction of our life is planned and that our steps are directed. Otherwise in a world which is full of perplexity and where our way would be through a trackless desert we should be filled with fear, for we do not know the course, nor the perils. But God is a willing, skilful guide and is ready to conduct us through moor and fen, over crag and torrent till the night has gone.

But the indispensable requisite for a guided life is a meek and quiet spirit. To acknowledge that we do not know the way is the first necessity; then to believe that Someone does know it is the second; and to trust the One Who knows is the third. Happy are the meek who are willing to be guided. All this sounds so simple and logical that it would appear the most reasonable thing in the world to trust the Lord implicitly, but the human heart, yes the redeemed heart, finds it much easier to plan one's own life, to devise one's own way.

Our eyes are to be upon the Lord our Guide. That means that our hopes are to be centred on Him, that we confidently look to Him to lead us. It means also that instead of merely looking at the track we are to look up to the Guide Who will guide us; His eye meeting ours and conveying His approval and encouragement, or otherwise His disapproval and correction. As we look to Him the Spirit of God Who indwells, each true believer will witness with our spirit that we are in the way, or will give us those other inward monitions that we are missing the path that is planned.

We lack both knowledge and wisdom, but these God has promised if we will but ask, and then wait to receive the gift. So often we impatiently plan the way and in our impatience set out upon it only to discover unexpected difficulties, and the Lord's own hindrances to turn us back. The meek, rather than the clever, will He guide in judgment: the meek, rather than the shrewd, will He teach His way.

Despising Danger

Be not afraid of them that kill the body.—LUKE 12: 4.

To the child of God is given the high privilege of witnessing to the Saviour's dying love and risen power. All the world must hear the news and therefore we must not hesitate to go into all the world to preach it. As a Christian I am under orders, and if it should mean witnessing in highest places I must speak before kings and not be ashamed, or if it means testimony in the common way I must not fail there also.

This testimony is to be given in an antagonistic world and an alien atmosphere for the world of men lieth in the evil one. There are many churches and noble institutions, and, thank God, many Christians in our land, but once we begin witnessing to the crown rights of Jesus Christ then we find ourselves up against real resistance.

Many things we can do without estrangement or objection, but the enemy of souls summons his resources to resist the witness of a godly man. And this means persecution, secret or open, sometimes reviling and false representation; it may mean in some places tribulation, distress, famine, peril or the sword. It is a good thing to ask ourselves if Christ means so much to us as to make us willing for these.

There have been saints all down the ages who have stood firm and scorned such threats. They have said, I will not fear what man shall do unto me. They have been able to rejoice and be exceeding glad and proved themselves more than conquerors.

> They met the tyrant's brandished steel,
>   The lion's gory mane,
> They bowed their necks the death to feel:
>   Who follows in their train?

Is Christian courage a thing of the past only? The church in other lands answers, No.

God Loves to Pardon

Turn unto the Lord your God: for He is gracious.—Joel 2: 13.

We human beings whose knowledge of God must always be limited by our restricted abilities are only able to think of one attribute of God at the same time. Here we are reminded of His mercy, His delight in forgiving sinners. The quality is best illustrated by our Lord's unforgettable portrait of the Father in the parable of the Prodigal Son. When he was yet a great way off the Father saw him, and ran, and fell on his neck and kissed him. The words suggest that the father, grieved and lonely, had been looking out every day in the hope of the prodigal's return, and when the time came all thought of what was decorous and fitting was forgotten in giving his wandering son a father's forgiveness and welcome.

God is ready to pardon in the same way, because He is gracious and merciful. He is longsuffering and waits to be gracious. No impatience spoils His holy love, He can wait and continue waiting until a sinner sees the folly of his sinning. That ability to wait without becoming angry is our salvation, and is a divine quality.

Each one of us is an example of the merciful patience of God and exemplifies His willingness to bear with our folly and delay, and when at last we repent, to forgive us freely and without reproach. This makes us wonder how we could ever appear so callous and unresponsive. But we did behave in that manner, and when sometimes now we are tempted to despair of men or to become impatient with them as they continue in their sins, let us remember the longsuffering of God with us, and our own folly.

And should any reading these lines be still in heart away from God with no assurance of His acceptance and forgiveness, the words read shew us the way we are to "rend our hearts", that is, we are to be genuinely concerned about our sins, and hating them, we are to turn from them to the Lord Who bore them and waits now to pardon.

All One in Christ Jesus

The whole family in heaven and earth.—EPHESIANS 3: 15.

WHAT a glorious fact has been brought before us in today's readings! The children of God form one family. All who everywhere call on the name of the Lord whatever their colour or language, whatever their origin or background, whether they be cultured or otherwise we are one in the Lord—and not merely one army of the Living God, as we sometimes sing, but one family. We have one Father, the God and Father of our Lord Jesus Christ and we have one Home to which we travel.

Each became one in the family by the new birth, by faith in Christ. We were not made members by our first birth. Such a natural birth made us members of our earthly family but not of the heavenly. Only when we were born again and received God's life did we become God's children and members of His family. It is being possessors of the same divine life which makes us one family and causes us to love each other.

The family consists not only of the total number of Christians on earth but also of the redeemed in heaven. It is "the whole family in heaven and earth". Some of its members serve in the higher and some in the lower spheres, some in the eternal and some in the temporal, but one day the family will be complete in heaven, when the redeeming processes are complete and God has gathered together in one all things in Christ.

In the meantime we are to love every member of the household and while doing good to all men are to have a special responsibility to our brethren in Christ. There is a family likeness and a family badge. The likeness is our resemblance to Christ, the badge is that of mutual love.

There are lonely souls in the world, but should any Christian be really lonely if we enjoyed our family privileges and accepted our family responsibilities?

Trouble May be Near but God is Nearer

Lo, I am with you alway.—MATTHEW 28: 20.

TROUBLE is never far off from any one of us. Our frail human nature is very liable to attack; on any of the three planes of our being we may soon be in serious difficulty. Some spiritual problem, some mental care, a physical sickness or, as most often, a combination of attacks on two or three levels. And the trouble which was not far away comes nearer. The day of trouble has begun. No matter how privileged and apparently sheltered a life may be, every Christian must see trouble. "Man that is born of woman is of few days and is full of trouble."

When such a day comes it may be short and very severe; and its passing leaves us shaken. Or it may be long drawn out and make for great weariness under a prolonged strain. We cry, How long, O Lord? We think ourselves forgotten; it appears as though God was angry with us and had forsaken us.

But God has made promises to His tried and tested servants. "I will be with him; I will deliver him; He will save them; I will not leave you comfortless." He is with us now in the present trial for He is faithful to His promises.

God is faithful; not He has been,
Nor He will be; both are true,
But, today, in this sore trial
God *is* faithful *now* to you.

He means that we should take hold of His promise and remind Him of His covenant, telling Him that our souls wait only on Him for deliverance.

When such an attitude of faith and expectancy is taken then victory and deliverance have begun. Faith may be strained to the limit but it will be strengthened; the heart may be made sore but it will be more tender. The Christian who has been through real trouble is mature and his life and influence take on a new power.

At Peace with God

Lord, Thou wilt ordain peace for us.—ISAIAH 26: 12.

AT the basis of our faith, and affecting both our character here and our destiny hereafter, is our view of the nature of Jesus Christ. Merely believing in Him being a good man is completely inadequate, accepting Him as the best man is equally insufficient. He is, and must be so received—the Son of God, God Incarnate. A Christ Who is less than "Very God of Very God" would be unequal to the great task of redeeming mankind and would break under the weight of the burden of man's sin. But He is the Son of God, in Whom dwells divine fullness, so that the work of reconciliation was the act of God in Christ.

An appreciation of such Scriptural views of Jesus Christ makes the death of Christ a very different, and more majestic thing than could otherwise be. The Godhead is involved, sin is being grappled with and settled by a person of the Godhead. God Himself is doing something with the estranging principle of sin in order to make possible a righteous and enduring peace between the offended God and offending man, and in removing the barrier to the fullest fellowship.

Now the reconciling work is finished, it is an historic fact which is to be preached and believed. God would have all men know that He has loved them so as to give His Son to be a sacrifice for them. His thoughts of us are of peace and not of evil, of fellowship and not of judgment; and He invites erring and estranged men saying, "Come now let us reason together, though your sins be as scarlet they shall be as white as snow."

And when the heart has believed and entered into the joy and peace of forgiveness, what can it do but bow and worship saying, Who is a God like unto Thee? Life must henceforth be concerned with pleasing such a God, with enjoying the fellowship made possible and in witnessing to one and another of Him Who has redeemed us to God by His blood.

God Listens to the Lowly

Give ear, O Lord, unto my prayer.—PSALM 86: 6.

THE fact that God is high and holy is too often forgotten today. We have so gloried in His nearness as to forget His greatness, with the result that we weak men and women do not bow sufficiently low before His power, nor do we as sinners deserving judgment sufficiently humble ourselves before His holiness. The spirit of contriteness and meekness is with God of great price. God dwells with such as are lowly, and promises to hear their cry and deliver them.

Our drawing near to God must therefore be with becoming humility; we are to submit ourselves, we are to humble ourselves under God's mighty hand. In such a case the Lord will have respect to us and give us grace and exalt us. Indeed as soon as ever we seek Him in a right spirit we shall be heard. The answer may not come immediately but the prayer will be heard immediately. There are no delays in our prayers reaching the throne of God, though there may be delays in the answer reaching us, but God's delays are not to be interpreted as denials. The Lord is good and full of mercy, and His goodness and mercy are as active when He denies as when He supplies, when He delays as well as when He hastens.

All this is meant to encourage us to draw near to God Who is good and ready to forgive, who is full of mercy when we call. This will be a day of trouble for some, indeed for many. Today some will be bereaved or stricken with grief on some other account; some Christian will be in financial straits or pressed in difficult circumstances; some who read these lines will be almost ready to break and yield, but the situation will be relieved and the burden lifted if we call on Him. The first requisite for receiving the Lord's help is a broken spirit and the second is that we call for it.

Great Facts with Great Consequences

Christ both died and rose . . . that He might be Lord.—ROM. 14: 9.

THE basis of the glorious gospel we proclaim as well as of the Christian life we seek to live lies in the historical and accomplished facts of the incarnation, death, resurrection and ascension of the Son of God. Ultimately Christianity is dogmatic and doctrinal, and a faith which is not grounded on solid teaching and is sentimental or emotional will neither save the soul nor establish the character.

The doctrinal facts face us today in these Scriptures. They are cold facts in the sense that they remain true when men reject them, but they are anything but cold when rightly apprehended. They humble the mind, melt the heart, and cause the spirit to bow low and worship. For the death of Christ is not a subject for mere discussion and controversy; it is a display and an act of the mighty love of God which moves man to repentance and faith. Nor does it only work in bringing sinners back to God, but the truth makes its imperious demand on the devotion of the redeemed. Christ died and rose that He might be Lord as well as Saviour, Master as well as Friend.

Moreover if Christ is our Substitute and Representative His death to sin was our death to sin. In Him we have died to our selfish purposes, to our self-rule; now we live only to God. The Cross is not something which we only believe intellectually, or about which we sing with emotions which are moved. The cross of Christ, that is His redeeming work, calls us to a life of redemptive service. We can, of course, never do anything to atone for sin, our own or any other person's, but we can and must live to introduce others to His redeeming love. The acceptance of our own salvation purchased at such a cost, involves us in the obligation of both living and preaching so that others may be won to the Redeeming Lord, for Christ died and rose, not only to become Saviour but also to become Sovereign.

Our Defence is Sure

The Lord is my rock and my fortress.—2 SAM. 22: 2.

TODAY'S Scriptures almost entirely consist of pictures of safety. They illustrate with great variety and kindness how God protects His people; He is to them as a fortress for the soldier, surrounding mountains to a city, and the wings of a mother-bird to her young. And thus would God teach His children how much He cares for and shields His own children.

The truth of all this assumes, in the first place, that we have an enemy or enemies always on the watch, stealthily surrounding us and waiting for an opportune moment to attack and destroy us. This is certainly the teaching of Scripture which warns us that Satan is continually on the alert to destroy the people of God or to bring them down in shameful defeat. He goes about as a roaring lion or he appears as a serpent or an angel of light.

Whatever be his guise he is known to God Who is our defence, and our safety is to abide under the shadow of the Almighty, as the Psalmist puts it, or to abide in Christ as the New Testament expresses it. In fellowship with God, not living apart in self-will or carelessness, we are kept safe from the attacks of our malign foe. God may suffer us to be tempted but not above what we are able to bear; He may allow us to be attacked in order to be made stronger and more skilful, but He will not suffer us to be defeated.

Because of all this we may live this day in quiet confidence. We need not to be always looking out for the enemy but we do need to be always on the look out for the Lord's directions and corrections. Therefore we can sing about our work because the Lord is watching over us in love. We need not fear but rather we can rejoice. The foe is strong but our God is stronger, the enemy is subtle but the Lord is wiser and in His wisdom and skill we find our peace.

It is of the utmost importance, therefore, that we follow in the way which God appoints for only in His will is there safety.

Diligence in Appointed Service

Whatsoever ye do, do it heartily. . . . —COL. 3: 23.

HALF-HEARTEDNESS is unChristian. The Lord Jesus could say, The zeal of Thine house hath eaten Me up; and the same quality of whole-hearted devotion to the Lord and to His service is expected of all who name His Name.

There are many reasons why we should live and serve the Lord with zeal. The first has been given namely, because it was the way the Master lived. Then upon us the last times appear to have fallen; evil is gaining strength and evil-doers stalk unabashed. This means that what may have been understandable, if not permissible, in quieter, better days is unthinkable now; we must gird up our loins. And for our own sakes, we must not look back or hesitate, but press on with zeal; otherwise we may be overtaken with the spirit of the age in which we live and succumb in the atmosphere of ungodliness. The enemy is subtle and may too easily succeed in getting us into By-path Meadow or immobilised on the Enchanted Ground.

This whole-heartedness is to characterise us. If we cannot do a thing well and with zeal, we should question whether it should be done. If we are master, we should be diligent in our attention to all that which concerns the fair name of the Master Whom we serve and the men and women who may, in turn, serve us. A Christian grocer should be the best grocer, and a plumber who names Christ's name must do good plumbing. Whatever may be our vocation, if we are in the will of God, good service is expected and zeal in the appointed task is glorifying to God.

The Christian is in every form of service a servant of the Lord Christ, therefore good work, zealously and cheerfully done, becomes a testimony to men and a pleasure to God. For such service God reserves His own suitable reward.

Rejoicing and Righteousness

To declare . . . at this time His righteousness.—Rom. 3: 26.

God's nature, whatever it may be must obviously be the ground of all our thoughts and hopes. If God be good then ultimately the end of His plan and work must be good; if He is wise then ultimately all creation must praise His wisdom and His goodness. It is the fact that our knowledge of God's character is fundamental in our life which makes biblical theology so important. Many lives are wrecked and many more distorted for lack of a true knowledge of God.

If God is truly known in His Word, if His character be really appreciated then the saint can rejoice all the day. Above the petty disturbances of life, beyond the noise of earth's ten thousand voices, the child of God sees the wisdom and the love of God and His heart rests and rejoices.

In days when righteousness seems so scarce and its pursuit so rare; the righteousness of God is that to which the troubled soul turns again and again. Public life is corrupted, people are oppressed, dictators rule without mercy and there seems no barrier to the flood of iniquity. Then the righteousness of God is the Christian's solid rock and refuge. The Judge of all the earth will do right, even though at present He stays His judgments.

This righteous character of God is the subject of the Gospel. It is available for unrighteous men, first as a garment to fit us for judgment, and then as a quality to fit us for conduct. The righteousness is both imputed and imparted. Oh! blessed Gospel.

We may therefore, we must, rejoice in such a Lord. We have not seen Him but we know Him revealed in Christ and in His Word.

Pardon and Cleansing—Both Are Ours

Jesus said . . . This is my blood of the new testament.—MARK 14: 24.

THE life of the flesh is in the blood, that is to say, the blood is the seat and the vehicle of life both in man and beast. In the sacrifices it was given upon the altar for others represented by the sacrifice. In the case of our Substitute and Sacrifice, the Lord Jesus Christ, His divine-human life was in His blood, and that has been shed for us men and for our salvation. In the Bible, therefore, the blood of Christ means the spotless life given up on the behalf of sinners, or in other words, the death of our Lord Jesus with this particular interpretation that it was substitutionary.

This death of the Saviour was the sealing of a covenant between God and believing man. In the covenant God undertakes to pardon the other party, and to write His will on the heart and put it in the mind, thus guaranteeing both pardon and holiness. Such blessings are given in covenant grace and are to be received and enjoyed by faith. We are to believe the promises and to trust the Promiser to do and give just what He says.

Moreover the water enforces the thought that cleansing is also ours in Christ; we are meant to enjoy a conscience free from guilt and accusation and to live a life which pleases God.

Here then is our heritage, or at least a basic and most important part of it. Pardon and holiness; pardon for the past and holiness in the present, while heaven awaits us in the glorious future. These have been merited and secured above by our Lord Jesus, they are ours if we will receive them. Have I pardon? If not I may receive it as I read; it is in Christ and He offers Himself to me. Am I holy? In Christ I may be so in intention and purpose now, and in practice increasingly so each day.

Sufficient Is Thine Arm Alone

If God be for us, who can be against us?—ROM. 8: 31.

THERE are many and varied enemies which seek the downfall of the servant of God. Their ways are subtle and they have had long experience, while behind them all stands the devil, directing and inspiring them, for he it is who is our arch-enemy, and that because we belong to Christ against whom all his attacks are ultimately directed.

These enemies may sometimes use craft and sometimes display wrath but the Lord has promised to keep His saints and we may therefore dwell confidently in His shadow. He has promised to keep our feet from being taken, and He will surely enable us to sing with the Psalmist, He delivered me from all my fears.

It is sometimes overwhelming to realise the power of the world without, the flesh within and the devil below. This trinity of evil is more than a match for our frail spiritual strength and is far too wise to be evaded by any trick which we may be able to practise. But, no, our safety is in the power of God Who has promised to make the wrath of man to praise Him, and to restrain the remainder, to turn the heart of kings and rulers to serve His own purposes of good, to make even our enemies to be at peace with us.

Therefore our eyes must be only upon God; not too much upon our subtle foes, certainly not too much upon our friends or ourselves, but upon Him Who is faithful and has promised. In His Word we hope and in Him we trust. He is the refuge into which we may run and His strong hand supports us. In view of all this why should we fear; we must not be over-confident or proud, but we need not fight our battles in doubt of the issue.

The Intentions of the Heart

O, how I love Thy law!—PSALM 119: 97.

IT WAS good that it was in thine heart, was God's message to David concerning his desire to build the temple in Jerusalem; and though the king was never allowed to fulfil his desires yet the Lord commended his intentions. The desires of the heart, when they are good, are precious to God our Father. He finds pleasure in them as an earthly father delights in the good intentions of a son, though the execution of those purposes may be very blundering or may never be fulfilled. We Christians are very prone to bemoan the evil of our hearts, so we should take comfort from the fact that God Who trieth our hearts not only uses unsuspected evil but also unsuspected good.

Our portions today are mainly concerned with the attitude of our hearts towards God's word and will. It is one of the marks of the truly converted that the Bible is loved; the book which before the great event which inaugurated our Christian life was dull and uninteresting becomes interesting and alive; it speaks personally to us. We begin to delight in it, and find it the joy and rejoicing of our hearts. We treasure its truth, we underline its promises and it becomes as necessary as our daily food.

But the words before us bring home the further truth, namely that the true Christian rejoices in learning and doing God's will. It is possible to study the Bible with zeal but the purpose of Bible study must be to know God and His will, then to seek to please God by doing what He commands. When the heart is disposed to doing the will of God then the Bible enlightens the eyes, feeds the soul, and is the first of books. We delight in it in our hearts, even though our minds may be limited.

Open Thou mine eyes that I may behold
Wondrous things out of Thy law.

Plenteous Grace

Of His fulness have all we received.—John 1: 16.

By God's mercy we who are Christians are united to Christ by a double union; He first joined Himself to us in incarnation and died for us as a Substitute, then we were enabled to join ourselves to Him by a faith which is the gift of God. Being united with Christ we are now treated as one with Him; the love the Father bestows on Him is bestowed on us, the graces given to the Son of God are given to the sons of God. Behold what manner of love, for ours is not merely the gift of forgiveness but of life in Christ and all that means.

If Christ is heir of all things, we are joint-heirs; if Christ is one with the Father so we are one with Him also, and the God and Father of our Lord Jesus Christ has become our God and Father. This means that the Church of Christ, the godly company of all faithful people, is enriched with all the riches of Christ, is given access to the Father to ask, as His children, the things which are requisite and necessary for the body and the soul as well as for the work which he has committed to our hands. We are rich indeed for our Lord is heir of all things and we are in Him and partakers of all.

This means that life is to be lived on a royal level; we are to behave as saints. The unclean and unworthy are not for us; they are to be shunned as things to be avoided by the sons of God. We are to cleanse ourselves not only from practices which defile the flesh but from all bitterness, anger, jealousy which defile the spirit and may be the more dangerous because they are more fashionable. For all this there is plenteous grace, grace upon grace. As grace is used so fresh grace flows in. Plenteous grace with Thee is found.

Whom and What Shall We Fear?

The Lord is the strength of my life.—PSALM 27: 1.

THERE is much to disturb the traveller to the Celestial City, there are obstacles and foes sufficient to turn the stoutest pilgrims back again. The only way to meet these fightings without and fears within is to have a heart fixed on God, and that requires first of all a knowledge of God as a trustworthy Lord and Master. To this all the pages of the Bible and all the many characters it portrays bear witness. Throughout the long stretch of human history which its sixty-six books cover we see God keeping watch over His own, working out His glorious purposes in spite of men and devils. Moreover His character and ways are such as to give us absolute confidence in Him and then we can say, "This God is our God for ever and for ever"; our heart is fixed.

But not only must a deliberate decision be taken in the calm of one's church or home, it must be reaffirmed when trouble comes, "what time I am afraid", I must say, "I will trust in Thee". In the time of trouble the steady attitude must be maintained. We must refuse to be disturbed by bad news for we must relate it all to the God Who rules and is trustworthy. Our mind must remain stayed upon Jehovah or (as it may be translated) our mind must "stop" at Him, that is, not wander around looking at second causes and seeking explanations which omit the wisdom and love of God.

To those whose hearts are established and fixed, trusting in the Lord, songs will be given in the night and they will come to know the more and praise the better the God of all grace, who uses the worst of experiences to stablish, strengthen and settle us before He calls us to His eternal glory.

Satisfied with His Provision

Godliness with contentment is great gain.—1 TIM. 6: 6.

THE Lord Jesus Christ has completely upset the world's standards and ideas. Among men strength is the most desirable thing, but in the Kingdom of God it is a recognised weakness; for weak we are and when we acknowledge it we are making way for the power of God. Honour and position loom large in the world, but in Christ's teaching we are to be meek and lowly in heart. And so we might go on shewing the complete reversal of earth's standards. Our portions today emphasise the difference between the Christian and the non-Christian views of wealth, between the false and the true riches.

In the first place we are reminded that our life is not to be judged by its accumulation of goods or its reserves of money. There are times when wealth may be of the greatest use, but there are times when it is the greatest weight and danger, as many have recently found in lands where the political systems have been changed. In any case wealth means responsibility and often anxiety, so that if a man has simple tastes and these are met, he is truly rich. Real wealth according to Scripture economics is sufficient to meet life's simple needs with God's blessing. The dangers of too much or too little make the wise man pray to be delivered from both extremes.

The basis of the godly man's contentment is that he has a rich Father in heaven, Who carries riches without a burden and uses them without a danger. This good Father has promised that His children will lack no good thing. With such a Father and such promises let us refuse to be anxious about the future, and let our conversation be without any trace of covetousness. If God our Father sees that more will be better for us, we may trust Him to send us more.

Let There be Hope Today

Why art thou cast down, O my soul?—PSALM 43: 5.

How often we are tempted to despair! Things go wrong, very wrong; and there is apparently no way of rectifying the mistakes. Sin is on the increase and all attempts to arrest it appear vain. Earnest prayer is made and the word of God is preached, but there seems to be neither interest nor response. With the result that the servant of God feels himself forgotten and forsaken and he is tempted to feel hopeless—and sometimes succumbs. But no good can ever come of abandoning hope. In the first place, it casts doubt upon the purposes and promises of God. Then it takes the nerve for any further endeavour away, and we tend to become powerless and perhaps even cynical and sour.

To all who are tempted to think themselves forsaken and who are tending to become hopeless the word of God is addressed to-day. There are here some promises on which to take hold. Has not God said that He will not forget us? Has He not even explained Himself to us in that He has hid his face from us for a moment, and for a purpose? But does He not also say that He will have mercy and revive us again? Then surely we may believe that He will do so and begin to hope in His Word and praise Him again.

There is not only a word from God here but also the example of others. Jonah says that though he is cast out of sight, yet he will look again towards God's temple. The Psalmist pulls himself together and determines to expect God to work, saying, "I shall yet again praise Him". Hopelessness paralyses, hope renews. If we abandon our expectations of the Lord's working, our hands will hang slack and our knees become faint.

Let there be hope today, Lord.

Guest and Guardian

I am with you . . . unto the end of the world.—MATTHEW 28: 20.

THE Lord's promise to be with His disciples unto the end of the age has brought unspeakable comfort to millions who have been tried and tested during the whole history of the church. It is a firm foundation for faith and a good basis for hope. It covers all the days whatever they may hold and wherever they may be spent. The "alway" eliminates exceptions and scatters doubt.

The promises before us, however, not only assure us of Christ's presence but of His presentation of Himself to us. As He journeys with us He has undertaken to manifest Himself to us. He may not, indeed, will not, always explain His ways, but He will reveal Himself which is better. It is better to walk with Him in the dark than walk alone in the light, while most of us are unable to take in His manifestation when the days are easy and the mind is occupied. Think of the terms of the promises here. Both the Father and the Son will make their home with us: They will not be with us as Visitors but as permanent and intimate Guests. Our hearts will become royal palaces, and we, who apart from grace would have been nobodies, become friends of God, heirs of God and joint-heirs with Christ.

And our royal Guest becomes our royal Guardian for He promises to keep us from stumbling. The road is rough; there are pitfalls and traps; but He knows the way He is leading us and all its dangers so that we may travel in confidence in His glad company today, and look towards the glorious end when He has brought us to the presence of His glory with exceeding joy. He will be glad to have us there—and we shall certainly be glad too.

God Ruleth on High, Almighty to Save

He removeth Kings, and setteth up Kings.—DANIEL 2: 21.

GOD'S power is sovereign and absolute, and yet it must not be divorced in our thinking from His other attributes. Here we are reminded of His handling of kings and princes, times and seasons, as He sways the destinies of empires. Yet at the same time He is the God of the odd sparrow and the individual human being. God is an authority which is supreme and just, yet loving and beneficent.

But the great views of God which were held by our forefathers, and which went to make them the strong characters which they were, have tended to diminish during the last few decades. Human triumphs in the realms of science and organisation have made man think more of himself and less of God. Today we have the salutary reminder that behind all the election campaigns God is disposing the rulers of nations, beyond all the wars and revolutions of nations the Lord on high is putting down one ruler and setting up another. He is at work when least we can detect His hand, and an attitude of humble trust and reverent submission toward God is becoming on the part of all men both kings and subjects, presidents and princes.

What comfort we draw, however, from the ensured beneficence of this Sovereign Lord God; He is Himself good and always good. His rule is good and the end is good. Moreover it is not with Him as with so many earthly rulers that the individual is either forgotten or despised, or sacrificed for the mass. Every single human being—and indeed sparrows too!—are under His eye and in His infinite mind, and nothing comes to us except He first knows and permits it. The Lord reigneth, let the earth tremble; The Lord reigneth, let the earth rejoice, said the Psalmist and his words we would echo today.

Compassion and Cleansing

And . . . the leprosy departed from him.—MARK 1: 42.

THE infirmities and sicknesses of the human soul are here illustrated by one of the worst of physical maladies, leprosy. The disease is constitutional not local, it is contagious and spreads from one to another. In this it is like evil in its many forms.

Sin is a deep-seated condition of the human soul by virtue of which the heart is defiled, the mind is degraded and the will is deposed. Every part of our intricate nature is affected, and though we may be subjected to educational and social restraint the moral disease remains. There is no human cure for this human curse, the remedy must be with God.

The way in which He has dealt with it is such as to cause the believer to bow and worship. It is provided by God and satisfying to God; it saves man and gives God all the glory; it is equally free and accessible to rich and poor for no money is involved; to learned and ignorant for one does not need to know much to be cleansed. It is open to those who, by human standards, are morally good and morally bad, indeed all the fitness He requireth is to feel our need of Him.

The disease is dealt with by God Himself becoming man and taking the disease on Himself to death. Himself took our infirmities, and bore our sins, He was made sin for us; so that we may now be free from its power and hear Him say to us, "Be thou clean". Jesus is still moved with compassion for us in our sins and infirmities, He wants to be gracious and only longs for us to come. By one bird the penalty was paid in death for the leper, by another the pollution was carried away into an unknown land. By Christ all has been settled, so trust Him with all and rejoice.

There is No Alternative

He saw that there was no man, and wondered . . .—ISAIAH 59: 16.

MEN of ability and willing to undertake responsibility are scarce; but there are a few. But for one supreme task, namely of saving mankind from sin, there was and is only one Man, the Man Christ Jesus. To make the need and the alone ability of Christ vividly clear, it is suggested in the principal text here that God looked everywhere for such a man, hoping to find one but was unsuccessful. The fact is that God knew that no man could save men, so His own arm, His own Son, brought salvation.

Willingly the Son of God left heaven saying, Lo, I come. And willingly He laid down His life, though none of the ransomed ever knew how dark were the waters which He passed through to visit and save; His loneliness, rejection and abandonment when He was despised and rejected of men and at the same time rejected of God, because He was bearing our sin. But He not only laid down His life but took it again, and now He lives on high to save.

In that office of Saviour and Lord He remains alone, and invites men to look to Him, to turn to Him for deliverance, for there is no alternative. Many schemes have been tried and many more theories await their trial but there is none but Jesus can do helpless sinners good. The economist and the politician grappling with the questions of supplies and administration leave the heart of man sinful still, and, we repeat, none but Jesus can do helpless sinners good.

Then let us remember the obedience towards His Father's will and the disposition toward us which brought Christ down from the heights of glory to the shame of the cross.

The More We Know the More We Love

He is altogether lovely.—S. OF S. 5: 16.

THE Lord Jesus Christ completely satisfies the longings of the heart and the ideals of the mind. He is all that could be desired both as a Master and a Friend. There is nothing in Him which one could wish were not there and there is no quality absent which is desirable. He is, in Himself, balanced and beautiful and in His ways with men both true and understanding. He is completely satisfying—and so much more that the heart not only goes out in love but in humble adoration.

Compared with the best of men He is altogether beyond comparison, the chiefest among ten thousand. All other human beings, even the most saintly, have their failings and limitations; at one time or another their faith fails or patience is exhausted, but Christ is ever and everything perfect. He is fairer than the children of men and there is no clearer evidence of this than in His speech. To friend and foe He spoke in grace and truth and when it was best to be silent He never spoke at all.

One's every thought of Him is glad and only when we are following our own devices or cherishing some sinful way does the thought of Him challenge us and make us sad. The only trouble is that we do not think sufficiently of Him. We need to be more in our Bibles where His portrait is so skilfully drawn and where His Spirit specially works. Let us cultivate the habit of turning to Him today by praying frequently and spontaneously. Any price which may be necessary to know Him better will be gladly paid if only we realise His true worth—and, thank God, we do already know something of Him and love Him.

Waiting in Patience and Hope

Rest in the Lord and wait patiently for Him.—PSALM 37: 7.

THE Christian is often tried by the apparent absences and the seeming delays of the Lord. God withdraws the sense of His presence that we may learn to trust His word of promise without feelings of His nearness. He loves us to trust His simple statements and promises. Or in the matter of answers to our prayers, He keeps us waiting as a healthy exercise that faith may grow stronger by being used. But these experiences are trying to our nature. We are tempted to ask if God has really withdrawn Himself and if the prayer is really unheard.

But God's presence is assured by His promise that He is with us all the days until the end. To faith the question of His nearness and help is settled for ever by His word. Whether He appears to be near or far, the fact remains the same. And prayer will be answered though not necessarily in the way we expect. He has not forgotten to be gracious; He will avenge His own elect; the wicked will not triumph for ever.

Our great need therefore is of a patient and expectant faith; that is that we should really be looking for an answer but quite prepared for a delay if God sees that is best. The timing of His answer may concern others as well as ourselves, and His ways are the best for all. So wait for Him, rest in Him and refuse to be anxious and impatient. He has assured us of an answer and a harvest, if we hold on in hope, and it may be that we often fail of the full and glorious end because we faint and tire too soon. Lift up your hearts, the Lord on high is also near and planning a timely and wonderful answer.

Thine is the Power and the Glory

Not by might . . . but by My Spirit.—Zech. 4: 6.

The double negative "not by . . . nor by" is an emphatic way of stating that there are some methods by which God does not work or accomplish His ends; and these very methods are unfortunately most respected and used by most of us. We find it easier to use and to expect blessing from numbers, organisation, eloquence, prestige etc.; we find it makes less demand on our faith if the church is led by men whose names are well known or if the Convention speaker is a man of repute. But, God's emphatic word to us is "not by might, nor by power".

We have only to read God's word to see how true this has been. Humble men with no standing, ordinary folk with little equipment, unknown individuals with no social advantages have been, for the most part, the instruments God has used. They have been "not many wise, not many noble" but God has deliberately preferred to work with those who might have been regarded as weak and unlearned, and He has chosen such; and such a fact may well inspire hope in the hearts of all of us who are ordinary or even less.

The reason for God's method is given very clearly, "not by . . . nor by" "but by my Spirit", saith the Lord. That the excellency of the power may be of God and not of us. To save us from foolish and sinful pride, to give the glory to Himself to Whom it is due and Who can bear it, God works in the way which has been described. By the gentle working of His Spirit, by the quiet but disturbing influence of His Word, using the feeble testimony of His servants and the stumbling words of His weak children, God saves men, calls out His church, changes the face of the world. The work is God's, the glory must be His also.

Servants, Suppliants, Worshippers

Blessed is the man that heareth me, watching daily at my gates.—Prov. 8: 34.

There is an attitude of mind and heart which is precious to God and of inestimable value to us. It is described here in terms of Eastern servants, and may profitably be considered by us. The servant is seen waiting at his lord's door, listening for any command or expressed wish and ready to meet the same with alacrity. Or it is described as the attitude in which both men and women servants looked towards their owners and employers as being dependent upon them and willingly subject to them. In that same attitude we wait upon God expecting Him to shew us mercy.

Modern ideas of freedom and equality have done much good but with the good some harm also. The old courtesies have tended to disappear, and the sense of dependence upon and humility before God has not been preserved. Whatever views we may have of men, we need to remember that before God we are sinners needing mercy, and servants who must do exactly as they are bidden.

The cultivation of this spirit of humble worship and service is to be a continual concern. We need to offer our burnt-offering every day and to pray without ceasing. To those who are of such a spirit God makes promise of His continual presence. He engages to meet us. As we look to Him for guidance He is under promise to give it, as we depend upon Him for light and wisdom He will most certainly dispense these mercies. There is a spirit of humility and worship, an attitude of dependence and trust which is to God of very great price.

What Would Jesus Do?

Ever follow that which is good.—1 THESS. 5: 15.

THE believer has both an example to follow and an objective to attain. The objective is pleasing God in doing good and living holily; the example is our Lord Jesus Christ Himself. It is clear therefore that by following His example we shall inevitably follow the course He took and arrive at the same end as He achieved, Who said, "Lo, I come to do Thy Will."

For the last fifty years or more there has been an emphasis on the salvation which Christ offers at the expense of the example He affords. This has appeared necessary because many have tried to save themselves by following the example. But in many cases the result was that there has been lost the sense of need to follow Christ. Some have scorned such valuable books as "Christ our Example" by Caroline Fry or "What would Jesus do?" by C. M. Seldon. This is a serious mistake which today's page of "Daily Light" may help to correct.

We are to follow the Lord Jesus. His devotion to God, His words of truth, His transparency and sincerity, His fear of God rather than of men and His going about doing good. Let us consider Him. Let us study His words and deeds and His manner of life and seek to emulate Him. If His life pleased His Father and He has now imparted His life to us, should not our lives do the same and reveal the same characteristics?

There is need for us today to refuse the evil and to choose the good, to think on the lovely things and refuse the selfish and unkind. When we are undecided as to the course to pursue or the attitude to adopt let us think which would most be like following His steps, Who did no sin, Who was guileless and trustful.

Teach Me Thy Way, O Lord

The ways of the Lord are right.—HOSEA 14: 9.

GOD's ways are right, that is, they are the very best ways and are established in equity. They are not unjust to any, and in them, all things work together for good to those whose lives are lived in His will. They who are wise observe this and make it their chief concern to learn the will of God and do it. In doing so they find their peace and discover that they are included in a softly-moving scheme of things with God at the centre and in control.

To all who sincerely seek to know and walk in God's ways the promise is made that the way will be shewn. If life be one of single purpose then it becomes simple and devoid of conflicting aims and claims. But to all who are determined to go their own ways, even when persuading themselves that their ways are God's will, the discovery of the right ways, the smoothly working will of God is impossible, for the eye of the soul is darkened by self and the light cannot shine.

The ways of the Lord are therefore the test of our motives. Are we seeking to please God or ourselves? And His ways also are for our blessing or judgment depending upon whether we are in right relation with God or not. To the obedient child of God the path lies straight ahead and there is the Lord's companionship in it, but to the person of self-will there is nothing but sorrow and confusion ahead.

Not my will but Thine be done.

Temporary Trials, Enduring Glory

Now for a season . . . ye are in heaviness through manifold temptations.—1 PETER 1: 6.

"NOW for a season, if need be"—that puts our present trials, whether they are fiery or just smouldering, in their right perspective. They are only passing and temporary, and they are only if necessary. They are permitted for a purpose and in order to yield peaceable fruit in righteousness if we receive them aright and profit by them. They are only for a little while. Weeping may endure for a night but joy cometh in the morning, and the night is short even though it seems rather long.

We are warned to expect such trials. They are described as manifold temptations, that is, they are of many and varied kinds. They come from very different sources and we are attacked in many different points. Pain of body and of mind, or anguish of spirit are our portion; the failure of friend or the treachery of foe bring their sorrow of heart; or we may be affected financially or socially. But the temptations which are manifold and the trials which are fiery are—"if need be". They are allowed because they will be God's instruments of bringing blessings which success and comfort could never bring.

Moreover, in heaven we have a High Priest Who feels with us and for us. Our life is linked with His and He has undertaken to bring us through. He will limit the strength of the temptation. He will temper the keenness of the flame. He is able to succour them that are tempted—and our light afflictions which are but for a moment, are even now working for us an eternal weight of glory.

Anointed with Fresh Oil

He which . . . hath anointed us is God.—2 COR. 1: 21.

OF the many types and illustrations of the Holy Spirit, the wind, the dew, the fire, the dove, etc., that of oil is certainly one of the most suggestive. It indicates in the first place the ability of the Holy Spirit to make things work smoothly. Here is the answer to difficult personal relations, the way in which different personalities fit in and work together. The Holy Spirit, as it were, oils the wheels of life and relieves the friction. Our need is more of God's Spirit in the individual life.

Also in Bible times oil was the indispensable and almost the only source of light. It was held in a simple vessel and a piece of pith or grass sufficed as wick, but it was the oil which made possible the light. And for our testimony as well as in our personal relations we need to be filled with the Spirit.

But the oil which is often envisaged in Scripture is the anointing oil which was compounded of sweet spices as well as oil. It was used for anointing priests for their intercessory ministry and was not in any way to be copied. It was holy unto the Lord. Such an anointing oil represents the Holy Spirit Who in Himself as God, possesses all the attributes and qualities of the Godhead and Who, dwelling in us, produces the gracious fruits of the Spirit.

Every Christian has received Him in his new birth, but we all need to be filled and controlled by Him, receiving of His fullness and living in His power. Let us today place our whole beings once again at His disposal and trust Him to bless us.

That Will Be Glory for Me

When He shall appear we shall be like Him.—1 JOHN 3: 2.

EYE hath not seen, ear hath not heard neither hath it entered into the heart of man to conceive what things God hath laid up for them that love Him, but by some illustrations and metaphors He hath at least begun to reveal these unto us by His Spirit. Our limitations of knowledge, the confines of our experience and all the handicaps of time and the flesh, greatly restrict the possibilities of our understanding and appreciating the glories of heaven. They are so far beyond anything of time because they are eternal, they surpass everything known in the flesh for they are in the Spirit, that thought and language are baffled to describe the place which God has prepared for them that love Him.

All this so utterly wonderful life awaits the believer when Christ appears. It is part of the inheritance of those who share His risen life, to share also His risen glory. They were baptised into His death, they were one with Him in His burial, they have shared in some small degree His shame (alas, how little), they will share His glory.

They suffer with their Lord below,
They reign with Him above.

But the most wonderful thing of all is that we are to be like Him. All the awkward traits of personal character which give us and others so much sorrow and concern will be for ever gone. The sin, the unsanctified temper, the uncontrolled tongue will be for ever gone. We shall think like Jesus, speak like Him, act like Him. It is this complete conformity to Christ rather than the pearly gates which will be glory for us.

How Good is the God We Adore

O taste and see that the Lord is good.—PSALM 34: 8.

THERE is nothing which the enemy of souls seeks to challenge, and to cause us to distrust, more than our confidence in the goodness of God. It is more important to him that we should doubt His mercy than that we should doubt His miracles; but both are true and we respond to the Psalmist's request to praise the Lord both for His goodness and for His wonderful works to us.

If there is a lurking doubt concerning God's care it is best that the matter be decided personally and early. In the old and beautiful language of the Bible we may "taste and see", that is, we may ourselves put God to the test and personally prove His care. Are we praying definitely, then let us definitely expect an answer. Nothing encourages both confidence and praise so much as specific answers to prayer. For this our prayers must be definite if the answers are also to be definite.

It is God's will that we should be aware of and appreciative of His goodness. To this end we should look around for evidences of His love. We shall find them in our lives, our families, our church and nation, if only we are prayerful and observant. The very search for them will cause us to look out for the blessings, where sometimes we seem to look most naturally for the difficulties and dangers.

And it is God's will that we should praise Him for His goodness. Praise is comely for the upright; it changes the whole tone of life; it brings victory to us as it did for Jehosaphat and Judah in II Chronicles 20. Therefore let us praise God for His goodness today. Let us greet Him now with praise and lift our hearts often to give Him thanks during this very day.

Hope Filling and Guarding the Mind

Putting on . . . for an helmet, the hope of salvation.—1 THESS. 5: 8.

A HELMET is a cover for the head, not for days of peace but for days of battle; it is not mere head-dress but a piece of armour. This may serve to remind us again of the stern conflict in which the Christian is engaged. He is fighting the world, the flesh and the devil; and the fight is in deadly earnest. If it is necessary that all the body be protected, it is of greatest importance to see that the head is covered, for it is the head which governs the body and its actions. From this we may learn two lessons.

First of all, our thoughts need to be protected. There the conflict is really fought, and today the battle is for the mind. The claims of world religions and ideologies are being propagated with such skill and insistence that the mind of the Christian is in serious danger, and there is evidence of the fact that too often the helmet has been missing. Once the thoughts are disturbed or poisoned by false teaching the whole life is endangered. We must put on the helmet, we need to gird up the loins of our mind; this is something we must do. The helmet is provided but the warrior must put it on, and such an act will affect our choice of reading and make more necessary our study of Holy Scripture.

The second lesson is that for the protection of the mind there is the Christian grace of hope, that is, that we cherish the expectation of God's better day. The Bible promises such, and the Lord Himself will appear to establish such. It is for that reason the New Testament speaks of the Second Coming of our Lord as "the hope". Blessed hope! Christ will come and bring in the reign of God and righteousness. We may be perplexed about the details, but let there be no doubt about the fact, and today let us protect our mind against doubt and despair by wearing the helmet of salvation, a completed salvation, and holding the bright hope of the coming of our Saviour Jesus Christ.

Knowing Our Frame, Meeting Our Need

One God and one Mediator . . . the man Christ Jesus.—1 TIM. 2: 5.

THE Bible is clear in its teaching that there is only one way of salvation. It is not a case of choosing the Bible way from among other choices; for there is no other way given under heaven among men whereby we must be saved. With an imperious exclusiveness we are told that we must be saved in God's own way or in no other. If the message seems harsh it is also full of comfort, for we are not left with the awful torture of confusion; the wayfaring man, though unlearned, need not err therein. There is one God, one Mediator, one Saviour and no more.

This saving God is a mighty God. He does not shut us up to Himself and then leave us in doubt as to whether or not He can actually save us. The God Who saves is the God Who creates and governs and judges. He Who sets the standards and pronounces the judgment also delivers from the condemnation and makes possible the meeting of the standard. Through the centuries He has been proving His power in countless lives of young and old, moral and immoral, and of every class and temperament.

But this mighty God has come near to us men, not only in leaving heaven to live on earth but, in the Person of His Son, has taken our nature and joined it with His own, so that we have a Saviour Who is both God and Man in two distinct natures but one Person for ever. He knows God for He is God; He knoweth our frame and remembereth that we are dust, for He was made man, and now He lives to save to the uttermost.

Hallelujah! What a Saviour!

The Two Feet on Which We Move Forward

Fruitful in every good work, and increasing in the knowledge of God.—COL. 1: 10.

GOD is good in His nature and in His ways; He is good to all and His tender mercies are over all His works. And the child of God is also good, following the Master, of whose life the writer of the Acts says "He went about doing good." Our aim should be to be good to all, especially to them who are of the household of faith.

But the first step into a life which is full of good works is to present ourselves and our members to God. As goodness is a Fruit of the Spirit, He must needs possess us and our faculties if He is to impart to our minds the disposition to do good, and then to use our gifts to express the inward disposition in actual and practical good works. It is well, therefore, that we should pause and ask ourselves whether we have fully and unreservedly given ourselves to God. If not let us do so now, that we may be filled with the fruits of righteousness.

Our life, however, is not to consist only of good works, but also of a true knowledge of God; otherwise we must needs become only a philanthropist. There must be an inward and intimate acquaintance with God through Jesus Christ which will be both the basis of the goodness and its guard from becoming vague and purposeless. Our knowledge of God comes to us in various ways and by various means all of which we should assiduously cultivate. There is the reverent reading of Scripture, for instance, which is of fundamental importance if we would know God. And there is the illumination of God's Spirit which we should earnestly request in prayer. Then there is the ministry of others who are learning God's ways which we must seek. Good works and increasing knowledge are the two feet on which our spiritual progress moves.

A Guide and Not a Map

He led them on safely.—PSALM 78: 53.

THE Christian life is represented by many metaphors, but the picture which comes before us today is that of a traveller through a wilderness; this is suggested by reminding us of God's people journeying from Egypt to Canaan and it is certainly a true description now. We are pilgrims journeying to the Celestial City but the way there is humanly speaking, unchartered. Every traveller travels a different way though every true Christian will reach the same end. This means that instead of travelling by a map we must trust a guide, and such the Lord has promised to be; and who, knowing the Guide, would not prefer Him to a map.

The Lord has undertaken to lead us through, and to do so by the right way, that is, the way which is best for us and for others. This is no rule of thumb but a divinely and distinctly planned route for each of us; the way has been chosen with our own personal temperaments and needs in view. The great comfort is that He is with us to check and encourage, to correct and to guard.

But the way the Lord is leading us is not only to a sure end and by the right way but has a worthy purpose, namely, to make Himself a glorious name. He will so guide us as to add to His reputation as a Guide and Friend. In some way His honour is involved in the success He makes of our journey through life: let us respond to His leading and correction lest we spoil the reputation of such a Lord and Guide.

The Grace of Repentance

Godly sorrow worketh repentance, not to be repented of.—2 Cor. 7: 10.

There is a sorrow which worketh death. Its effects spiritually, mentally and physically are destructive. It produces a haggard countenance, grey hairs and bent back, and brings no good with it. It is called the sorrow of the world—and how much there is of it everywhere. But there is also a godly sorrow which weeps over personal sin and failure, which sees sin in its real light and character. Such sorrow weeps over the dishonour brought to God's name and the affront which sin has made to God's love. It takes sides with God in judging sin in the life, in short it worketh repentance which is a grace to welcome and not to shun.

Such true repentance is the work of the Spirit of God. It is not a mere human state of mind, for only God can enable a man to take sides against his own sin and judge himself as worthy of eternal judgment. But God worketh this grace in us, causing us to grieve over our sins, as Peter did over his, and to confess them frankly and fully and without offering excuse. Such come to God in penitence, with a broken and contrite spirit; they hang their heads in shame rather than holding them high in pride. They cry for mercy and ask that it may be shewn early.

To all such God delighteth to shew mercy and dispense pardon. Instead of despising them He welcomes them; He pardoneth all them that truly repent and unfeignedly believe His holy Gospel, and with such an attitude of mind and heart God is well pleased. If therefore our conscience is tender and our heart is sorry for sin, let us thank God that we are not forsaken and rejected, but assured of both a welcome and a pardon as we come and confess our sins.

Loved and Made Worthy

Christ loved the Church . . . that He might sanctify and cleanse it.—EPH. 5: 25, 26.

CHRIST loved the Church. While it is true that God loved the world yet within the scope of that general love there is a more intimate love between the Son of God and His Church. For the Church the Lord Jesus gave His life; now to the Church, Christ gives His attention as He corrects and perfects it. This sanctifying of the people of God takes its place with the salvation of sinners as the chief interest of the Lord during this dispensation of grace, for the Lord is not only bringing sinners to Himself but also doing something in them when He has brought them, that is, He is engaged in cleansing and developing them.

Our personal and corporate holiness is therefore not a matter of preference but of fundamental importance. We are to walk before God, we are called to walk in love. The Word of God is to be to us what the cleansing laver was to the priests in the Tabernacle, an instrument for keeping us free from defilement. The daily use of Scripture and the careful adjustment of our life to its precepts are of greatest importance and a sheer necessity for the nurture and cleansing of the soul.

James likens the Bible to a mirror in which we see ourselves. The purpose of this self-revelation is that we may know what manner of persons we are, and that we may seek for full supplies of grace in order that our lives may be renewed in power, and lived in holiness and true righteousness. Christ has loved us and loosed us from our sins in His own blood, now He is engaged in washing us from their defilement by means of His own Word. Let us read, mark, learn and inwardly digest.

His Presence Helps Me Sing

Thou shalt compass me about with songs of deliverance.—PSALM 32: 7.

THE Christian's journey from this world to that which is to come is taken a step at a time. Sometimes the steps are swift, sometimes slow, and sometimes there are necessary pauses with no steps at all. It is reassuring, therefore, to be reminded that the Lord Who planned the route in general has also arranged the steps in particular, and the stops in addition. True faith rests in this fact of the loving-kindness and supervision of God and refuses to be anxious.

But in the way we meet with difficulties. Some are personal and due to our own wilfulness, sinfulness or weakness. For all our failures there is abundant grace and we do well to refuse to excuse ourselves, but rather to make our plea for help. There are foes without as well, some roaring like a lion in the way, others subtle like a serpent in the path. Let there be no mistake in this, that the Lord, our Saviour God, can give us the victory again and again. Should we fall through our ignorance or even carelessness the Lord will lift us up again. We need not be afraid of either the way or the foes. And the difficult and intricate situations in which we may be found are not too much for His skilful hands. He Who is in us is more than all that are against us.

For these reasons we may sing as we travel on, we may sing aloud that others may hear. And this is to be the subject of our song, that the Lord is nigh to us and strong on our behalf; we are to sing songs of deliverance.

His Faithfulness is My Solid Ground

He is faithful that promised.—HEBREWS 10: 23.

CHANGE and decay marks all that is around us; independability is too often the characteristic of all that is human about us, but God is faithful, He changes not. Were it possible for Him to change, then our last hope of some dependable person or thing on which we could rely would be gone, then hope would have no anchor and faith no objective. But God is faithful.

This faithful God has bound Himself to His people in a covenant relationship. In the New Covenant which cannot fail He has promised to be our God, to dwell in us, to forgive our sins and to write His law and will in our hearts. On the ground of what He has engaged Himself to do and the fact that He is faithful, our hearts are at rest, and we have true fellowship with the Father and with His Son Jesus Christ.

This faithful God has bound Himself to us by His promises. In them He undertakes to keep us, to feed us, to make us holy, to give us the victory, and He is dependable Who has promised. Each promise is guaranteed by God's faithfulness and backed by His omnipotence. Therefore whatever our need, His faithfulness and our faith meet, in a word of promise to which He holds and on which we depend.

God is faithful, not He has been,
Nor He will be, both are true;
But today, in this sore trial,
God is faithful now to you.

The Cleansing Power of the Word

Sanctify them through Thy truth: Thy word is truth.—JOHN 17: 17.

As the laver, filled with water, in the Old Testament Tabernacle was that in which the priests were daily cleansed as they went into the sanctuary, so the Holy Scriptures provide the means of our daily cleansing from the defilement of the flesh and spirit and from anything of this world which may defile our hearts through our daily contact. The daily reverent use of the Bible is indispensable if the believer is to walk in holiness and righteousness before God. It is God's appointed means of correcting the judgment, stimulating the conscience, checking the conduct and purifying the motive. It must therefore needs be applied to us by the Spirit Who wrote it, and most of us know the meaning of what our forefathers called "the applied word of God."

The Word of God therefore is meant to keep us set apart from the present evil world, not living in isolation and at a cold distance, but, while necessarily mixing with people every day yet, having our hearts weaned away from its pleasures and practices, and with our standards of conduct still intact. It is necessary therefore that the Scriptures should be in our heart and memory if they are to sanctify us daily.

This means that we must use the Scriptures daily, reading them carefully, reverently and obediently. We are not only to be skilful in such matters as date and authorship, nor to be acquainted only with the outline of the books, but we must set ourselves to know the meaning of the text and to allow its meaning to have full effect on heart and conscience. Then we must assiduously set ourselves to obey what is revealed and so continue in His Word. In doing so we live in perfect freedom.

A Deep Where All Our Thoughts Are Drowned

How unsearchable are His judgments.—ROM. 11: 33.

GOD'S thoughts and plans are a deep where all our thoughts are drowned. We are human and finite; God is divine and infinite. Our knowledge is limited while He is all-knowing. Our foresight is small and unreliable whereas to Him the past and future are all spread before Him in an eternal NOW. The limits of human knowledge of divine things are very real and it ill becomes us to be unduly dogmatic and uncharitable on many things, even though we must hold tenaciously the things which are revealed to us and to our children for our salvation.

The depth of God's thoughts should produce in us a spirit of true worship.

> Where reason fails with all her powers,
> There faith prevails and love adores.

Our worship often begins where our reason stops and our wonder grows. Mercifully however, the deep things of God are not meant to mystify us but to provide a sure ground of confidence and a wide circle of enquiry and delight. At the centre of all stand the simple facts that God is, that God is good, that God loves us and in Christ has redeemed us. From such a centre we may move out in ever-increasing circles of enquiry. The Apostle prayed that the Christians of the first century might be filled with the knowledge of God's will, and we should surely pray and ponder with the same desire for knowing Him Whom to know is life. Let us therefore gird up the loins of our mind, and let us gladly accept the fact that always God's thoughts are higher and deeper than ours.

For His Mercies Still Endure

He stayeth His rough wind, in the day of the east wind.—ISAIAH 27: 8.

THE east wind of cold adversity is allowed to blow on all God's children at some time. It is necessary for us in order to quicken our sympathies with others, and it is good for us in strengthening and refining. It may come to us in the ways of physical suffering, mental anguish, loss of home and property or perhaps most bitingly when friends misjudge us and accuse us. The east wind is permitted.

But its severity is limited and allayed, for in such a day the rough wind is restrained. Did we have both the keen edge of the one and the terrific blast of the other then our faith might well fail. But no, God will not suffer us to be tested beyond our strength. His correction is measured, and Himself takes us under His own protection when the storm and blast beat upon us. When Satan makes direct attack upon us, and lays his subtle schemes to bring us down, then our risen and sympathetic Lord enfolds us in His intercessions so that we may be safe and secure from all alarm.

All this reminds us afresh of the loving kindness of the Lord. Like as a father pitieth his children so the Lord. He knows our frame and how much we can bear, He remembers that we are dust and pities our infirmities. It is His nature to guard and keep us and when, in His inscrutable wisdom, He ordains the biting east wind of criticism to cut us, then, just then, He holds back other temptations that we are not brought down in failure, or swallowed up in grief.

An Unfailing Law and a Reliable Test

By their fruits ye shall know them.—MATT. 7: 20.

A TREE produces only fruit after its own species, and human life follows the same universal law. As surely as a vine produces grapes and a fig tree bears figs so does a godly man display a godly character and an ungodly man fails to do so. The fruit indicates the tree.

For a time a man may pretend to be other than he really is. Judas may pose as a true disciple saying the same things as the other eleven, but a day comes when the real Judas is revealed. He has been stealing out of the bag for the poor, secretly for long, but the self-appointed treasurer in due course reveals his selfish ambitions and he sells His Lord for thirty pieces of silver.

This is a tremendous challenge to genuineness of profession and to real godliness of life. It is not what I now appear to men in the office or the church, but what I really am before God, for ultimately that which I really am will be revealed. Some slow process is at work which will bring the evil to light: God has made the world so; or if it should be that in this life the matter remains hidden then the day will declare it. This calls us today to an honest facing of our true character as we know ourselves to be. Is there hidden sin? Is some unrighteous conduct being covered up in the life? Are we pretending so be other than we are? Let us deal drastically with the matter, let us confess our sin, without in any way cloaking it, let us seek pardon from God through Jesus' blood, and God will grant us a clean heart and a right spirit and the joy of honest profession.

A Divine Companion and a Sure Guide

When I sit in darkness, the Lord shall be a light unto me.—MICAH 7: 8.

NOT all life is to be described as darkness, waters, rivers or fire. Life is wonderfully varied by the mercy of God. There are days of light as well as darkness, indeed many more are light than dark. But for all men, and for all saints, certainly there are experiences which are aptly described as darkness, flood or fire. At such times we are acutely aware of our inability to discern the way, we are fearful lest we are carried away with the temptation, or our hearts feel the scorching heat of sorrow and trial. It is at such times that we need special help and for such experiences God has given us special promises, when . . . when . . . I will . . . I will.

And what does the God of promise engage Himself to be and do when we are in such sore straits? He first promises to be with us in them; His presence is assured. It may be that we feel most lonely and forsaken, but whatever our feelings may be, He is with us according to His word. Let us repeat the promises and reassure our own hearts. Then secondly, He has undertaken to guide us lest in the darkness of the hour we miss the way and run into disaster. Though the darkness is so acute that it is as though we were blind, yet, He will bring us by a way which we do not know. Thirdly, He has promised to temper the flame, and stay the flood so that we shall come safely through and profit as a result.

None of us want such dark and shaking experiences, but it is in heavenly love they are permitted. Let us then trust Him Who cares for us too much to allow us to be swept away. Indeed let us rejoice in our God Who makes such occasions to minister to our good.

His Tender Mercy

Him that cometh to Me, I will in no wise cast out.—JOHN 6: 37.

GOD placing Himself at our disposal! The Infinite waiting for us poor creatures! The Eternal listening attentively while we pray! Such thoughts are humbling indeed. And we can only say, Who is a god like unto Thee? It should, of course, be just the opposite in us placing ourselves at His disposal, waiting His time and listening for His Word. Indeed so it is when grace has truly worked in us, but at the beginning, yes, and often on the way, the situation is that God is taking the humble place and we standing on our dignity or unaware of our poverty.

Here then is a fresh reminder of the Lord's disposition to His children. He waits to welcome, He listens to answer, He refuses to cast them away when they rebel, because He loves them still and engages in a covenant with them. Love so amazing, so divine!

But the verses are mainly ones of entreaty, Come, let us reason; let the wicked forsake his way. Is there any way of wickedness in us, then let us abandon it today. Have we a controversy with God or is there a distance between us and Him, then let us draw near to talk it over with Him. The Lord understands, we have not a High Priest Who cannot be touched with our infirmities, He will generously interpret any stumbling approach we make. As parents add lavishly to the intention and attempt of a child to please them, so the Lord will give fullest weight and more, to our words of explanation and of contrition. Come let us to the Lord our God with contrite hearts return. He will support and help the faintest flicker of repentance and love.

The Spirit Who Teaches to Pray

Praying in the Holy Ghost.—JUDE 20.

GOD is a Spirit, and it is through the working of His Spirit we have acceptance with Him and access to Him. It is the Holy Spirit who draws us to Christ for pardon, it is the same Spirit who draws us to the Father in prayer. As we yield to His promptings and gentle drawings He will lead us more and we shall be enabled to live in the Spirit of prayer. It is as we live in this attitude of subjection to the corrections and enablings of the Spirit that we are able to pray in the Spirit and thus to pray according to the will of God.

Such prayer will be costly for it will mean the setting aside of personal interests and feelings, it will mean saying,—Not my will, in things both great and small, but in so doing we shall find the Holy Spirit praying through us by taking our minds and causing them to think His thoughts, and by taking our hearts and enabling them to express His desires. Because of this, a confidence will be given us which can only come to those who have been enabled to renounce their own wisdom and plans, and be taken up with the purposes of God. This is a confidence which usually only comes in a life which is disciplined by the Spirit of grace and love, and it necessitates that we watch and pray.

But we shall only learn to pray in the Spirit by praying. This is an art which is taught to the obedient; it is not learnt by reading text-books on prayer, valuable as they may be, but by praying. Guarding our spirit lest it be hindered in its greatest ministry by overmuch talk, or work, or indulgence, let us give ourselves unto prayer, watching with diligence for any signs of flagging or failing.

The House of God is Fear-Proof

Your life is hid with Christ in God.—COL. 3: 3.

IF OUR dwelling place, that is, the place where we are really at home, is in the Lord's presence, then we shall live in inward peace, and be delivered from fear of what the future holds. For if we continue to abide in the secret place then the future can bring with it nothing which can disturb us. We shall still be under the protective shade of the wings of God, with our hearts garrisoned in Christ Jesus. This is a simple but transforming truth which we need to accept in all its simple grandeur and then practise as a daily exercise. Shall we not today reaffirm the fact that our real life is hid away from our foes and is safe, because we are united to Christ and Christ is God.

There are times when faith must be active, when it must take the sword and stand its ground, when it must venture out from the shelter which our fellowship and comfort affords, and go out alone to fight. But in some situations too much action would rob us of the victory. These are occasions when we must stand still and see what God will do, and when all we can do is to take refuge in the character and promises of God. In such cases He is our strong tower and has promised to defend us for we are exceedingly precious to Him.

This is meant to give us confidence; we are to be glad since God is God and we are in Christ, God's Son. He will keep us safe from danger and He can keep us safe from anxiety and alarm.

Since God is God and right is right,
And right the day must win;
To faint would be disloyalty
To falter would be sin.

It is Obedience Which Brings Blessing

Blessed are they which hear the word of God and keep it.—LUKE 11: 28.

THE fundamental difference between the truth of God and any other knowledge is that it makes demands on obedience. A man may be most learned in astronomy but his knowledge of the heavens does not necessarily challenge his sinful behaviour. When once a person comes to know any truth about God, immediately moral decision confronts him. Let us take a seemingly abstract feature of God's self-revealing, say, His holiness. No one can truly apprehend the holy character of God without loathing his own sin and quitting it. No one can begin to understand the truth of God's majesty and remain unaffected, he must bend low and humble himself before his Maker.

It is on this principle of obedience to truth that the spiritual life deepens and the life becomes increasingly blessed. Those nearest to the Lord Jesus are those who, knowing His will, do it. We are His friends if we do what He asks or commands, we are His happy disciples only as we trust and obey. On a number of occasions He warned His hearers that only as they obeyed would they enter the Kingdom, and the faith which is not obedient is not a living faith nor a saving faith.

Here then is a basic principle of our spiritual life and growth. The knowledge of God and the blessings of fellowship with Him are not dependent on great intellectual gifts (though when these are sanctified they are great gifts) but on a willingness to obey, just to do God's will and do His Word. This opens the blessed life up to all, whatever our education or qualification, for a simple soul who obeys God's Word will know God more intimately than a well-educated man who refuses to obey.

Liberated and Enslaved Again

Being made free from sin, ye became the servants of righteousness.—ROM. 6: 18.

THERE are two masters to whom or to which men may be enslaved; they are sin or righteousness, Satan or the Lord. Slavery to sin is bondage indeed but enslavement to God is largest liberty.

Our birth into the human family brings with it our entry into a race which is under bondage to sin. Our first parents sinned and our race has been dominated by a sinful nature and sinful tendencies ever since. These evil tendencies have borne fruit in our life in evil deeds and we are conscious of a bias to evil, and of a fight if we would do good. Generally speaking the tyranny becomes stronger and we become less able to set ourselves free.

But the coming of our Lord Jesus Christ into the world, His union with our human nature and His suffering for our sins, has made possible a glorious break with our sinful heritage and the beginning of a new race of men who are united to Christ. We have been set free from sin, we are justified from it, our love of it has gone and we desire holiness. But the participation of His holiness in daily experience is governed by our subjection to Him in heart and will; we are to be bond-servants of God and of righteousness, accepting our directions and standards of life as dictated by them.

It has been the experience of all who in every age have accepted Christ's Lordship, that "when the heart submits then Jesus reigns and where Jesus reigns there is rest." His yoke is indeed comfortable and His burden is light. Therefore we rejoice and are honoured to be the servants of the Lord doing His will from the heart.

The Lord's Crown Jewels

They shall be Mine . . . in the day when I make up My jewels.—MAL. 3: 17.

WHILE we have often thought of our inheritance in Christ, of those treasures and pleasures which are made over to us by grace because we are the Lord's, Paul was also occupied with the reverse side of the matter. In praying for the Christians at Ephesus he asks that they may know what are the riches of the glory of God's inheritance in the saints, and we might well pray the same for ourselves and for Christians today. The fact is that God has found something which is to Him of great value; the Saviour has found a hidden treasure; we are the Lord's jewels.

For that reason we may look back at His ways with deep appreciation; He Who created us as children of men also redeemed us that we might become children of God. His delights and interests in the sons of men lay chiefly in His plan that they become the sons of God. To effect such a change was and is a mighty work. In the past it meant nothing less then the divine act and suffering of Calvary; in the present it means in each case the mighty working of the Holy Spirit, but the result is a child of God, loved of God.

This deep love and appreciation of His children, which is revealed in these Scriptures, ensure us that nothing which is necessary for life and godliness will be withheld. Food and clothing, friends and home, correction and instruction, work and play, all will be given in love by the Father Who pitieth His children and rejoiceth over them with joy. We are so dear to His heart and so present to His mind that He never forgets us. We are His jewels and, though at present in the stage of polishing, we shall one day be set in His crown. Until then let us pray that not only we may know our inheritance in Him, but His in us.

We Beheld His Glory

The glory of God, in the face of Jesus Christ.—2 COR. 4: 6.

ALL through the Old Testament men had longed to see the glory of God. Moses had prayed, "I beseech Thee shew me Thy glory," and to Isaiah had been given by the Spirit to prophesy, "And the glory of the Lord shall be revealed." Now and again by one and another something of God's glory had been revealed as when Isaiah saw the glory of the Son of God and spake of Him. But the full revelation was left until the fullness of times when men saw the glory of the Only-begotten of the Father, full of grace and truth.

What is this glory which men longed to see, and afterwards saw so clearly? While it is so high and deep, so transcendent and profound, some attempt must be made to understand the words we use. It may be regarded as the perfection of God's character, the combined qualities of His perfect love, wisdom, power and purity. All the rays which shine forth from God's being combine to make up the glory of the Lord. Sometimes in the Old Testament men saw one quality with special clarity, sometimes to another was revealed another attribute; but the sum total of all perfections is the glory of the Lord and such has been finally and fully revealed in Jesus Christ, God's son.

This self-revelation of God in the life and death of Christ is the focal point of history, the greatest fact of the world. But yet more wonderful to us who are His children by grace, is the fact that the glory has shone into and illuminated our hearts. The darkness of our souls has passed, the light now shineth and such light is nothing less than the glory of God which shines in the person of Jesus Christ.

Faith and Love Are Proved by Act

Faith without works is dead.—JAMES 2: 26.

THERE are almost always in the Bible two sides to a truth. Paul must needs write of justification by faith since the Jews were seeking to establish their acceptance with God by works. Then James must needs warn men of the danger of a merely intellectual acceptance of truth which is not faith. Both together, as inspired messengers of God, join to say that we are saved by faith but it must be a faith that works.

There has always been a danger of men becoming attached to a school of thought without a change of heart; of saying and not being and doing. To such our Lord said, "Not every one that saith . . . but he that doeth the will of my Father." Our merely saying certain things does not save us, does not sanctify us. Real holiness of heart and life is the work of God in the soul, often received through differing presentation and terms. We are in danger of stopping at the terms without knowing holiness itself.

Today we are called by these Scriptures to a faith which works and grows, which is ever adding to itself by claiming and practising other graces. Such faith is living and is the true gift of God. By it we are saved and by it we are made holy. There arises, therefore, a challenging question as to whether there is proof of such faith in our personal lives. To such as possess an active faith in the living God all things are possible; the trees that are in the way will be removed, the mountains which obstruct will become a highway, either being levelled by the power of God or climbed by the servant of the Lord, who is made strong by a grace which is only and always received by faith.

Filled, Abundantly Satisfied

They shall be abundantly satisfied with the fatness of Thy house.—PSALM 36: 8.

THE statement seems too wonderful, the promises too good to be true. Do they really mean that our thirsty souls with so many deep longings can be really satisfied and our empty earthen vessels really filled? That is precisely what is promised. Satisfied with goodness, dwelling in God's presence, filled with good things, abundantly satisfied; so the words of promise run and they are meant for me.

The thirst we have is a sign of life; hungerings after holiness is an encouraging feature even if the hunger be acute. The worst thing is that we have no desire for God and holiness, the best thing that we long intensely to be conformed into the image of His Son. To all such the promises apply and are meant to be fulfilled.

It must be remembered that God hath fulfilled His word to those who have gone before. The long story of the Church of Christ bears witness to this. God's saints have borne witness to the complete satisfaction of spirit which has been theirs; they have sung in prison and triumphed on beds of affliction, utterly satisfied with the goodness of the Lord.

The promises are ours to-day, and each of those two words must be emphasised. No experience of the fullness of Christ was meant for the saints of old and not meant for us. We are meant to experience the presence of God as Brother Lawrence did, and the intimacy of Christ's love as Samuel Rutherford. And they are meant for today, this very day and hour on which I read the precious promises. Let us go out into this day believing that we are satisfied with the living, indwelling Son of God.

Thy Still Dews of Quietness

The Lord of peace Himself give you peace.—2 THESS. 3: 16.

OUR hearts are often more set on God's gifts than on Himself the Giver. It is because the Lord is Himself the Lord of peace that He gives peace to His people. This He is able to do at all times and in all places, and it is well to remind ourselves that "at all times" means at this time, today. Moreover, the Peaceful Lord bestows His peace by all means. Innumerable and various channels are at His disposal, any one of which He may use to give peace to a disturbed saint. It may be a word of Scripture, a verse of a hymn or poem, a thought from a sermon, the visit of a friend, the receipt of a letter: but when there is need of peace the Lord of Peace can Himself impart His own peace.

This peace is adequate to answer all our disturbances: it is eternal, being given by Him Who is eternal: it is beyond thought or description and is related intimately with our sense of the presence of God. How could one be hurried or worried if God were present: before Him we should conduct ourselves with seemly and restrained behaviour. But is He not present? Everywhere? Always? Then if God's promises of His presence are true and we accept and claim them, should we not live daily and hourly as if God were visibly standing near?

God's presence is assured us today and all the days. His peace is offered now and always. It is pleasing to Him and speaks well of Him to others if we live serenely as we pass through this disturbed world. Let us ask for and expect to receive a full supply of peace to meet today's duties and the Lord of peace Himself will impart His own inner rest.

A Shelter in the Time of Storm

Thou art my hiding place.—Psalm 32: 7.

Wind and tempest shake the life of every Christian at some time or other. To some the shattering experiences come more frequently than to others: in some experiences the blast is short and almost overwhelming, in others it is lasting and strong, but in every instance the stability of life and the qualities of faith and endurance are tested. What is our resort in such experiences?

God's provision and protection from these terrible blasts is *Himself*. Our help is not in a formula or creed, not in a Church, nor indeed in mere human will-power, our help is in the Lord Who made heaven and earth, and Who made us, redeemed us and keeps us. He it is Who shields us from the withering heat of life's tropical sun or storm, and because of His presence and love we may be assured that we shall not wilt or fall.

Is there not wonderful comfort in the fact that the Lord Who is our shelter in the time of storm is not only God but Man. The Second Person of the Blessed Trinity has become man and continues to be both God and Man for ever. This helps us to understand a little as to how intimate and friendly His presence is: He is partaker of our nature and He is God's fellow or equal: He is one with us and at the same time one with the Father. How adequate is our stronghold! The wind blows but the refuge stands, the storm sweeps but the anchor holds.

And yet, alas, how often we stand against the storm alone and we do not seek Him: we fail to take refuge in the warm security of His love until the storm is passed. At such times may God graciously remind us of His promised shelter and help us to run into it and be safe.

Our Helper, Teacher, Guide, and More

The anointing which ye have received of Him, abideth in you.—1 JOHN 2: 27.

GOD'S greatest gifts to us are all beyond our feeble apprehension. Who can understand the giving of His Son? And who can enter into the giving of His Spirit? One of our greatest dangers is to become so familiar with words that we lose the sense of wonder and therefore lack the spirit of reverent enquiry. Today we contemplate the gift and ministry of God's Spirit.

Will it not be well for us once again to reaffirm our faith in the fact that after the ascension of Christ God poured forth His Spirit upon the waiting disciples, and that ever since the Comforter has been dwelling in the members of Christ's mystical Church and working in the world. He it is Who convicts and converts: He alone imparts the life of God to the soul of man. Pause and recollect that the third Person of the Blessed Trinity dwells in your body as in a temple, if you are a true Christian. Pause and worship.

Now from that inner shrine of the human spirit God's Spirit works, strengthening where there is weakness, teaching where there is ignorance and helping us in prayer by drawing our hearts to the presence of God. And as the Son of God was anointed with the Holy Spirit and with power, so we may be, indeed must be, also. Our need of the Spirit's power and teaching is known to us all in varying degrees. Let us bring our need to God now, and ask that the Spirit of Grace and Power Who rested on Jesus Christ our Head, may rest also upon us who are His members. It is not only true that we need Him but it is just as true that He desires to work in us. Not with impatience but yet with importunity let us seek the Spirit's help and power.

Living Only Unto God

I would seek unto God, and unto God would I commit my cause.—JOB 5: 8.

THE Christian's dealings are with God; it is the Lord alone with whom we must be primarily concerned. Once our motive to please God becomes adulterated with a desire to please others or the fear of man, then life becomes more complicated and confused.

This is particularly true when the way we are called upon to take is unpopular, and unlikely to commend itself to all concerned. Having reassured our hearts before God that the decision reached is not according to our own plans (and for this we may need to seek the counsel of some godly man or men) let us seek unto God and commit ourselves wholly to His hands. The letter which saddens us, the speech which bites let us bring to the Lord, that in His calm presence our hearts may find rest. Let us cast this present care upon God asking Him to look after it and us, as we seek to pursue His appointed path.

And while we are committing our care God is taking it over; while we are praying He is listening and working. The answer He is already giving may have demanded that the work should have been begun long ago, but that He anticipated as the God of eternity. The consistent continued prayer of a man who is right with God is mighty because it helps the mighty God to set free His power.

When the answer is seen, and the way of obedience is vindicated, then others will be blessed and our own faith confirmed and deepened. We shall love the Lord all the more because of this fresh and intimate experience of His mercy, and our desire to live only unto God will be strengthened.

Wisdom for the Asking

If any of you lack wisdom, let him ask of God.—JAMES 1: 5.

EVERY DAY there is the occasion which makes us aware of our need of wisdom. Yesterday's action leaves its aftermath and today we are made to realise where we failed through ignorance, impatience or frailty. We meet those who seek our counsel, we are brought face to face with problems for which there seems to be no answer, and our most natural question, though often clothed in other and more modern terms, is, "Where shall wisdom be found?" We know we need wisdom, though if we were asked to define it we should be baffled. For it is not mere knowledge but knowledge what to do and how to behave; it is not just understanding but the understanding of a situation and the additional quality of knowing how to handle it.

In our daily lives and in our difficulties our first need is to realise our need. We are shortsighted and ignorant; we can neither rightly interpret the past nor can we assess the present. Our vision is limited, our knowledge restricted, our best intentions too often warped. We are children in wisdom and there is no reason for us to be conceited. So long as we trust ourselves we shall fail and fall and hurt others as we do so.

But wisdom is available to those who ask, for the Master has not only given us the open cheque of His promises to give whatsoever we ask according to His will, but He has specially promised wisdom, the ability to assess a situation and the knowledge of what is best to be done. Then why should we stumble along and frequently fall when, renouncing our own weakness, we may receive the wisdom that cometh from above? But it must be sought, we must needs make frequent request for it, and as we do, God, Who is the only wise, will communicate His wisdom to us.

A Method of Teaching

It is good . . . that I have been afflicted, that I might learn Thy statutes.—PSALM 119: 71.

ANY good method of teaching must first take the pupils into account, and in this case the Saviour and His people are the pupils. In the case of the Lord Jesus it is at first somewhat difficult to understand that He should need to learn anything, but it must be remembered that in the divine idea of knowledge it is not only a question of intellectual information but experimental acquaintance also is included. Therefore the Lord from heaven, though a Son, must learn obedience through suffering.

And God teaches us in the same way, though in this instance the pupils are very different, for they are sinful; the mind is slow to apprehend and the will is often rebellious. But the ministry of correction and instruction is often the way of suffering. We learn as we are afflicted, for the lessons God is teaching us are concerning Himself and concerning our own dependence upon Him. They are lessons regarding character and relations and these are not taught in text books but in trial. It is for this reason that the most afflicted saints are usually the most advanced in the intimate knowledge of God. They have learned how weak they are and how strong He is.

One of the intended lessons of our past life, whether it be forty years or more, or less, is the knowledge of our own hearts. It is good to ask ourselves whether or not we have learned the lesson. If not, shall we not go over the pages again that we might begin more faithfully to do God's will, to walk in the ways He chooses and to hold Him in reverential awe.

The Unfinished Work of the Spirit

It is God which worketh in you.—PHIL. 2: 13.

WE are so often aware of our difficult circumstances that our prayers are necessarily concerned with the need that God should work *for* us. But the greater need is that God work *in* us; indeed some of the outward and difficult circumstances would not arise if we were better and holier than we are.

Here is a reminder, the encouraging reminder, that God is actually working in us, working in our inmost being to conform us to the image of Christ. It was God Who first began to change us; He, and not a preacher, convicted us of our sin; He, and not an evangelist, directed us to Christ: He imparted faith; He regenerated us and gave us the witness of His Spirit. God began to work in us or we would never have begun the Christian life, and now He continues, day by day, working towards the one end of making us like His Son.

Apart from Him we can do no more to sanctify ourselves than we could to save ourselves.

And every virtue we possess,
  And every victory won
And every thought of holiness
  Are His alone.

But the virtues, the victories and the desires after holiness are His gifts to us, and in that fact we may find encouragement. Be assured that the Spirit Who now indwells you as a believer is able to continue and deepen His work in you. He has really only just begun; there is a great deal more He will do; there is nothing He cannot do in transforming the life. But we must come to Him and come again and again. He is able to save to the uttermost those who come.

The Work was God's—The Praise must Be

Who, His own self, bare our sins . . .—1 PETER 2: 24.

IN our salvation God took the initiative and carried through the work. Had it been left to us frail sinners either to begin, continue or complete it, our case would have been sad indeed; "but God"—the words occur frequently in Scripture—loved us and lifted us. Today we are forcibly reminded of this, for we read, "He hath made Him to be sin for us." The Lord hath laid on Him the iniquity of us all. Who His own self bare our sins. God was active in redeeming us.

This meant for God the most acute suffering, for it made it necessary for Him to deal with sin, and in so doing to judge it Himself. Into that awful and profound mystery we can only see a little way, it is too deep and great for the human mind; but it meant the Cross where the Son of God cried, "My God, my God, why?" The bruising of Christ's body, painful though it was, did not compare to the bruising of His sinless soul when He was made a sin-offering. The rejection by men was nothing compared with the rejection by God in those dark hours. And what shall we say of the Father's suffering when God in Christ reconciled us to Himself? Is this not in some faint way suggested by thoughts of Abraham as he bound his son for sacrifice?

But the work is finished and the results are glorious. By this one man's obedience to death many, yes millions, are justified and given a place in glory. The kindness and love of God is revealed in the forgiving of our sins and in our being regenerated by His Spirit. We are able to stand before God without fear because of Christ's righteousness and rejoice in God through our Lord Jesus Christ by Whom we have received reconciliation. Eternity will be too short to sing His praise for such redeeming love.

The Badge of Discipleship

By love serve one another.—GALATIANS 5: 13.

"ONE another"—the words recurring so often in the Epistles remind us of the prominence given to our personal relations in New Testament instructions regarding the Christian life. We are being constantly reminded that while our relation with God is of the first importance, our association with our brethren is not far behind. Indeed the Bible never separates the two and always assumes that the real Christian is rightly adjusted to God above and man around. Here the emphasis is particularly on our relation with fellow-believers in our Lord Jesus Christ.

The one thing which stands out clearly is that we are to love them; that being done the rest will follow. Now love to the brethren was the badge of discipleship in the early church, "By this shall all men know that ye are my disciples," said our Lord Jesus. While a Christian was to love every man for Christ's sake yet his fellow-believer stood in a special relation with him, and between them there was to be a real bond of love. They were born of the same Spirit and loved by the same Lord, and as they possessed the same eternal life being indwelt by the same Holy Spirit so they were to love one another. This love would be expressed in serving one another, that is, in actual deeds, in helpful ministries. Loving each other they were to restore any who fell by the way being caught in some snare or falling into some sin.

Our frail and sinful nature gives us great and frequent opportunities of shewing our love to one another. The strong may help the weak, those who remain standing may lift the one who has fallen. And as we do these deeds of mercy our love will flourish, and our Saviour will be glad.

Creed Expressed in Conduct

Behold, to obey is better than sacrifice.—1 SAMUEL 15: 22.

THERE are always two great dangers confronting the people of God, the first concerns an indefinite faith, and the second a faulty conduct. In the first instance all the emphasis is on our personal behaviour and our social conduct; it doesn't much matter what we believe if we behave rightly; conduct is more important than creed. Such a view we must reject, for taken to its logical conclusion it is just salvation by works and it gives the honour to man. The other view stoutly rejects that which has already been set forth, maintaining that man is a helpless sinner who cannot help or save himself, and that salvation is entirely by the grace and power of God. Therefore faith, which ultimately includes doctrine, is important.

The latter view is that which was held by the Reformers and Evangelical leaders of the last three centuries; it is the treasured faith of their successors today. But to such the words of today's portion come as a timely reminder that our faith must not be mere intellectual assent or mental conviction; it must include the will and be demonstrated in obedience to God. Doing the will of God, keeping the commandments of the Lord, keeping justice and mercy, obeying God's voice, these are the real tests which Scripture applies to our faith. It is necessary that we should rightly believe in our hearts and minds, but it is also necessary that we should outwardly express our Christian faith in Christian conduct. In order to do this we are reminded that God is at work in our hearts first to help us desire it and afterwards to enable us to fulfil the same.

An Indissoluble Union Nothing Can Separate

The Lord will preserve me unto His heavenly kingdom.—2 TIM. 4: 18.

GRACE united us to Christ when first we believed. The union was vital and reciprocal so that our Lord could say, "Ye in me and I in you." And so we are able to sing

And round my heart still closely twine
These ties which nought can sever,
For I am His and He is mine
For ever and for ever.

This deep and satisfying assurance that the Lord will keep us is fundamental for a true Christian life. We shall meet foes without and the foe of sin and unbelief within; it is necessary therefore that we should not be in doubt regarding the possibility of someone or something breaking the bond which grace hath forged. This is not meant, however, to make us prayerless or presumptuous but to save us from fear and anxiety. We do well to say to ourselves "I . . . am persuaded He is able to keep . . . against that day." This is a good persuasion.

A long catalogue is here given of the things which might conceivably break the union and sever our souls from the Saviour. Is death, which breaks so many other bonds, able to break this one? Can life, which strains every relation, sever our relation with Christ? Are evil powers on earth or Satanic powers from hell able to do it? To all such questions there comes the ringing answer, No, and the explanation given is that our life is hid with Christ in God. The believer's eternal life is the life of God and is thus beyond the reach of death or life and of powers human and Satanic. We may be poor and ignorant, frail and unworthy, but our spiritual life is the life of God communicated to us by the Holy Spirit, the Giver of life, and as such is eternal and divine.

Let these truths comfort us, reassure and strengthen us today, as we go out to live our life in a sinful world.

Walking Carefully

Let not your good be evil spoken of.—ROMANS 14: 16.

"A WISE man does not tie his shoe-laces in a strawberry garden." So runs a Persian proverb, and it is a useful comment on the command of Holy Scripture to abstain from all appearance of evil. Obviously there is nothing wrong in tieing a shoe lace, indeed it is a positively right and necessary thing to do; but to do it in a strawberry garden will give rise to real suspicion which explanation will not remove. Here then is a principle of conduct which all Christians must accept and follow, if we would wish to obey the Scriptures and live blamelessly before our fellows. We must not only do the right but do it in the right way and place, otherwise our good may be the ground for evil speaking.

Many are looking on at our lives; each servant of God is the centre of a larger or smaller world of interest; within that circle his influence extends and in it his conduct must be circumspect. What of my own circle of influence, which includes home, office, shop, street and church? In this circle, is my life exemplary so that younger and less mature Christians can safely follow me? Or is my behaviour a cause of stumbling to some? Solemn words are spoken here to those whose lives prove a stumbling-block to others; but also, let it be noted, words of reward will be spoken to those who have helped and lifted others.

The Christian is called to a life of liberty; he is only under bondage to Christ's law of love; but no more engaging law is possible for it outlaws all conduct which is unworthy of a disciple of Christ, or which will prove unhelpful to another. We are committed to obedience to such a law.

The Lord is Near

Fear thou not, for I am with thee.—ISAIAH 41: 10.

THE Lord is nigh at hand and not far off, that is the message of these Scripture portions. It is difficult to keep before us the two complementary truths that God is high and He is nigh. Thinking of His nearness it is not easy to avoid forgetting His great power and sovereignty; while meditating on His supremacy we may easily forget that He has promised to be near His people. Think today of this comforting and comfortable truth, that while God is the Creator and Controller of this vast universe and the Centre and Soul of every astronomic sphere, yet He is at the same time closer than breathing, nearer than hands and feet.

God is in the midst of his people. In Old Testament days He was in the midst of Israel, at first as their King ruling through the patriarchs; He dwelt in tabernacle and temple and they gathered together unto Him, Who was the centre of their national life. Though the token of His presence left them on account of sin, the cloud lingered as though unwilling to depart and as soon as there was longing He revealed His presence again.

But now in the dispensation of the Gospel, God is not only among His people as He was among Israel, but by the Spirit of His Son He actually indwells each believer and has made a temple of every redeemed soul. Think of this, that the spirit of the living God is dwelling in your body, is thinking through your mind, acting and expressing Himself through your whole personality; this will transform today or any day.

Moreover a day is coming when all the people of God will be gathered home and when the Lord will be in the midst in another and a special way! He will be in the midst of the throne and we shall worship and serve Him for ever. Break, day of God, O break!

Strong in the Strength Which God Supplies

Be strong in the grace that is in Christ Jesus.—2 TIM. 2: 1.

THE Christian is to be gentle to all men but utterly strong against all sin: he is to be loved by children but at the same time he is to be unyielding when tempted to falter or fail. The course of the world is against us and we must needs stand firm rather than drift; this calls for moral courage and we must possess it. The days are marked by a fashionable lack of principle, when it is easily considered an affront to refuse alcoholic drinks, but the believer knowing that the Christian is not to stumble others, must needs refuse for Christ's sake. Much that is done in the world around us is neither desirable nor permissible to us, and we need strength to stand alone—yet not alone for God is with us and our brethren, who are making a similar stand are with us too.

The strength which is needed is also available; it is in Christ Jesus and we are in Him. This means that the first duty of the Christian is to abide in Christ, to keep in constant touch with Him. Prayerlessness, disobedience and unbelief tend to stop the supply of strength, and the opposites prayer, obedience and faith keep open the heart to receive adequate power. The Word of God is food for the soul without which we must faint in the day of adversity.

Each Christian, then, is standing on good ground, he is sheltered in a trustworthy refuge, he has good supplies of food and a mighty Captain. There is to be no parleying with the foe, no yielding of ground; rather we are to advance to win the victory and to gather the spoil, at no time afraid of the enemy.

Te Deum Laudamus

I will praise Thee, O Lord my God, with all my heart.—PSALM 86: 12.

THE Lord is worthy; all His attributes unite to call forth our praise. The Father is to be praised for His eternal love and wisdom, the Son for His redeeming work; and the Spirit for His saving and sanctifying grace. All God's ways with man call to us to laud and magnify Him; from every point of view and on every consideration the Lord's name is to be praised.

Praise is a sacrifice which we should offer to God Himself. The Lord rightly expects it from His people. There is little we can give to God, but praise from a redeemed sinner's heart is precious to Him. He has loved us in our sins, He has loosed us from our sins, He has put upon us the garment of salvation and within us the Spirit of holiness. In return for such mercy He looks for a spirit of true thankfulness which is warm and vocal and active. Let us offer this sacrifice to Him continually.

The praise should be offered that the Lord may be had in honour by others. It is not only acceptable to God but evangelistic among men. A heart to praise our God and full of love divine is the first requisite for helping to turn other sinners to the saving grace of God. If only we praised God more, and more spontaneously, then the world around, unsatisfied and grumbling, would surely take note that we have a Friend Who means much to us.

For these and other reasons let us decide to praise God, to give Him His just due. The Psalmist says repeatedly, "I will praise Thee, O God," and we take up the sacrifice and service and say, "We will praise Thee"; we purpose to do it, let us begin now and sing our personal Te Deum.

Jesus First Others Next

Bear ye one another's burdens.—GALATIANS 6: 2.

THE critical experience which makes a person to become a Christian called conversion, regeneration or by other names depending on the aspect of the matter, shifts the centre of life. Before conversion a person is self-centred: life's considerations and programme revolves round self, and whether the self be kind and courteous or aggressive and assertive, the centre of life is the same. But on conversion Christ becomes the centre, and as life moves round this new pivot it takes in others as part of its circle. Where Jesus is really first, then others come next and self last.

We are to bear one another's burdens, and we all have them. It is better that I help you with yours and as you are able you help me with mine, than that we both struggle alone with our own. There is fellowship and help in the former method but only loneliness and despair in the latter. Such sharing of another's burden draws us closer together, and closer to the Lord Who Himself is the great Burden-bearer.

What opportunities life affords for obeying this law of Christian conduct. There is hardly a life around without its burden, which means that there is scarcely a soul at hand which is not open to a kind approach, and ultimately open to our giving the Gospel, if only kindness and compassionate interest has come first. Alas we are so often too anxious to give the Gospel first and it is resented, but where kindness has done its work then heart and mind are more open to listen and to learn. When Jesus sat down at the well He asked first for a drink and afterwards told of living water.

I Am His and He is Mine

I pray . . . for them which Thou hast given me.—JOHN 17: 9.

"MINE"—that is how we are described by the Lord Jesus. It is a humbling thought that such sinners as we are should be dear to Him, for all our merit is demerit; we were once estranged by nature and practice, but now we are His friends. His own, it appears to be with pleasure that He thinks of us and prays for us as "mine". And what mercy it is that we can take up the same word, as we think of our Risen Lord, for by grace He is ours and each true believer can say or sing:

Mine! Mine! Mine! I know Thou art mine.

It is better to be sure that He is ours than that we should have Deeds and Covenants which made half the world our own. To know ourselves possessed, supported and guaranteed by the Son of God is life and peace indeed.

Now it is one thing to know that He loves us now, but supposing we fail and fall, supposing through weakness or folly we have a bad patch of road when our testimony is poor or worse than that; Will He love us still? Will He still say, "Mine"? The answer is in the affirmative. He loved Peter when He followed afar off, yes, and when he stood by the fire, and while warming his hands his heart grew colder. Whatever be the condition of the reprobate, the one who has utterly renounced His Saviour, the position of the one who has fallen is surely that the Lord loves him still and wants to lift him up again. And in the meantime, as the Saviour bends over him in tender concern and prays the Father for such an one He says, "Mine."

There are many things which are insecure, many friends who may fail us when we fail, but one Friend remaineth and He saith, "I pray for them, they are mine," for He loves us to the uttermost and to the end.

The Spirit Giveth Life

The words that I speak unto you, they are spirit and they are life.—JOHN 6: 63.

WHETHER the need is for the first imparting of life or of that continual renewing of divine life in the soul, we can only turn to God the Holy Spirit Who is the Giver of life; He it is Who is alone able to quicken us, but He is able. And we are as needy as He is willing; for as with the Psalmist, our hearts cleave to the dust and we need to pray continually "Quicken Thou me according to Thy word." The answer to such a prayer is our ability to call upon His name, that is, to pray for ourselves and for others; and the evident lack of the spirit of prayer proves beyond doubt our urgent need of spiritual quickening or reviving.

It is the Spirit Who quickeneth; this is a lesson which is easy to forget. In a day when the whole tendency is to regard what man can achieve, at a time when our evangelistic ministry has available for its use all the latest products of electricity and advertising, it is all too easy to trust in the aids rather than in the Spirit, or if not in the aids then in the man who uses them. But only the Spirit of God can impart the life of God.

The means which the Spirit uses in His renewing work is the Word of God; "Thy precepts" as they are called here—and this means the Old as well as the New Testament. The Spirit may use any part of the Scripture to give life to the spiritually dead or to renew the heart of a fainting or weak believer. Let us therefore not fail in our careful use of Scripture, for here is the means which the Spirit uses, and it is well to be in the right attitude to receive the enlivening which God loves to give to the spiritually hungry and thirsty. My soul, wait thou only upon God.

Let Us Draw Near

Let us come boldly . . . and find grace . . . in time of need.—HEBREWS 4: 16.

MERCY for past failures—and how much we need it; grace equally necessary for future victories; and peace in present circumstances; these are the gifts of God's love dispensed to those who ask and receive, and all may be ours if we come for them. Today the emphasis is on the necessity of our coming.

We began our Christian life by coming to the Lord. Grace drew us and we followed. We came to Jesus labouring and heavy-laden as we were and we found rest. And the Christian life has been maintained as we have continued coming. To whom coming, Peter says, as a Living Stone, ye also as living stones, are built up—the tense is in the present continuous. We keep on coming to the Lord Jesus, we continue to draw near to God in Him, and in so doing we become like Him and share the same qualities of living stone, that is, of life and strength.

Here then is a fundamental principle for our spiritual life, we are to draw near to God habitually; we are to come to the throne of grace regularly. Instead of being careful and anxious and in need, we are to come and make known our requests. There are many things to hinder us coming but none so effective as our own natural disinclination to come. It is far more natural to worry than to come; as a pungent proverb puts it, why pray when you can worry? Life's engagements, sometimes very trifling, keep us from coming. But in the heart of the child of God dwells the Holy Spirit of God and it is by Him we draw near. He prompts us to come, leads us to the throne of grace; let us respond to His gentlest leading, and the way to God's presence will become an increasing delight.

Light After Darkness

When I sit in darkness, the Lord shall be a light unto me.—MICAH 7: 8.

DARKNESS for the Christian; can it be? With all the promises of light which God makes, is it possible for one of His children to be in darkness? The answer is that God permits us to find ourselves in darkness in order that He may train us and develop our character. It is in darkness that faith becomes necessary and strong; there is little to exercise it in the light. In dark periods and experiences we discover whether we do really trust the living God or not. The prophet speaks about us walking in darkness, that is, having to take steps or make decisions with no light. This is perhaps the greatest test of faith. Now what is the message of God to His servants who are in darkness?

First of all light is promised; the period of darkness is distinctly limited. The time when it is permitted may be longer or shorter but it must give place to light as soon as God's loving purposes are fulfilled. The Lord Himself will be our light. His law will be the lamp and we shall be brought forth into the full light of day and see God's righteousness, which means we shall see how right His ways in the darkness were.

The second thing is that we are to trust God to send us light; we are not to try and create it ourselves. This is the place for passive faith if any faith can be passive. It is the occasion to say that we mean to rest wholly upon God and wait quietly for Him. The adopting and maintaining of such an attitude of confident faith is really very active but the activity is in standing firm against fuss and scheming.

To all who wait for God, light will appear, the whole life will be flooded with it and we shall know that it is God's light.

A Deep Where All Our Thoughts Are Drowned

God hath from the beginning chosen you to salvation. . . . —2 THESS. 2: 13.

THE deep subjects of election and predestination are both full of difficulty and comfort; they are made the subject of bitter controversy and contention, when they are meant to be the cause of praise and adoration.

In the first place let our emphasis be on the God Who has performed these great acts which initiate His saving operations in our souls. If we have rightly appreciated His character as revealed in His Son and in His Word, then anything which is clearly stated that He has done or is to do, must be both good and wise. Nothing unjust or unloving can be attributed to Him Who is good and Whose mercy endureth for ever. He is the God and Father of our Lord Jesus Christ of Whom His Son said, "He that hath seen me hath seen the Father," and concerning Whom all creation will sometime say, "He hath done all things well."

Then let us acknowledge the limitations of our knowledge. We are creatures of time and we necessarily think in time processes where event succeeds event. On the contrary God is the God of eternity with whom the past and future are one in an ever-present Now. There are great dangers therefore in seeking to reduce the ways of God to a series and system which fits in with our limited knowledge.

But let us draw our comfort and receive any necessary correction from the fact that our salvation is not something which is haphazard or doubtful. God hath saved us and hath called us to holiness. We were predestinated to be conformed to the image of His Son and to Him we must look for the performance of all that is necessary for true holiness. He hath begun a good work in us, He will perform and perfect it.

That Will Be Glory for Me

The days of thy mourning shall be ended.—Isaiah 60: 20.

In the world tribulation! It is not always that; there are times when the way is easier; it may be that if we were better Christians there would be more difficulty; but no life which is really Christian can escape the tribulation. It may come from those without the church in forms of persecution or slander, or it may come from those within, in which case it is all the more painful; but come it certainly will for it is written, "In the world tribulation." We ourselves groan within ourselves.

But the promise lifts up our eyes to the horizon and to the day break. The days of mourning shall be ended; the present sorrow is a temporary experience sent to work in us a holiness and grace which is precious in God's sight, then when patience has had her perfect work we are to enter a land which is fairer than day and a city which is four-square, where there is no night, no sorrow, no sighing, no crying but where all sin and its results are left behind for ever.

We are meant to look forward to such a time. It is to be the joy set before us to help us endure our cross and despise our shame. We are intended to sing about it and why should we not do so today? Let our hearts, if not our voices, take up some such song as the Glory Song—"When by His grace I shall look on His face, That will be glory for me." "Sing on, O blissful pilgrim, Nor think the moments long"; weeping may endure for a night but joy cometh in the morning, and when the morning cometh it will be the beginning of a day which shall never pass away. Lift up your heart—and your voices.

Faith Working by Love

Faith, if it hath not works, is dead, being alone.—JAMES 2: 17.

SAVING faith is active; it is not a passive receptivity but actively moves out towards God Who is its object. It deals with promises by or statements (facts) concerning God; God speaks a promise, faith receives it, and God and the believer are bound together, He by His faithfulness and the Christian by his faith.

The genuine character of the faith of any man is demonstrated by the fact that he proceeds to act upon it. If certain truths about God are believed, then certain conduct on the part of a believer must follow. If we really believe that God is holy then we desire to walk in holiness of life and it is the latter which proves that our faith is real, otherwise we may merely hold God's holiness as a mental persuasion and not in living faith. Similarly if we believe God is Almighty, we shall desire to live our lives, and conduct our service, as those who are joined by grace to almightiness; such a truth should deliver us from both low levels of life and diffidence in our active service.

Faith works by love; if it be the faith that pleases God and affords Him an opportunity of doing His will in our life then its activity is in the atmosphere of love. It is not brusque, nor aggressive, nor thoughtless but rather considerate and kind; its works are not only in the realm of miracle but of mercy, and sometimes the mercy is as acceptable as the miracle. When faith grows exceedingly, love abounds towards each other and men of faith are almost always and equally men of love.

Let us examine ourselves today in the light of these words of Scripture. Is our faith an active faith? Does it enable us to do and suffer for Christ? And does it make us loving and considerate of others?

Peace, the Gift of God's Love

Let him take hold of my strength, that he may make peace with me.—ISAIAH 27: 5.

THERE is no message which the Gospel brings which is so desirable and welcome as that of peace. The hearts of men long for it without often knowing what it is they desire. There is an inward tension which makes men restless even if there is no other person to disturb them. Then there is misunderstanding and intolerance between a man and his fellows; and there is the fundamental lack of right relations with God. All these produce a heart unrest which makes peace so desirable: and the Gospel is a message of peace, peace with God through our Lord Jesus Christ; also inward peace, because the contending faculties of the personality are harmonised, and there is peace with our fellows. By the blood of Christ Jesus we are not only made nigh to God, but to others, for of Jew and Gentile, of cultured and unprivileged, God makes one new man.

And all God's thoughts for us are of peace and not of evil. Whatever may be the appearance of the present, or indeed of any circumstance, it is meant to bring peace and not unrest, to minister good and not evil. If only we learn to receive the dispensations and providences of God aright we shall live in peace, proving that Christ's yoke is comfortable and His burden is light.

But today we are reminded that peace does not stand alone. Here it is related to strength, for peace is a gift and a product. To make it possible Jesus Christ put forth His might in wrestling with the prince of darkness, and bearing the load of sin; the Father exerted His power in raising Christ from the death; so peace is only possible because of God's strength. On that strength we are to take hold in order to find peace; we are to rest on the reconciling work of Christ and his resurrection. And finally, it is only as we rely on the power of God to meet all life's problems and to control all life's movements, that we shall know peace, the gift of God's love.

Dying to Sin, Living to God

They that are Christ's have crucified the flesh with the affections and lusts.—GALATIANS 5: 24.

IN the day that thou eatest thereof thou shalt surely die, so said the Lord to Adam in Eden; but the word of divine warning went unheeded and Adam began to walk alone and shun God's presence, for death had begun to work. Sin, when it is finished, brings forth death; this is a law of the universe, a law which was established in the beginning by the Law-maker. The same law operates still, for sin is still followed by death which works in every realm of human life.

This law should be remembered by the believer who is called to live in obedience. If, by the enabling of God's Spirit we put to death the sinful tendencies of our natures, then we really live unto God, but if we are governed by selfish motives, dominated by selfish indulgences, we die; a process which limits and enervates our spiritual life sets in. A choice is before us; it is whether we desire life or death, the enthronement of self or of Christ, the diminution or enlargement of Christ in our lives. A choice may be made critically and definitely in some quiet spot or in some large convention, but the thing which most matters is the daily mortifying of the deeds of the body and the daily strengthening of the spiritual life with the food of God's Word, with the fresh air of prayer, and with the exercise of obedience and service. These are all daily recurring engagements which need to be cultivated.

As the spiritual life is cultivated in obedience and faith then it grows, and bears fruit in Godly behaviour, and the graces which adorned Christ's life will adorn ours similarly. In order to bring us this full salvation the grace of God has appeared to release us from our sins, to quicken and fulfil our longings. With such a coming behind us, with such a Christ within us and with such an appearing before us, what manner of persons ought we to be?

Love Incarnate, Love Divine

When the fulness of the time was come, God sent forth His Son.—GALATIANS 4: 4.

IN the Gospel the righteousness of God is revealed; He is seen in relation to sin and so dealing with it as to display His character as holy. But in the particular aspect of the message which Christmas emphasises we are reminded of the condescending love of God, the love which stoops, draws near and blesses. In this was manifested the love of God because God sent His only begotten Son; the kindness and love of God our Saviour toward us being manifested.

This great display of the divine heart was given in the fullness of time, when the time was ripe. All things had been carefully prepared through four thousand years. A people had been separated from the other nations and a family chosen out of the people. The Greek language was diffused abroad so as to make the message clear and Roman armies, laws, and transport, were all at the disposal of the Lord of Glory and His servants. And finally a Roman emperor, finding his money spent, sent out a decree that the whole empire was to pay taxes, an edict which brought Joseph and Mary to Bethlehem. And thus the prophecies were fulfilled; "And thou, Bethlehem, in the land of Judea, art not the least of the princes of Judah, for out of thee shall come a son who shall rule my people Israel," and many other promises also had their fulfilment in that country inn. But most important of all, God appeared in human flesh, born of a woman, drawing near to us all to share our lot before He carried our sins.

Before that first Christmas it might easily have been thought that God was far off and mighty, but now we know He is also near and understanding, full of grace and truth.

Abounding in Labour and in Fruit

Ye know that your labour is not in vain in the Lord.—1 COR. 15: 58.

WE are to be labourers together with God; and as Jesus said of His Father, "My Father worketh hitherto and I work," we need to be continually abounding in the work of the Lord. He does not work by fits and starts but is always busy caring for His world, blessing His people, saving souls, so we must be consistently doing the works of Him Who sends us, remembering that the day of opportunity will end.

This calls for a persistence and prayerfulness lest we faint by the way. The years come and go and our early devotion may too easily depart; middle age with its tendency to self-indulgence comes upon us, and we are tempted by its comforts and the plea of self-preservation. Many churches are in a poor state because its older members have slackened off in their devotion to the Lord; they have the feeling that the younger folk are earnest and that they, therefore, may relax. Or even into the life of the younger Christian, things and affections may enter which interfere with the first claims of Christ; it is to be regretted that engagements too often spoil the discipleship of young men and women who profess faith and whose friendship is intended to stimulate their Christian devotion. Let us watch and pray.

But it is not in the mere abundance of work where true success is found in the Christian life; indeed we need to beware of being too busy. "Beware of the barrenness of a busy life" lest in our rush, the fruit of the Spirit has no chance to grow. We are to be fruitful as well as busy, and this means that we must make time for the cultivation of our fellowship with God in Christ; we have need of unhurried time for communion. Let us then hold before us these two needs, first, that we are consistent in our work, and secondly, that we are careful about our times of communion.

A Blessed Contrast

The things . . . seen are temporal, but the things not seen are eternal.—2 COR. 4: 18.

HERE is a page of sharp contrasts; things seen are set against things unseen, the transient is over against the enduring; light affliction becomes exceedingly light in the assurance of an eternal weight of glory.

This world is meant to be for God's children a place of discipline and training; we are not meant to have an easy time here and settle down. God knows we shall be burdened while we are in this tabernacle. The difficulty is that the present often eclipses the future; we easily fall into the snare of the proverb, which in earthly things may sometimes be true, but in heavenly things is often untrue; namely, "a bird in the hand is worth two in the bush". Future glories though they be never so great, do not glow sufficiently to counterbalance the almost trivial inconvenience we suffer here. We too easily take a short term view of God's work in the soul and feel discouraged.

But the Bible does not make this mistake; nor did the martyrs. The Book sets things in their true perspective regarding time as very short and eternity as very long; it speaks of suffering here as light, and the glory there as exceedingly heavy. This means that if we can only think more of heaven and get its glory into our souls we shall easily despise the passing baubles, and the dazzling sights will lose their attraction. For that reason preachers should preach more about heaven; a generation of men in the pulpit have succumbed to the taunt that we preach "pie in the sky when you die, when what we need is a little more here", and the Church has become materialistic. Let us lift up our heads and set our hearts on the heaven and glory of God.

The Joyful News of Sins Forgiven

I will remember their sin no more.—Jeremiah 31: 34.

It may be said that there are three fundamental needs of the human heart, namely, pardon, peace and power; pardon for the past, peace in the present and power in the future. The first of these in order of experience is pardon, and it is on this one that the other two are built.

We are reminded in the first place that forgiveness is a divine gift and prerogative; no one is able to forgive sins otherwise, neither prophet, priest or king. Kings may pardon crimes, that is, offences against the laws of the land, priests may claim to pronounce absolution in the Lord's name, but ultimately only the God against Whom we have sinned can say to us, "Thy sins be forgiven thee"; and this He does for the sake of His name or character.

There are two things necessary for forgiveness. One is that the sin which is to be forgiven must be punished, it must be judged; for divine forgiveness cannot be based on any mere disposition of clemency as an indulgent father might forgive his son without regard to authority or character. God, Who desires to forgive, must do so while upholding the moral government of His universe, therefore, sin which is rebellion must be punished. This God accomplished when He came in the Person of His Son and bore the sin of the world and the sins of His people on the Cross. The death of Jesus Christ is the righteous basis of God's loving act of pardon.

Then there is something we must do, namely, we must repent and confess our sins and trust the promise of our pardoning God to relieve us of the guilt. This He does the moment we truly believe. And more, He begins His gracious work of introducing us into a life where we experience deliverance from the yoke or dominion of sin. Praise be to His name!

Knowledge is Meant for Obedience

Understanding what the will of the Lord is.—EPHESIANS 5: 17.

KNOWING and then doing is the chief end of the Christian life. On many subjects the Lord's will is revealed with sufficient clearness that we do not need to be in doubt. For instance it is clearly not God's will that we should sin; it is God's will that we should be holy. It is the will of the Lord that we should rejoice and not that we should be overcome by grief. And so from definite statements of Scripture we could gather together a number of important matters on which there need be no doubt as to the will of God.

In the many personal details of life, however, we are cast upon God without having specific texts of Scripture which settle the matter. God may use texts to guide us but this is done by the Spirit of God applying a general text to a specific instance, in which case we need to be sure that we ourselves are not making the application to please ourselves. In all such personal matters where guidance is needed, where to live and work, what to do, where to go, which house to buy, whether to become a missionary or a minister or not, etc., we need to understand the will of the Lord. This means the use of our mind, to which faculty is committed the ability to understand anything. A sound and active mind, therefore, is of fundamental importance, though in divine things it must be subject to the word of God.

But God means us to know His will. Either for the sake of necessary discipline from Him, or because of mixed motives on our part, the time necessary to discover it may be long. However, we may be sure He means us to know it. But it is only revealed to our understanding that we may do it. Is our present darkness due to unwillingness to obey?

Blameless Now, Faultless Then

Now unto Him that is able to keep you from falling . . . be glory.—JUDE 24.

BEFORE that wonderful work of grace in our souls which we call regeneration or conversion we were enemies of God characterised by wicked deeds. The strong statement of Scripture on the matter will be resented unless we have really begun to understand the nature of sin, but once we have seen that sin is our disposition towards God by nature and is not necessarily concerned with any particular form of outward deeds, we shall readily accept such statement is truly descriptive of us.

Then we were reconciled to God and a new nature was imparted to us and Christian life began as "the life of God in the soul of man". This made, and continues to make, complete demands upon our life and loyalty. We are to renounce all sin and seek to walk in holiness before God all the days of our life. Anything dark and doubtful is to be refused; we are to shine as lights, walk as examples and with the utmost diligence endeavour to be found in Christ without spot and blameless. Here then is our ideal for the coming year. We have not attained it yet but no lower standard is acceptable to God than that we walk before Him and before men blameless. This means avoiding even the appearance of evil and shunning things which may not necessarily be evil in themselves but which have doubtful associations. Blameless and harmless even here—what a standard!

But the climax of all God's work in us is to be achieved when the Lord comes and we see Him as He is and are made like Him; then we shall be faultless. At present this is impossible but it then will be revealed and the last trace of sin will have disappeared; ignorance and habit and limitation of every kind will be done away. When by His grace I shall look on His face that will be glory for each saint—and it will be glory for Him too.

Here We Raise Our Ebenezer

Hitherto hath the Lord helped us.—1 SAMUEL 7: 12.

THE year is drawing to a close and thoughts of the past as well as hopes and plans for the future are very much upon our minds. Such thoughts of the year may well gather round two centres, first our personal failures, and secondly God's merciful care. Let the latter subject fill our minds today.

Throughout all the past, whether it be long or short, the Christian is able to trace the mercy of the Lord. He has borne with our slowness to learn, our unwillingness to follow Him. In spite of our unyieldingness He has borne us up and carried us along; by His grace we remain standing today. He has trained us like a father trains his son; He has taught us to trust Him like an eagle teaches her young to fly and trust the air. These lessons were not easily learned on our part, but His mercy and patience are greater than our slowness, and He Who loved us enough to redeem us has carried us through.

Moreover our experiences of His grace during the past year are meant to encourage us to hope in Him during the future. Even down to old age, when our faculties become less active and our dependence on others increase, He has promised to be with us and proved Himself as trustworthy to keep such promises by His love in the year now closing. Therefore we may with increased confidence cast our burden on the Lord, and refuse to be anxious about the future. The unknown tomorrow can bring with it nothing but that He will bear us through. Our Heavenly Father knows our needs of every kind and will supply, and as to the past "He is Ebenezer—Hitherto hath the Lord helped us"; while for the future He is "Jehovah—Jireh, the Lord will provide."